D0879422

DAILY NEWS, ETERNAL STORIES

The Guilford Communication Series

Daily News, Eternal Stories

The Mythological Role of Journalism

Jack Lule

gp

THE GUILFORD PRESS
New York   London

070.4301
L955d
2001

44.00

© 2001 The Guilford Press
A Division of Guilford Publications, Inc.
72 Spring Street, New York, NY 10012
www.guilford.com

Printed in the United States of America

This book is printed on acid-free paper.

Last digit is print number: 9 8 7 6 5 4 3 2 1

Library of Congress Cataloging-in-Publication Data

Lule, Jack, 1954–
    Daily news, eternal stories : the mythological role of journalism / Jack Lule.
        p.   cm. — (The Guilford communication series)
    Includes bibliographical references and index.
    ISBN 1-57230-608-4 (hardcover) — ISBN 1-57230-606-8 (pbk.)
    1. Journalism and literature.   2. Journalism—Social aspects.
    3. Mythology in literature.   I. Title.   II. Series.

PN4759 .L85 2001
070.4'3'01—dc21

                                                                    00-049498

To Mom and Dad;
John, Nick, and Joe; and Gregorie

Contents

Acknowledgments

I am not the kind of person who quotes Shakespeare often. But I remember this scene well. Hamlet has entered morosely, head down, paper in hand—"the poor wretch comes reading." Polonious asks him, "What do you read, my lord?" Hamlet's answer: "Words, words, words."

I don't know why the line stays with me. But I do know that I've spent much of my time trying to understand the timeless and enduring power of what are really only . . . words.

Many words—spoken and written, said and unsaid—have shaped me and this book. Friends and colleagues at Temple University, the *Philadelphia Inquirer*, and the University of Georgia first helped forge these thoughts. At Georgia, Al Hester and Jim Carey, who fortuitously was visiting for a semester, offered early direction. Though we worked together later, I first met John Pauly at Georgia, and have always benefited from his thinking.

I never thought I would acknowledge academic organizations. But the Association for Education in Journalism and Mass Communication, especially the Qualitative Studies division, put me in touch with many good people, especially Richard Campbell and Ted Glasser. The International Communication Association and National Communication Association gave me forums to pursue these ideas. Most of the case studies were originally published, in different form, in organization journals, including *Journalism and Mass Communication Quarterly, Critical Studies in Mass Communication*, and the *Journal of Communication Inquiry*. Those publications also led to my connection with Peter Wissoker and the good people at The Guilford Press.

My home for the last 10 years, Lehigh University, has been remarkably encouraging. The administration, faculty, and staff have supported me personally and professionally. Students have become friends—and teachers.

Long before all this, however, friendships formed from kindergarten through college shaped me in deeper ways. My family, including the Lalor family, which I married into, keeps me rooted in the world outside the university. My mother and father, especially, provided me with models of happiness and hard work. My wife, Gregorie, and three sons, John, Nick, and Joe, became the reasons in a life that had many reasons. These words are for them.

Introduction

Front-Page Myths

The News Story

Story 1: Elders of the Choctaw tribe of North America told of a time when total darkness covered the earth. Tribal leaders searched endlessly for daylight. Finally, light was seen coming from the north. The tribe rejoiced, but a few wise families understood danger could be found in the light as well as in the dark. These families built themselves a vast raft while the rest of the tribe dismissed the possible danger as they waited for the light to arrive. Then a great roar resounded. The light was revealed to be the headwaters of a huge flood that carried off the tribe, except for the wise families on the raft, who survived to create the tribe anew.

Story 2: Chief priests of the Inca taught their people about the disaster of the Pachachama era. It was a time of corruption and barbarity. Only two humble shepherds and their families remained true to their gods. One day, the shepherds were warned by llamas that a great flood was approaching. The shepherds and their families sought refuge on the highest mountain. They watched as the world below was subsumed beneath roiling waters.

Story 3: Genesis tells the story of Noah and the ark. The Lord saw that wickedness and corruption was great on the earth. But Noah, a good man, found favor with the Lord. The Lord told Noah to build an ark and to fill the ark with living things. Then the floodgates of the sky were opened and rain fell upon the earth for 40 days and 40 nights. Only Noah, his family, and the animals in the ark survived.

Story 4: The *New York Times* told of the devastation of Central America in 1998. Immense poverty plagued many nations. Impoverished people erected poorly built homes dangerously close to rivers or precariously perched on mountain slopes—areas forsaken by the wealthier classes and corporations. The nations' leaders looked away. A hurricane came from the east. Rain fell for days. Floods and great mountains of mud swept away entire villages. Thousands of people died. The scene was a vision out of Dante, a deluge of biblical proportions, the *Times* reported. "It's a punishment from God," said an elderly Honduran carpenter on the front page of the *Times*.[1]

The four stories summarized above are, in many ways, the same story. Tales of the great flood have been told in countless societies. The tales have a remarkable similarity across centuries, continents, and cultures. They are stories of birth and renewal, death and apocalypse. They portray people who have done grave wrong, people who have sinned against their gods, people who have strayed from the right path. They depict gods or fabulous forces of nature that punish and purify. They culminate, always, with the same image: the devastating, humbling, cleansing waters that sweep away a people.[2]

The flood tale is just one of humankind's *eternal stories*, the age-old myths and ageless archetypes that have chastened, challenged, entertained, entranced, and instructed people since people first were. Those stories were told around prehistoric campfires, in ancient Greek dramas, in epic Roman poems, in Hindu verses, in native American myths—and are still told today, in the news.

Our society calls the flood stories told by ancient societies "myth." Our society calls the flood story told by the *New York Times* "news." This book is about connections between myth and news. It suggests that similarities between flood myths and news stories are one example of a much larger phenomenon. It suggests that ancient myths have taken modern form on the front page.

In fact, I will argue that archetypal myths can be found every day within national reports, international correspondence, sports columns, human interest features, editorials, and obituaries. I will suggest that any discussion of journalism that does not account for storytelling and myth will miss a vital part of the news. Because this argument might seem curious, I will identify seven master myths and, through case studies of the *New York Times*, I will attempt to demonstrate how these myths take shape in the stories of news.

THE NEWS STORY

The news *story*: We run the words together so often that their meaning gets lost. News comes to us as a *story*, the telling of a happening, the dictionary says, written or spoken with the intention of entertaining or informing. Journalists are part of a long storytelling tradition that includes fleet-footed messengers, minstrels, troubadours, carriers, couriers, criers, poets, chief priests, missionaries, rabbis, and medicine men. They draw their tales from a deep but nonetheless limited body of story forms and types that long ago proved their ability to hold audiences. The storytelling tradition is significant, probably even crucial—as we will see—to human lives and human societies.

We don't often think of news in this way. Our understanding of news is shaped by our times. We act as if news was invented for our modern era. We think of news as information for an information society. News, for us, is details and data about politics, products, crime, celebrities, technology, sports, and stocks. News gives us reports about candidates, companies, teams, movies, school boards, neighbors, and the weather.

Our understanding of news is also shaped by where we live. We act as if news was invented in the United States for U.S. democracy. We think of news as enshrined in the First Amendment, created by Jefferson, Madison, and the other framers of the Constitution for the proper instruction of an informed public. News, for us, is crucial to the smooth functioning of democratic life. Without journalism, there is no democracy, writers say. And without democracy, there is no journalism.[3]

Seen as enduring, abiding stories, news can be understood in different, though not incompatible, ways than now is common. Eternal stories do convey information. Eternal stories can be useful for democratic life. For example, the flood tale often assigns blame to a people. Was the *New*

York Times suggesting that Central American people and governments were being *punished* by the flood? An emphasis on stories helps us think about news in different ways. We ask different questions. We get different answers. We arrive at a new understanding of news.

That's good. We are in desperate need of a new understanding. No doubt: News—the reporter of world crises—is in crisis. Critical issues face journalism. The issues are many and actually have achieved a kind of urgency in our times. People express immense dissatisfaction, even cynical disgust, with the news. They detest the arrogant attitude of reporters and broadcasters, as well as the dispiriting negativity in much coverage. They deplore its sensationalism, tawdry gossip, and lack of fairness. They charge that serious subjects, such as education, health, and hunger, are ignored for tabloid drama, such as celebrity trials and the sex lives of politicians.[4]

Of great concern: The very role of news in our society is increasingly being called into question. Surveys show that people think the news media *hinder* rather than help the country. A majority of people say they do not trust the news media. Indeed, even journalists don't trust their fellow journalists. Surveys place journalists far down on the list of trustworthy professionals, a depth once associated with used car dealers, snake-oil salesmen, and pornographers—a far cry from poets and chief priests.[5]

Journalists and scholars have proved adept at identifying the news crisis but have been less adept at suggesting solutions. They try to refine campaign coverage. They swear to forsake sensationalism. They work to improve relationships with the public. Almost monthly, books and essays appear that seek to restore the role of news in democratic life.[6] These efforts are good and much needed. But they are destined to fall short unless they address the human hunger and need for stories.

Storytelling will never be in crisis (even if individual storytellers are) because storytelling is an essential part of what makes us human. We understand our lives and our world through story. Perhaps stories are so much a part of us because human life itself has the structure of story. Each of us has a central character. Each of us knows, better than we know anything, that life has a beginning, middle, and end. We *need* stories because we *are* stories.[7] Stories will stop, it is clear, only when humanity stops.

News? The outlook is not so deathless. In our time, we have embraced the notion of news as information. We deprecate storytelling. And now news has become less valuable, less central. News will survive if we truly recognize the significance and implications of storytelling. News will be in crisis to the extent that we ignore the roots of journalists as storytellers.

THE LANGUAGE OF NEWS

This book could pursue its goals in a number of ways. To study news as story and myth, many research methods could be employed. Interviews could be undertaken with reporters and editors. Surveys could be conducted of journalists and of the public. Scholars of myth could be asked to offer historical comparisons. Opinions of people in power could be sought. Scholars have employed all these approaches in studies of the news.

But, for me, the most direct way to study news is to analyze the articles themselves as illustrations of myth. My primary focus is the words, the language, of news. Ultimately, what is really at stake—for presidential candidates and protest groups, for princesses and terrorists, for heavyweight boxers and inner-city neighborhoods—is what the news *said*. The language of news is what matters. Readers—even journalists themselves—often don't have the time to really concentrate on the words of news, to fully understand *what is being said*, to probe all the possible meanings and implications of the language. Yet the news, as Hamlet told Polonious, is "words, words, words."

Where shall we find the words to study seven master myths in the news? The evidence for this perhaps unconventional argument will be taken from case studies of journalism. Case studies are a proven means of research in many fields. Rather than contemplate abstract principles of business, law, medicine, or journalism, research focuses on a particular incident, a case, that illustrates principles at work. Harvard Business School, for example, has long prided itself on teaching its subject through detailed case studies. In journalism, case studies often concentrate on news coverage of particular individuals or events—story by story, word by word.

Case studies can be a valuable tool. Sometimes issues are so large and so complex that abstract discussions founder on endless possibilities. For example, one could write—and I have—long and interminable treatises on news coverage of terrorism. The issues are large: What has been the news media's role in modern terrorism? How should the news report acts of terror? To what extent should the media cover victims of terrorism? The list of questions can go on. But the discussion of issues gets much more specific—and often much more worthwhile—by dramatically narrowing the focus and considering, for example, coverage of one incident by one newspaper: the terrorist killing of Leon Klinghoffer aboard the *Achille Lauro* cruise ship as reported by the *New York Times*. The issues remain the same but now the discussion is grounded, real, specific.

Cases might be drawn from various media, such as the *Wall Street Journal*, *USA Today*, the weekly news magazines, CNN, the evening news broadcasts, or even high-quality local news outlets. But more than any other U.S. news medium, the *New York Times* has become crucial reading for those interested in the news, national politics, and international affairs.

Understanding the *Times* has become a necessary part of understanding the times. Though not the biggest, it may well be the most significant newspaper in the world, "the last great newspaper."[8] Evidence of the *Times*'s influence is clear to the careful observer.[9] Studies confirm the influence of the *Times* in the White House, Congress, State Department, and Pentagon.[10] Some critics even charge that the *Times* serves as an instrument of the State Department and U.S. foreign policy. On the other hand, foreign dictators and prime ministers too strive to give information to—or hide information from—*Times* correspondents.[11]

People in the news media also acknowledge the importance of the *Times*. The newspaper has been awarded dozens of Pulitzer Prizes, far more than any other news organization. Rival newspaper editors and broadcast news directors make the *Times* required reading for their staffs so that the *Times* helps set an agenda for other news media.[12] Conversely, media commentators devote much time and space to critical examinations and heated excoriations of *Times* reporting. Right-wing commentator Rush Limbaugh and left-wing columnist Alexander Cockburn may share only one belief: The *Times* is dangerous to U.S. politics.

The stories are no more true—they may be more false—because of this relationship with privilege and power. But for critics and admirers, the *Times* has long been recognized as a key to understanding U.S. and world affairs.

THE STATE SCRIBE

For these reasons, the *Times* offers a premier site for case studies of news as myth. In many ways, the *Times* has the status and privilege accorded mythic storytellers of the past. For example, Homer was the leading scribe of his times. Elite and influential, he enjoyed access to the powerful and privileged. He produced knowing accounts of political intrigue, military conquest, personal struggles, and heroic triumphs. His words and works shaped the writings of others. The *Times* can be understood in similar terms. The *Times* can be seen as a State Scribe, as our society's privileged and preeminent storyteller. The *Times* is the connected insider, serene with position and power, flattering the mighty but also sometimes threatening them because of its status.

Such social, political, and economic success will prove to have large implications for *Times* journalism—and for my study of news as myth. Can the State Scribe and other national and local news media—now inextricably a part of the social, political, and economic system—really be expected to invest heavily in stories that confront this system? Can *Times* reporters and editors be expected to question a structure in which they and their newspaper have risen to the top ranks of power, prestige, and compensation? Can the State Scribe really write too far from the state?

These are the kinds of questions that arise from serious reflections on news as myth. Thankfully, we are not setting off over completely unexplored ground. Other writers too have considered news in mythic terms. Studies have come from an eclectic group of scholars, from French writer Roland Barthes to Canadian philosopher Marshall McLuhan.[13] Myth became an important concept in U.S. and British cultural studies during the 1970s and 1980s. Researchers adopted myth to study news coverage of politics, terrorism, assassinations, labor disputes, social movements, South African elections, presidential addresses, the *Titanic,* modern films, and other topics.[14] They argued that, consciously or unconsciously, journalists cast modern experience in terms of myth.

The research was highly suggestive. But the research mostly has stalled. Writers in the academy have moved on to other topics. Though the early work still makes bibliographical appearances, comparisons of news and myth are mostly cited and recited as research relics. With some notable exceptions, few recent works have appeared.[15] But I think we will find that myth lives on in the news, that news—perhaps now more than ever—needs to be understood as myth. The comparison at first might seem odd or strange. But I hope to show that the daily news brings eternal stories, that news is the true heir to humankind's myths, and that news—as myth—deserves critical attention and consideration.

Part I

The Story of the News Story

Chapter 1

Seven Master Myths
in the News

Eternal Stories

On a cool November night, a 59-year-old handyman, George Bird, was beaten to death a half-block from his West Philadelphia home. He was knocked down from behind by a gang of young males, then punched, kicked, and stomped to death. His killers, at least five young men, ran off with five dollars and five cans from a six-pack of beer.

I was working as a reporter in the city. Later, I was told the murder had been covered by the 11 P.M. newscasts, and had also appeared as a small blurb in one city paper, but I don't recall having seen it. I lived about 15 blocks from Bird.

It was only later when the man's neighborhood began to take action that I took notice. The police had arrested a number of suspects, but the neighbors were not satisfied. Some residents were linking the murder to a neighborhood corner store, which they claimed sold drugs to young people and which, in fact, had been the site of seven arrests for narcotics violations. The residents claimed they had tried to close the store through legal channels for more than a year. They were now urging that the neighborhood residents themselves close the store. Their plan was simple but potentially explosive: They would just stand outside the place and not let anyone, owners or customers, enter.

I began to follow the action closely. I interviewed grieving neighbors. And I covered the illegal picketing and sidewalk confrontations—which did eventually close the store without violence. The *Philadelphia Inquirer* wanted me to pull the whole story together as a cover piece for its Sunday magazine.

But I could not get started. I was stuck on the most basic question: Why was this a news story? From the beginning, the events seemed to have news value, yes. But writing about the events was a different story. What did those events mean to people, a lot of different people? The *Inquirer* Sunday circulation was then more than a million, scattered around the city itself and in its Pennsylvania and New Jersey suburbs.

I recognized early that readers did not need *information* about George Bird. His death had already been reported, even if superficially. Readers also did not need information about his neighbors. What the neighbors did had no real effect on the readers of the *Inquirer*. A straightforward summary news lead—"A West Philadelphia corner store, accused of being a site for drug sales, was closed recently by neighbors who demonstrated on the sidewalks outside"—seemed useless. Unless readers lived in West Philadelphia, why would they care?

I eventually came to believe that the events in West Philadelphia could not be presented in the form of news as *information*. The events were of interest as a *story*, a story with characters and a plot and a theme, a story that could be told to a city, a kind of public story. I proceeded very tentatively. Back then, I did not like this emphasis on story. For me, information always came first. The news story was simply the standard, implicit, assumed way in which information was reported. The story did not take precedence over the information. But this seemed different. Thus, the implicit became explicit, for better or maybe for worse. The somewhat melodramatic results crowned an introduction that the editors ran in large, bold-face type over the article:

> What these people did, and how they did it, may offer something for other neighborhoods, not that different, where others have surrendered their streets, their peace of mind and even the very dignity of their life in this city.
>
> Indeed these are times when being a neighbor is, more often than not,

a geographical circumstance; a good neighbor is defined by what he does not, and the best of neighbors is one who, in the name of privacy, leaves us alone. Perhaps this neighborhood has something to say, to a city of neighborhoods, about getting involved with the concerns of others and allowing others to get involved with our own concerns. Maybe then what will be surrendered is this false sense of privacy. Which is not privacy at all but fear.[1]

Despite my immodest hopes and the earnest overkill of my writing, the story was relatively successful. Editors and reporters had kind words. Radio shows discussed the story for a few days. The people in George Bird's neighborhood said I portrayed the events well. But I was left with a disquieting feeling. I had struggled mightily to understand the "news" in George Bird's death. And even after the story appeared, I wasn't sure I got it right.

Years later, I could see my problem. I did not have any model for understanding news. I did not understand the social role of news. I did not understand the relationship between news and other forms of storytelling. In truth, I did not understand much. And if someone had suggested to me that my struggle with the death of George Bird had led to a modern retelling of a classic myth, that I had reproduced a story told and retold in numerous cultures, that in my story George Bird became an archetypal figure, unheralded in life, sanctified in death, an innocent victim whose sacrifice and death brought a people together—I would have snorted with loud derision.

My questions about news continued. Despite years in the classroom and in the newsroom, I somehow had never thought too deeply about the role of news in society. I had vague ideas: News was congressional votes, stock prices, fires, election results, killings, sports scores, deaths, births. If pressed, I might have said news was information about recent events of interest to people. But I was already beginning to see the inadequacy of that conception. News wasn't always information, it wasn't always about recent events, and its interest to people was not always clear.

I was a drag in the newsroom. "What's the news in this?" I would ask other reporters. "Why are you writing the story this way?" I was a deadly presence at deadlines. Eventually, my questions took me out of the newsroom and back to the classroom.

My studies first led me through the usual theories of communication and models for news and society. But convinced that news was not simply information, certain that news was primarily a form of storytelling, I eventually wandered far outside the journalism curriculum. I was reading fairy tales and folktales, legends and myths. I studied histories of the penny press and morphologies of folktales. I followed studies of presidential press coverage with collections of Greek mythology.

Of course I continued to read the news. But strange connections began to suggest themselves to me. I was seeing myths on the front page. I found the Hero myth in stories of sports stars, politicians, and corporate executives, and in other "success stories." I saw the Victim myth narrated in accounts of senseless shootings, tragic auto accidents, and other misfortunes. I observed the Flood myth in stories of swollen rivers, storm-battered coasts, and other natural disasters. Each time I picked up the newspaper, I recognized stories told long ago. All the disparate readings seemed to come together. Many news articles seemed to have very little to do with information or politics or civic life. They seemed to have everything to do with storytelling and myth.

This book thus seriously considers a once outlandish proposition: Ancient myths are told in the news stories of today. In conceiving this book, I didn't want to offer a dry, academic treatise on news and myth. I've done those. I wanted to get the idea out of the classroom and into newsrooms and living rooms. Surely, some news readers will chortle at comparisons of local columnists to the great Greek Homer. Journalists themselves will disown comparisons of classical texts to front-page stories that end up wrapped around fish or placed at the bottom of bird cages. Chortling and disowning, however, may not be a bad start. At least a conversation will be under way.

MYTH DEFINED

At first, the connections between news and myth may appear to be the product of overly imaginative professors who have spent a bit too much time in ivory towers. In popular use, *myth* often means an untrue belief. Or myth can mean an ancient story about fantastic people and equally fantastic events. *News* usually means a report of factual events and real people. To compare news and myth may seem like comparing black and white or true and false. Indeed, myth is often contrasted with reality, as in the possible title: "The Ivory Tower: Myth or Reality?"

I will define myth in burdensome detail below. But I want to be very clear at the outset before I start to get unclear. For this discussion, myth is not unreality. Myth is not a false belief. Myth is not an untrue tale. To compare news and myth does *not* suggest that news regularly passes down untrue stories of doubtful origins. It does *not* suggest that news is inherently false, biased, slanted, spun, or spindled.

Instead, this book sees myth—and news—as telling the great stories of humankind for humankind. It follows the lead of scholars who see the stories of myth as a rich, essential part of social life. In this view, myth is defined, somewhat stiffly, as a sacred, societal story that draws from archetypal figures and forms to offer exemplary models for human life.

The definition emphasizes "archetypal figures and forms" and "exemplary models." I want to explain and explore further what they are. Archetypes are "original frameworks." In terms of myth, they are patterns, images, motifs, and characters, taken from and shaped by the shared experiences of human life, that have helped structure and shape stories across cultures and eras. They are fundamental figures and forces, such as heroes, floods, villains, plagues, patriarchs, pariahs, great mothers, and tricksters. Given life in narrative, they help create the fundamental, archetypal stories that are at the heart of human storytelling.

Myth enters the picture when these stories represent important social issues or ideals. Not all archetypal stories are myths, after all. Archetypes influence much storytelling, from the imaginative play of children to day dreams to romance novels to Shakespearean plays.[2] *Myths are archetypal stories that play crucial social roles.* We will see later that this seemingly simple definition can have numerous social, cultural, and political implications. It places myth near the center of social life. It sees the stories of myth as much more than interesting, entertaining, well-known tales. It sees myth—and perhaps news—as an important way a society expresses its prevailing ideals, ideologies, values, and beliefs. A hero can represent strength or bravery or compassion. A flood can represent the wrath of an angry god or the humbling power of nature. Used in this way, archetypal stories offer exemplary models. That is, they provide examples of good and evil, right and wrong, bravery and cowardice. They are models *of* social life and models *for* social life. Myth draws upon archetypal figures and forms to offer exemplary models that represent shared values, confirm core beliefs, deny other beliefs, and help people engage with, appreciate, and understand the complex joys and sorrows of human life.

Archetypes are often associated with the theories of psychologist Carl Jung.[3] Though Jung provided many insights, his psychological framework, such as the "collective unconscious," is not necessary for an appreciation of archetypes, models, and myth. In fact, a staggering number of theories and theoreticians have explored this terrain. I draw most frequently upon the work of Mircea Eliade, a philosopher and historian of religion. Eliade studied myth in hundreds of societies. A Romanian who lived for years in France and the United States and taught at the University of Chicago, he had a breadth of experience that allowed him to see links among myths from many different cultures and eras, including our own. Eliade's political positions, which seem to range from far right to far left, have troubled some. But he is a towering figure in modern studies of myth.

In his studies, Eliade found that archetypes and exemplary models were the key to myth. He stated that:

> religious life, and all the creations that spring from it, are dominated by what one may call "the tendency toward an archetype." However many and varied are the components that go to make up any religious creation (any divine form, rite, myth or cult) their expression tends constantly to revert to an archetype.[4]

Myth, Eliade argued, uses archetypes, such as heroes and floods, as models. He believed that myth is sacred, exemplary, and significant because it "supplies models for human behavior and, by that very fact, gives meaning and value to life."[5] For Eliade, myth is often about origins and beginnings. Myth provides models based on these creations. According to Eliade, "The foremost function of myth is to reveal the exemplary models for all human rites and all significant human activities—diet or marriage, work or education, art or wisdom."[6] We get married in ceremonies based on age-old, archetypal models. We get educated in institutions based on age-old, archetypal models. These models often are handed down in myth.

Eliade argued that myth uses archetypal models to guide all kinds of activities, including "the act of procreation, 'the cheering of a despondent heart, the feeble aged and the decrepit,' inspiring the composing of songs, going to war." Myth thus "provides a *model*, whenever there is a question of *doing something*."[7]

For example, parents often want to instruct children to be kind to others. They may find that such instruction goes well if they can tell stories of extraordinary and successful people—heroes—who engage in acts of kindness. In Babylonian society, parents may have called upon the story of Sargon the First. In ancient Greece, parents may have told tales of the great Ulysses. In my baseball-crazy house one day, I found myself calling upon news stories about Mark McGwire, who broke the home run record of Roger Maris, and then, instead of doing some self-celebratory, chest-pounding dance or strut, jumped into the stands and embraced the Maris family. Like Eliade, then, we will find that myth is best conceived as a sacred, social story that draws from archetypal figures to offer exemplary models for human life.

MYTH IS ESSENTIAL—EVEN TODAY

Seen in this way, myth is not ancient or old, fantastic or false. Myth is essential and always alive. The stories of myth are necessary to human lives and the societies they construct. Eliade argued that "certain aspects and functions of mythical thought are constituents of the human being."[8] He wrote:

> It seems unlikely that any society could completely dispense with myths, for, of what is essential in mythical behaviour—the exemplary pattern, the repetition, the break with profane duration and integration into primordial time—the first two at least are consubstantial with every human condition.[9]

Another great researcher of myth, Joseph Campbell, agreed. "No human society has yet been found," he said, "in which such mythological motifs have not been rehearsed in liturgies; interpreted by seers, poets, theologians, or philosophers; presented in art; magnified in song; and ecstatically experienced in life-empowering visions."[10] Jung too saw myth as essential. "Has mankind ever really got away from myths?" Jung asked. "One could almost say that if all the world's traditions were cut off at a single blow, the whole of mythology and the whole history of religion would start all over again with the next generation."[11] Every society needs stories that confront the ultimate issues of the human condition. Every society needs myths.

Modern societies, though, have modern conceits. They especially like to pretend that they are more "advanced" than other societies. They believe myth is for ancient or primitive societies. They believe they have no need of heroes, villains, exemplary figures, portrayals of good and evil. They believe they have replaced myth with scientific knowledge, technological advances, and objective reports of the real world. They fool themselves.

Eliade, as I noted, studied myths in hundreds of societies. He raised his gaze to the modern world—and saw classic myths all around him. He wrote that "an adequate analysis of the diffuse mythologies of the modern world would run into volumes: for myths and mythological images are to be found everywhere, laicised, degraded or disguised; one only needs to be able to recognise them."[12]

He called these disguised mythologies "the survivals and camouflages" of myth.[13] And he and other writers revealed the "survivals and camouflages" of modern myth in many places, from cars to suburbia to modern art—but especially in the mass media. Comic books, plays, mystery stories, radio shows, romance novels, movies, television programs, and other forms of mass media continually reaffirm the truth that modern society too needs to hear the stories of myth.[14]

MYTH IN THE NEWS

With this background, we can take an arresting step: We can recognize in news stories the siren song of myth. These news stories offer more than a retelling of common story forms. These news stories offer sacred, societal narratives with shared values and beliefs, with lessons and themes, and with exemplary models that instruct and inform. They are offering myths.

There is no need to overstate the case for mythic stories in the news. Many news stories have no relation to myth. Many news stories are derived from rudimentary story forms; professional conventions of the trade; or easy formulas for writing speeches, sports results, or fire stories: Official gives speech. Home team wins. Fire destroys building.[15] Even Sigmund Freud warned against the danger of overanalyzing, of seeing symbolic content in every object. "Sometimes a cigar is just a cigar," Freud is supposed to have said. Well, sometimes a fire story is just a fire story.

But sometimes, in describing some experience, in reporting some event, reporters and editors draw upon a fundamental story of earthly existence, a universal and shared story of humankind, and they use that story to instruct, inform, celebrate, or forewarn. Like myth tellers from every age, journalists can draw from the rich treasure trove of archetypal stories and make sense of the world.

Sometimes reporters do this consciously. They make explicit references to Icarus, infernos, Oedipus, or plagues. Sometimes they do this unconsciously. Their eyebrows raise when an observer points out ancient heroes, modern tricksters, and archetypal deluges on the front page. Consciously or unconsciously, however, journalists take their place among the generations of storytellers who tell and retell the myths of humankind.

MYTH: *ESPECIALLY* IN THE NEWS

I want to extend this argument still further. I have come to believe—and hope to show—that, more than any mass media, the daily news is the primary vehicle for myth in our time. News, of all things, has become the inheritor of humanity's essential stories. Other mass media possess the ability to tell myths. But the news, when studied carefully, will reveal numerous, numinous links to myth. Though ties between news and myth will be explored throughout this book, I can suggest some preliminary connections that first grabbed my attention.

News and Myth Repeat Stories

First, like myth, news offers the steady repetition of stories, the rhythmic recurrence of themes and events. Eliade noted that societies need to have their myths told again and again. Myths, he wrote, offer an "exemplar history which can be repeated (regularly or otherwise), and whose meaning and value lie in that very repetition."[16] In more difficult language, he wrote: "What is involved is not a commemoration of mythical events but a reiteration of them. The protagonists of the myth are made present, one becomes their contemporary."[17] Myth, he argued, thus invokes

> the prodigious, "sacred" time when something *new, strong*, and *significant* was manifested. To re-experience that time, to re-enact it as often as possible, to witness again the spectacle of the divine works, to meet with the Supernatural and relearn their creative lesson is the desire that runs like a pattern through all the ritual reiterations of myths.[18]

News too surely offers stories that are "new and strong and significant." Yet, like myths, news stories are not really new. More than any other mass medium, the news thrives on the ritual repetition of stories. The news tells us the same stories again and again. Like myth, news tells us not only what happened yesterday—but what has always happened. Flood and fire, disaster and triumph, crime and punishment, storm and drought, death and birth, victory and loss—daily, the news has always recounted and always will recount these stories.

For readers, this connection between news and myth may help explain the almost formulaic recurrence of stories in the news, the strange sensation the reader has of reading stories already read before, the odd ability to glance at a story and know precisely what it says. For journalists, myth may help explain the peculiar feeling of writing stories that already have been written, the dim awareness of telling stories that already have been told. "It's an old story," reporters will sometimes explain. It is.

News and Myth Tell "Real" Stories

News and myth also share an emphasis on "real" stories. News, of course, places special significance on "the real." Distinctions are drawn, and mostly observed, between fact and opinion, between nonfiction and fiction. Journalists are punished, sometimes even fired, for making up facts, for straying from "the real." Other mass media tell "stories." Sometimes they tell *real* stories. But only news places such a heavy emphasis on being "real." Only news is first and foremost supposed to be a report of real events.

Myth too, oddly enough, has privileged "the real." Modern societies equate myth with unreal stories. But for centuries, societies have always been careful to distinguish between the "real" stories of myth and the false stories of fiction, fable, and legend. Myth, after all, explains origins, promotes order, represents social beliefs and values. Myth needs to be seen as real and true. Eliade wrote that "myth tells only of that which *really* happened, which manifested itself completely." He added, "The myth is regarded as a sacred story, and hence a 'true history,' because it always deals with *realities*."[19] The philosopher Ernst Cassirer also argued that the images of myths "are not *known* as images. They are not regarded as symbols but as realities."[20]

News and Myth Are Public Stories

News and myth also share a tradition of *public* storytelling. Stories are everywhere. Some stories are told by one individual to another. Children, couples, friends, and neighbors share stories with one another. Other stories entertain an audience. Plays, radio shows, movies, and television programs offer stories to engage and entertain audiences. News and myth too address individuals and audiences. But, as we will see, they also offer stories that inform, instruct, and enlighten *a public.* They address people not just as individuals, not just as audiences, but as members of a social, civic group.

As Mitchell Stephens made clear in *The History of News,* news stories were told to publics even before the advent of writing.[21] Tribes gathered to hear news of battles and births from well-traveled messengers. Later, towns scheduled times and places for news criers. The Roman Empire distributed copies of the *acta*—proceedings and transactions—and posted them in cities. News was understood as information of *public* interest. Myth too has addressed its audience as members of a public. As social charter or sacred story, as account of origins or geography of the underworld, myth speaks to a society *as* a society. It is a social narrative, a civic text. Myth and news are, after all, stories of public interest.

News and Myth Use Fundamental Stories to Instruct and Inform

News and myth thus will be shown to bear the closest social similarities. They offer and repeat stories. They draw stories from real life. They tell stories that confront issues of social, public life. And they use these stories to instruct and inform. They are moral tales. They warn of disaster and disease, of degeneracy and decay. They tell tales of healing and comfort, of righteousness and reform. They offer dramas of order and disorder, of justice affirmed and justice denied. They present portrayals of heroes and villains, of models to emulate and outcasts to denigrate. News and myth speak to a public and offer stories that shape and maintain and exclude and deny important societal ideas and beliefs.

Again, there is no need to overstate the case. Other mass media at times repeat age-old stories. They draw from "the real," they address a public, they instruct and inform. But only news regularly and daily shows its allegiance to myth.

SEVEN MASTER MYTHS IN THE NEWS

Trying out my tentative ideas before colleagues, friends, reporters, or students, carried away by arguments and archetypes, I was sometimes taken aback when an engaged listener would nod, hand me a newspaper, and say: "Show me!" But of course. If news is myth, then we should be able to consistently find myths in the pages of the newspaper. We should be able to point to a set of recurring myths that normal, nonprofessorial readers can regularly identify and consider. Without such concrete examples, the discussion is doomed to remain safely suggestive and academically abstract.

The task, however, is more than a bit presumptuous. Identifying a set of regularly occurring myths in the news will necessarily be a subjective enterprise. No statistical package isolates and quantifies myths. The list offered here is thus impressionistic. It is derived from three decades of reading, writing, editing, and studying the news. It cannot be considered exhaustive or complete. In fact, as readers identify other myths in the news, the argument will be enhanced.

With that prologue, I will offer and outline seven recurring myths below. Other chapters will take up each of these myths in detail and show how they are given modern form in particular news stories. Despite the subjectivity of the list, I am quite confident that these seven myths appear frequently, if not daily, in the news. They are primordial stories that have guided human storytelling for ages. And they guide the news stories of today.

The Victim

The Victim lies at the heart of many myths.[22] Myth reconciles people to the tragic and seeming randomness of human existence. Plans, careers, dreams, and lives can be shattered in an instant by a lightning strike, a rare disease, a betrayal. Life must be lived in the presence of death. Myth confronts death. Myth turns death into sacrifice. Through stories of the sacrifice of the Victim, myth offers reconciliation and elevates life in the face of death. From the ancient Greeks to the early Christians, stories about victims are told and retold. News continues such stories. News tells stories of innocent victims killed in car accidents, airline crashes, hijackings, fires, robberies, drownings. The news, as myth, elevates and transforms death into sacrifice. A life story is gathered and told. A passing is marked and mourned.

The Scapegoat

Myth plays significant social roles. It defends the dominant social order. It upholds the "social charter" of a group. It protects and proclaims core values and central beliefs. Indeed, some scholars of myth, such as Joseph Campbell, suggest that a primary function of myth is to bend and shape individuals to the prevailing beliefs and ideals of a particular society.[23] The Scapegoat, who embodies evil and guilt, often helps fulfill that role. Myths of the Scapegoat tell in dramatic fashion what happens to those who challenge or ignore social beliefs. Myths of the Scapegoat ridicule and degrade. They vilify and shun. People—and societies—seem to need scapegoats to blame and abuse.[24] Native Americans, the Mayans, and African tribes all had myths and rituals in which scapegoats, embodying various evils, were isolated and expelled from the group. As myth, news too degrades and demeans those who are deemed to threaten the comfort of those in control or those who stray too far from accepted social practice. Political activists, religious sects, criminals, radicals, and many others can be cast as scapegoats in the news.

The Hero

The Hero is one of humankind's most pervasive myths. As many writers from Jung to Campbell have made clear, people always seem to need stories of heroes.[25] Heroes remind people that they can succeed, that they can achieve greatness. Hercules, Karna, Gilgamesh, Ulysses, Achilles, and Samson are just a few heroes whose exploits are celebrated in myth. Heroes also subtly offer limitations by telling stories of *who* can succeed and *how*. As myth, news stories too regularly celebrate the exploits of heroes. From sports stars to movies stars, astronauts to artists, presidents to prime ministers, the news tells stories of heroic men and women. The news produces and reproduces the timeless pattern: the humble birth, the early mark of greatness, the quest, the triumph, and the return. The news daily brings us stories of the Hero, stories that proclaim—but also help define—greatness.

The Good Mother

Myths of the Good Mother seem to derive in part from the first deep bonds that develop between an infant and an adult, usually though not always the mother. Myths of the mother can vary from those about the Terrible Mother, a figure of fear and hate, to those about the Madonna, an icon of virginal innocence. Myths are told of Gaea, Mary, Diana, Isis, Kali, and many others.[26] The *Good* Mother offers maternal comfort and protection.

She represents kindness and gentleness. She often is acclaimed above all others, blessed among women. The myth nurtures and nourishes and offers people a model of goodness in times when goodness may seem in short supply. The myth can also confine and restrict, presenting rigid models of maternity and gender. As myth, news often brings us stories of the Good Mother. The news tells stories of good and kind people who comfort and care for others. Sometimes these are politicians, celebrities, or stars who volunteer (perhaps quite publicly) for relief work or holiday charity. Other times the news finds models among us. In features and human interest stories, the news suggests that models of goodness may be all around us. It's a comforting, consoling—but possibly confining—portrayal.

The Trickster

One of the most fascinating and complex mythological figures found in hundreds of societies is the Trickster. The title can lead people to think that the Trickster is simply a sly and cunning figure. The myth is much more formidable. The myth of the Trickster often portrays a crude and stupid figure, half animal and half human. He is senseless and unreflective and brings on himself and others all manners of suffering. He is a subject of mockery, contempt, and ridicule. The Trickster myth has been well documented in Native American tribes and in cultures from Asia to Africa.[27] News too often tells stories of crude, contemptible people, governed by seemingly animal instincts, who bring ridicule and destruction on themselves. In some stories, stupid criminals, dumb and dangerous athletes, hapless hit men, classless and crude rich people are offered up in the news as objects for mockery and contempt. In many stories, the selection and portrayal of a person as Trickster can raise troubling questions for the news.

The Other World

Humans seem naturally intrigued by lands different from their own, by those outside their social group. They compare and contrast. They listen and learn. Myth expresses how a group of people in particular historical circumstances sees itself. And often myth does so through the Other World.[28] Sometimes the Other World is a garden of delight, an exotic land of foreign charm. Sometimes the Other World is portrayed as a threat, as a dark and disagreeable land that harbors an enemy. Myths of the Other

World offer neat, dramatic contrasts that affirm a group's way of life, position, or place. As myth, news too tells stories of the Other World, especially in news of foreign countries. Contrasts, implicit and explicit, are drawn between our way of life and the Other's. The cold war brought news of an archetypal enemy for decades. In our times, the news often tells stories of diabolical dictators, strange beliefs, and "primitive" nations in its depiction of the Other World. These stories can have large implications for how our country acts on the world stage.

The Flood

The Flood is a myth that occurs in cultures around the world.[29] It represents an even larger set of myths portraying calamities and disasters. These stories depict the destruction of a group of people by powerful forces, such as the gods or nature. The Flood often comes because people have strayed from the right path. Humans can be filled with hubris and pride. The disaster humbles and reminds humans of forces greater than themselves. As myth, news regularly brings stories of disaster from around the world. Sometimes the only international news of the day will concern earthquakes, floods, volcanic eruptions, or hurricanes. Disasters close to home receive even more attention. As myth, news reminds humans of the humbling power of nature. The humbling can be horrible and yet oddly comforting. People seem to embrace submission to the superior powers of nature. They seem to take comfort in the thought that forces lie outside the grip of human control. And as noted previously, the Flood myth can subtly accuse and impugn peoples and nations. Disaster comes to those who have done wrong.

MASTER MYTHS IN THE NEWS

These seven "master myths," I hope to show, can be fully demonstrated in the news. The evidence will be taken from case studies of the news itself. The sacrifice of the Victim will be shown in news of the terrorist killing of Leon Klinghoffer. The archetypal Good Mother, who nurtures and cares for the unfortunate, will be discovered in reporting on Mother Teresa. Myths of the Hero will be revealed in stories of home-run king Mark McGwire. The crude and cruel Trickster will be uncloaked in articles on boxer Mike Tyson.

I will also emphasize that these individual cases represent many others. The sacrifice of victims, exemplified in *New York Times* reporting on a terrorist victim, can be found in local and national reports of accidents, crashes, and other tragedies. The degrading of a Scapegoat, exemplified in news reporting about Black Panther Huey Newton, can be found in numerous reports of people outside the political mainstream. Myths appear daily in the news. Like a plodding, laconic lawyer, slowly building a case for a jury, I hope to submit exhibit after exhibit until the verdict is inescapable: Our modern society would like to think it has no need of myth, but the great stories of myth are told and retold daily in the news.

My emphasis obviously will be on *stories*. We will be drawing connections among stories that span human history. We will try to understand the constructive and corrosive implications of these stories. Though we use the words easily, we don't often consider the cultural and political significance of the *news story*. But it is through story, the subject of the next chapter, that news becomes myth.

Chapter 2

The Mythological Role of Journalism

Stories for Society

In 1980, musician Bruce Springsteen was atop the world of rock 'n' roll. He was no overnight success. For years, he and his band had bounced through the bars of New Jersey, New York, and Pennsylvania until a series of albums in the 1970s earned him true rock-star status. To solidify that status, Springsteen began a world tour designed to coincide with the release of his album *The River*. As a concluding note to the U.S. leg of the tour, Springsteen would return to Philadelphia, not far from his Jersey roots and a place where he had long been a major attraction. He sold out the Spectrum, an 18,000-seat arena, for three straight nights.

News stories often are formed from many complex sociological and political factors. This story was not.

An editor at the *Philadelphia Inquirer* called me to his desk.

He asked if I had ever heard of "Bruce Springboard." He said that.

I corrected him.

"Whatever," he said. "He sold out the Spectrum for three nights. No one does that. We should do a story," he said.

27

"Actually, there's more," I said. "He comes from Jersey. Philadelphia helped give him a start. The local bars hired him. The local radio stations played his songs."

"That's even better," the editor said. "A local angle. Do it."

From this in-depth, philosophical consultation, the news story first took shape. Other consultations followed. The story on Springsteen was to run on the cover of the Sunday magazine in the midst of his sold-out performances. I needed to interview him on the tour before he got to Philadelphia. I flew out to Denver and viewed one of his legendary four-hour shows that left him and his audiences exhausted and soaked with sweat. I found my way backstage. Springsteen was giving quick, helpful interviews to local reporters scrambling to meet deadlines after the long show. Within a half hour, I was the only reporter left.

Springsteen looked at me quizzically. Why was I still there? What did I need? He was being open and generous and wanted to help. I explained. I gave him an idea of "the story." I wanted to talk about Philadelphia and the early days and the triumphal homecoming at the end of the tour. He nodded enthusiastically. Now he too understood "the story." With Springsteen's assistance, my story on the "local hero" ran during his homecoming.[1]

GETTING THE STORY—FROM STORY

News stories do not arrive fully formed on the dusty computer screens of journalists, though journalists sometimes wish they would. Stories are shaped by many forces. The process begins early. Even as the story is assigned, such as with my Springsteen story, editors and reporters make sure they have a mutual understanding of "the story."

Other forces too then begin to act on the story. Colleagues may suggest their own interpretations. The publisher may have expectations, well known in the newsroom. Previous stories found in databases or clippings files sometimes exert an influence. Conventions and traditions guide research and writing, such as codes of objectivity and inverted pyramid leads, which place the last and most important part of the story first. Sources have their own views of the story. Questions asked by competing reporters are noted. The expectations of the audience and even long-term circulation goals can have an impact.

The single news story can be forged from some or all of these forces.

Stories, in this perspective, take shape before a word is written. For each event—a homecoming, congressional battle, fire, baseball game, or concert—editors, reporters, sources, and audiences try to understand "*what's the story.*"

Yet for each event, editors and writers do not have to conceive of brand-new stories. They do not have to tell stories never before written or read. "There are no new stories under the sun," an editor was fond of telling me. Stories already exist. Journalists approach events with stories already in mind. They employ common understandings. They borrow from shared narratives. They draw upon familiar story forms. They come to the news story *with* stories. Sometimes the story changes as the journalist gathers more information. But the story doesn't change into something completely new and never before seen. The story changes into . . . another story. What are these stories? We can call them *fundamental stories* or *eternal stories*. They shape the work of editors and reporters every day.

FUNDAMENTAL STORIES

As I noted, *storytelling* seems fundamental to human life. Every people have left evidence of storytelling. Humans make sense of the world and their time in it through story. Even more intriguing, *some stories* appear fundamental to human life. Startlingly similar folktales, legends, and myths can be found in different cultures and eras.

For example, the folklorist Stith Thompson worked for much of the twentieth century on a wonderfully convoluted, stunningly byzantine, multivolume index of folk literature. It began with a compilation of the world's myths. Year after year, Thompson collected, collated, and catalogued thousands of myths from across centuries and cultures. Thompson did not organize the myths by country, culture, or time period. Instead, he organized the myths by *theme.* In other words, Thompson looked across hundreds of years and thousands of cultures and found—the same stories.[2]

How does that happen? Some anthropologists are convinced that direct connections among these stories can be traced. They argue that neighboring societies borrowed ideas, custom, tools, recipes, and stories from one another. They point out that great cultural centers of the ancient world were often great trading centers. Stories, they say, were traded too. Stories became part of an overall process of cultural diffusion.[3]

Early psychiatrists and psychologists also observed fundamental stories. However, they advanced a different reason for their widespread oc-currence. Sigmund Freud and Carl Jung, in particular, noted similarities between stories, folktales, myths—and dreams. They asked: How could a seven-year-old girl, an unlikely candidate for diffusion, have dreams with plots and symbols taken from ancient stories? Jung was especially in-trigued. He was, for a while, Freud's foremost student and colleague. When he broke with Freud, one of his primary interests became the study of the "collective unconscious." Jung pointed out that humans were born with bodily organs that had long evolutionary histories. He believed that the human mind too had its own long evolutionary history. This collective unconscious, Jung said, contains powerful, primordial patterns—arche-types—that lead to the creation of universal symbols, characters, motifs, stories, and myths.[4]

Definitive answers about fundamental stories are not likely to be es-tablished by the anthropologists or the psychologists. Perhaps the best an-swer combines the two. Some stories may be fundamental to humans, and are probably based on the shared experiences of being human. People are born into an almost infinite variety of circumstances. Yet we all still share some experiences. We share birth, the entry into the world as small and helpless babies. We share infancy and have hazy, half-remembered im-ages from childhood. We typically have families or relationships with mother figures and father figures. We share feelings of fear, love, hate, an-ger, compassion, jealousy, and joy. We share bodily, natural sensations of hunger, thirst, and sexual desire. We need to sleep. We need to move. We produce and understand, tell and retell, stories based on these experiences. And these stories sometimes have been, and will be, shared and spread.

These fundamental stories can be understood as "archetypes." As we noted, the word can be used in its original, broader meaning without the Jungian theory. *Archetypes* are original figures or frameworks, powerful patterns, models to imitate and adapt. The fundamental stories of human-kind are archetypal stories. They are patterns and models, born from hu-man experience, to imitate and adapt. The Flood that destroys and cleanses human society is an archetypal story adapted by hundreds of cultures. The Trickster, that half-animal, half-human figure lurching through society, is an archetypal story. The Hero is an archetypal story.

Once the fundamental stories are in place, they cast their influence on storytelling. Stories shape storytelling. As writers and societies attempt to understand and express their experience of the world, they consciously and unconsciously draw upon the special stories, the commonly shared, universally understood stock of archetypal stories. Writers find these stories within themselves and within their societies. A person may never have been told or taught the story of the Flood. But the person has experiences: with the unpredictable forces of nature, or with driving rain and wild winds, or with sensations of being submerged in a bath, pool, lake, or ocean. And the person can be led by those experiences to understand, and perhaps to tell, the story of the Flood. Born from universally understood archetypal stories, the particular telling of these tales can have great emotional impact on listeners in every time—including today.

NEWS: THE LATEST ECHO

News stories can be understood as the modern recurrence of these stories. Society after society has attested to the enduring power of the archetypal stories. Our society is no different. News is the latest echo of stories uttered long ago. Journalists, as storytellers, cannot help but call upon the fundamental stories.

Other writers have noted fundamental stories in the news. The historian Robert Darnton spent some formative years reporting for the *New York Times*. Only after his days in the newsroom did he appreciate the power of story. He left journalism and had undertaken research in early popular culture. He noted with wonder the "striking resemblance" between modern news stories and early English chapbooks, broadside ballads, and other historical stories. He noted that, "all purvey the same motifs, which also appear in children's literature and probably derive from ancient oral traditions." He continued:

> Of course we did not suspect that cultural determinants were shaping the way we wrote about crimes in Newark, but we did not sit down at our typewriters with our minds a *tabula rasa*. Because of our tendency to see immediate events rather than long-term processes, we were blind to the archaic element in journalism. But our very conception of "news" resulted from ancient ways of telling "stories."[5]

Darnton, somewhat defensively, rejected the idea that "primitive" myth might be at work. "Of course it would be absurd to suggest that newsmen's fantasies are haunted by primitive myths of the sort imagined by Jung and Lévi-Strauss," he said. But, absurdly enough, Darnton seemed to suggest precisely that. "Big stores develop in special patterns and have an archaic flavor," he said, "as if they were metamorphoses of *Ur*-stories that have been lost in the depths of time."[6]

Thoughtful scholars of mass media also have perceived the influence of story on news. David Eason has emphasized the distinction between events and "the possible forms which the story of that event may take within culturally provided categories."[7] S. Elizabeth Bird and Robert W. Dardenne suggest that "six crime reporters who leave the courtroom with the same story may be writing about reality, but their 'story' emerges as much from the stories that have gone before as from the facts of the case in court."[8] Michael Schudson also placed special emphasis on stories in news. Writing about conventions of twentieth-century U.S. journalism, he said:

> I will suggest that the power of the media lies not only (and not even primarily) in its power to declare things to be true, but in its power to provide the forms in which the declarations appear. News in a newspaper or on television has a relationship to the "real world," not only in content but in form; that is, in the way the world is incorporated into unquestioned and unnoticed conventions of narration, and then transfigured, no longer a subject for discussion but a premise of any conversation at all.[9]

Other scholars have gone further and identified specific motifs and plots that recur in the news. Herbert Gans identified "enduring values" that shape news stories, such as altruistic democracy, responsible capitalism, small-town pastoralism, and individualism.[10] Richard Campbell argued that one large, Middle American myth of individualism guided the television newsmagazine *60 Minutes* each week.[11] My identification of seven master myths in the news attempts to add to this tradition.

For now, I think it is important to understand that "the story" is an underappreciated yet essential part of creating and understanding the news. Stories make news easier. Stories make news *possible*. Without stories, editors, reporters, and their sources might find it impossible to recognize news amid thousands of daily events. Without stories, reporters might find it difficult to produce news under intense deadlines and competitive pressures. Without stories, editors might find it hard to prioritize and select items for the front page—the "top story" of the day.

The influence of the story does not stop there. Stories make news possible for readers and viewers. Individual readers approach the story armed with stories. Readers decide for themselves "what's the story." And readers bring their own personalities, prejudices, and predilections to the story. The reader can nod and smile at the writer's wisdom. The reader can curse and reject the writer's version of events. The reader can understand the story in precisely the opposite way that the writer intended. Or the reader can completely ignore the entire thing and decide there is no story here. On city buses, I've watched readers pull out the part of the newspaper that contained my story on the section's front page—and discard the entire section to the dirty, puddle-strewn floor of the bus. The story was not even worth carrying around. Stories thus, in some way, come first and last. Story has continually shaped the story.

STORIES FOR SOCIETY: NEWS BECOMES MYTH

Every telling of the fundamental stories does not result in myth, however. Stories have their own status. Some stories are important just for individuals or for small groups. If one of my children runs into the house crying, I will ask what happened to him. And my child will put events into a story of the tragedy. That story is important to me and to my child but probably not terribly important to society at large. Other stories, though, are meaningful and consequential for many people.

Just as storytelling seems fundamental to *human* life, storytelling seems fundamental to *social* life. Humans need stories—and their societies need stories. Through stories, a group of people define themselves. They tell stories of their origins. They tell stories of what they believe and what they do not believe. They tell stories of evildoers who threaten the group. They tell stories that ostracize some and celebrate others. They draw from the archetypal stories to pass onto their children and their children's children their ways of life, love, worship, and work. These societal stories attain sacred status. They become accepted and their value becomes assumed. They narrate and illustrate shared beliefs, values, and ideals. They are myths.

And here we can achieve some understanding of how news becomes myth. We have seen that fundamental stories shape storytelling, that editors, reporters, sources, and readers consciously and unconsciously draw upon the universally understood stock of archetypal stories. When these fundamental stories become *public*, when these stories are told to a people, when these stories are narrated on a societal level to render exemplary models and represent shared social values and beliefs, news becomes myth.

NEWS, MYTH, AND SOCIETY

Comparisons of news and myth are thus important not for *literary* implications but for *social* implications. The crucial relationship between a society and its myths is made clear in a famous quotation from Bronislaw Malinowski. An anthropologist, Malinowski approached myth differently from Eliade and others I have considered. He emphasized the functions of myth in "primitive" cultures. He believed myth was primarily a "social charter" for such societies. Many scholars have found fault with Malinowski's politics. But they still love the breadth of this quotation, which attempts to make plain the importance of myth for humanity. Malinowski wrote:

> Studied alive, myth, as we shall see, is not symbolic, but a direct expression of its subject matter; it is not an explanation in satisfaction of a scientific interest, but a narrative resurrection of a primeval reality, told in satisfaction of deep religious wants, moral cravings, social submissions, even practical requirements. Myth fulfills in primitive culture an indispensable function: it expresses, enhances, and codifies belief; it safeguards and enforces morality; it vouches for the efficiency of ritual and contains practical rules for the guidance of man. Myth is thus a vital ingredient of human civilization; it is not an idle tale, but a hardworked active force; it is not an intellectual explanation or an artistic imagery, but a pragmatic charter of primitive faith and moral wisdom.[12]

It may seem strange, but I can examine each affirmation from that classic conception of myth and see news in every one. Those affirmations, for me, point to the large social possibilities and responsibilities that open up from serious consideration of news as myth. To suggest that news is myth calls for more than an appreciation of reoccurring stories. Myth has been a "vital ingredient of human civilization." Myth has been a "hardworked active force." How and why does that force get used? In concrete terms: Which myths get told and why? This is not a small question. It takes us directly into the tangle of news, ideology, rules, politics, charters, order, and society.

Since the early 1900s, journalists and scholars have striven to understand the societal role of U.S. news. One clear finding has emerged: No one clear finding will emerge. The role of news has proved to be an especially subtle, complex subject. Yet to advance a discussion of news as myth for our society, myth will need to find a place. At least six models, some conflicting, for exploring the role of news in U.S. society have been identified.

1. *To watch over government.* The news serves as a "necessary guardian," a watchdog, over government. Building upon the thoughts of Madison and Jefferson, writers have argued that an essential role of news in society is to keep a watchful eye on those in power. As a "fourth estate" alongside the three branches of government, the press makes sure the interests of the people are safeguarded.

2. *To manufacture consent.* In contradicting the previous model, other writers have argued that the news has served to maintain established ideology. Noam Chomsky and Edward Herman, for example, suggest that U.S. news, rather than observing government and informing the public, is used by the government for manufacturing consent of the public.[13]

3. *To set the public agenda.* For other writers, a primary role of news is to serve as a "gatekeeper" for events, issues, and ideas. Building on gate-keeping insights, other researchers have examined the agenda-setting role of news, its ability to order and organize social issues for the public.[14] The news, they say, might not be able to tell people what to think but it does tell people what to think *about.*

4. *To inform public opinion.* The news serves mostly to inform and educate the public, other writers suggest, so that citizens can make responsible decisions. More strongly, many writers are convinced that mass communication, including the news, has powerful *effects* on people.[15] These models declare that news stories transmit attitudes, opinions, or information to people.

5. *To foster public conversation.* John Dewey argued that public opinion cannot be conceived in terms of correct or incorrect ideas, right or wrong information.[16] He and others saw public opinion as an ongoing conversation of issues and concerns. And they saw news not as information, correct or incorrect, but as part of the conversation and sometimes as a site for the conversation.[17]

6. *To enact social dramas.* None of the previous models for news— even taken together—grasp fully my own experiences of writing and reading the news *story*. None capture the possibilities of news as myth. They

see news primarily involved with political beliefs, opinions, and decisions. The models shed little light on nonpolitical (yet socially significant) stories about floods and fires, saints and princesses, home-run heroes and murdered neighbors—the stuff that makes up most news.

Kenneth Burke has advanced a different, especially spacious approach. Burke was a wide-ranging thinker writing in the middle of the twentieth century, a literary critic and social commentator, a maddening writer of genius who seemed to see connections between all kinds of stories, dramas, and social life.[18] His model starts from basic premises. First, "society" is an ambiguous, imprecise term. Instead, one can talk more accurately about "social order," that is, how a particular society is organized and kept together. *Social order* is the specific structure of all the things that make up a society: rights, authority, power, hierarchy, status, ways of worship, labor, property relations, means of production, means of having fun. Social order provides a way to talk about a particular society at a particular time.

Though the model emphasizes *order*, social order is not some kind of fixed, unmoving system. Social order is literally acted out each day in "social dramas," large and small. Social dramas are the large and small acts and interactions that make up life. They are written and spoken, official and unofficial, formal and informal—from congressional hearings to parent–teacher conferences. Social dramas give life to social order each day.

News stories fit easily in the model.[19] Life and social order are understood in terms of drama. And news—a kind of daily dramatist—enlarges, extends, and enhances these dramas. In this model, a primary role of news is to enact social dramas that *sustain social order.*

WHICH MYTHS GET TOLD AND WHY

To sum up the matter perhaps too simply: Reporters, editors, sources, and readers draw from a large, though limited, range of fundamental stories to portray and understand events. Which stories ultimately get chosen? Which myths get told in the news and why? *News most often tells stories that support and sustain the current state of things.*

This model does not conceive of news, myth, and social order in narrow political terms. With each passing election, news coverage doesn't support social order by simply shifting support to whatever political party is in power. Social order is more deeply entrenched. For example, U.S.

news stories may aggressively criticize abusive judges. But stories will seldom question the judicial system. Likewise, news stories will take differing perspectives on the particular economic policies of either party. But the stories will accept, even assume, the free market system.

There's room for change, though, in the model of social drama. Social order is dynamic and flexible, acted out each day. The world is not fixed in place. Social dramas sometimes can be used to challenge and even change social order. Great social dramas have brought change to women's rights, civil rights, and other parts of society. And news has participated in these dramas. News can sometimes foster fundamental change. But not often.

The links between news, myth, and society thus will make for intriguing study. But, again, I don't want to overreach. I don't want to completely negate other, traditional models for thinking about news. News has many political, social, cultural, and economic roles. But in carrying out these roles, *news tells stories*. And those stories, drawing from myth, often shape and maintain social order.

I want foremost to keep an appreciative sense of wonder for this perhaps jarring juxtaposition of daily news and timeless stories. I want to explore the ways in which myth takes modern form in a news story. I want to understand some of the rich political, cultural, and social implications of news as myth. I want to comprehend some of the troubling consequences. It is humbling to consider that some stories have engaged and enthralled humans throughout existence, that people of the twenty-first century share stories of the human experience with people of the first century. I want finally to appreciate that in our modern, high-tech, online world, we find stories and practices that date back to tribal times.

In *The Educated Imagination*, the literary critic Northrop Frye, drawing upon Aristotle, tried to make clear the role of the poet in society. He contrasted the poet with the historian. He wrote:

> The historian makes specific and particular statements, such as: "The battle of Hastings was fought in 1066." Consequently he's judged by the truth or falsehood of what he says—either there was such a battle or there wasn't, and if there was he's got the date either right or wrong. But the poet, Aristotle says, never makes any real statements at all, certainly no particular or specific ones. The poet's job is not to tell you what happened, but what happens: not what did take place, but the kind of thing that always does take place.[20]

The thought may be a bit inflated. But I think the journalist, through myth, can ultimately fulfill the social role of historian and poet. The journalist, at best, can get the date right *and* the meaning right. The journalist, at best, can tell you not only what happened but what always happens, what took place and what always does takes place.

The remainder of our project lies ahead: The following chapters use the *New York Times* to examine case studies of news as myth. Through studies of the *Times*—story by story, word by word—I hope to show how the news tells and retells seven master myths: the Victim, the Scapegoat, the Hero, the Good Mother, the Trickster, the Other World, and the Flood. And I hope to show the social import of these news stories as myths. The next chapter takes up *Times* stories that recount one of humankind's most consequential myths: the Victim.

Part II

Case Studies of
News as Myth

Chapter 3

The Victim

Leon Klinghoffer and News of Tragedy

On October 7, 1985, on the Mediterranean Sea near Port Said, Egypt, four men hijacked the *Achille Lauro,* an Italian cruise ship, with 400 passengers and crew members aboard. The hijackers, identifying themselves as members of the Palestine Liberation Front, demanded the release of Palestinians imprisoned in several countries. They threatened to kill hostages if their demands were not met.

After two days of negotiations, the hijackers surrendered to Egyptian authorities. Soon after, Italian officials announced that a U.S. tourist, Leon Klinghoffer, sixty-nine years old and confined to a wheelchair, had been shot and his body thrown overboard during the hijacking. U.S. officials demanded that the hijackers be prosecuted for murder. On October 11, U.S. jets intercepted an Egyptian plane bound for Tunisia with the hijackers. The plane was forced to land at a NATO base in Italy, where the hijackers were arrested and charged with murder.

On October 14, a body washed ashore near the Syrian port of Tartus. On October 21, Leon Klinghoffer was buried in New Jersey.

VICTIMS AND WIDOWS IN THE NEWS

For two weeks, the *Achille Lauro* hijacking dominated U.S. news. It was a compelling news story. Four hundred people were held hostage. Powerful political actors engaged in international negotiations. The story bristled with gripping moves, from the daring hijacking itself, to the brutal murder, to the midair interception of a foreign jet.

Yet perhaps the story's most dominant image was the face of Marilyn Klinghoffer, the widow of the victim, who received incredible international attention. She, rather than her husband, became the central story. Reporters and camera crews dogged her as she grieved. They awaited her phone calls from Egypt to her daughters in New York. They thronged about her as she left the *Achille Lauro*, forcing her back onto the ship where her husband had been murdered. They crowded the sidewalk outside her Manhattan apartment. Her tears and faltering steps were recorded and replayed as she met her husband's body at Kennedy Airport. Her grief was broadcast worldwide on the day she buried him.

Years after the superabundant news coverage, as memories of Leon and Marilyn Klinghoffer fade, stories and images of victims and widows continue to appear in the news. Not only martyrs to terrorism, victims can be found in coverage of airline crashes, hurricanes, bank robberies, bus crashes, floods, and other tragedies. Not only widows, the grief-stricken can be seen in stories of husbands, partners, children, relatives, friends, or coworkers.

Wherever tragedy takes its toll, news stories seem to select and sanctify those who have been sacrificed and those who have been left behind. Why does the news do this? Why such terror and tragedy in the stories of victims and widows?

Some practical concerns of daily news can be acknowledged. Relatives are often good sources for reporters. They have information about victims and often have had privileged contact with authorities. Relatives also are convenient: They are available to reporters, while victims and authorities are not. Relatives can "flesh out" a story, giving human substance to complex, far-off affairs.

Yet such pragmatic considerations fail to explain the intensity and power of such news coverage. To suggest that Marilyn Klinghoffer was a good information source or supplied a feature angle does no justice to the drama. And it does not help us understand the enduring, prominent role given to images of victims and widows. News people responded to the terrorist killing of Leon Klinghoffer with searching, gripping stories about his widow. Stories with powerful symbolic content attempted to explain and give meaning to complex, compelling events.

On one level then, study of *Times* reporting of the Klinghoffers may provide some understanding of the complex relationship among terrorism, news, and public policy.[1] But in that reporting, the study explores a deeper issue: the intense, sometimes saturation coverage that news gives to victims, to people who have been thrust into the news by tragedy.

Journalists and scholars—and victims themselves—have recently begun to consider and critique news coverage of victims. When they do, however, they usually concentrate on issues of privacy. Though invasion of privacy is an important issue, this chapter takes a different look at news and victims. Specifically, this chapter studies the ways in which news stories confront nothing less than the fate of human existence: death. My study shows that news reports used dramatic details of the death of a terrorist victim to develop a compelling myth: the sacrifice of the Victim. This study will also explore an intriguing aspect of news coverage of victims. The news often seems to elevate victims and their loved ones into . . . heroes. It's an odd portrayal. Victims are sanctified and exalted in the stories of news. Myth may help us understand why.

THE VICTIM

Societies have always told myths of victims. These myths play a crucial role. They attempt to reconcile people to the vagaries of human existence—to cruel fate, to bizarre happenstance, to death itself. From the ancient Greeks to the early Christians to the modern United States, stories about victims are told and retold. The myths are told, Eliade wrote, "because they are better than any empirical or rational means of revealing human destiny."[2]

Myth reconciles, comforts, consoles. Myth tries to explain life in the face of death, death in the face of life. It "discloses on the one hand, the fundamental *unity* of life and death," Eliade wrote, "and on the other, the hopes man draws, with good reason, from that fundamental unity, for his own life after death."[3]

In "Ancient Myths and Modern Man," Joseph Henderson, who writes in the tradition of psychologist Carl Jung, notes the blend of victims and heroes. He notes: "Over and over again one hears a tale describing a hero's miraculous but humble birth," his proof of great strength, his battle with evil, "and his fall through betrayal or a 'heroic' sacrifice that ends in his death."[4] Eliade found in such myths "man's eternal longing to find a positive meaning in death, to accept death as a transition rite to a higher mode of being."[5]

Reports of Leon Klinghoffer and his widow—herself a victim—thus may represent much more than U.S. news coverage of terrorist victims. In a broader sense, news coverage of victims can reveal the mythic role of news as it confronts what Freud called "the battle of the giants": life and death.

A PRELIMINARY PICTURE: FRONT-PAGE, LOCAL NEWS

Before making an in-depth analysis, it is often helpful to get an overall picture of coverage—simply to count the number of stories and organize them by dominant themes. My first step thus was a preliminary study of all *Times* reports about the *Achille Lauro* hijacking from October 8 to 22, 1985. The hijacking took place over just two of these days. Indeed, by the time the *Times* was able to publish word of the hijacking, it was almost over. But the story commanded coverage for two weeks because of the subsequent U.S. interception of the jet bearing the hijackers and the discovery and burial of Leon Klinghoffer's body.

Following sections offer an in-depth look at this coverage. But here I can point out some intriguing preliminary findings: First, *Times* coverage of the family was early and consistent. The *Times* turned out to be especially important for study of the *Achille Lauro* hijacking. It was the "hometown" newspaper of the Klinghoffers, who lived on East 10th Street in Manhattan. The local angle provided the *Times* with motivation, opportunity, and justification for covering the victim and his family. For example, the day *before* anyone off the cruise ship knew of the murder, a photo of the Klinghoffers appeared on the *Times* front page. Editors just happened to select the Klinghoffers, and to use a photo supplied by the family, to dramatize a story about the many New Yorkers held hostage on the *Achille Lauro*. After news of the murder, despite the many national and international actors who might have been written about, the Klinghoffers continued to receive steady coverage. In the first week of the hijacking, the *Times* published 10 stories about the Klinghoffers.

Another finding: The stories were given great prominence. In the first week, the *Times* devoted five front-page stories to the family. Mrs. Klinghoffer's photograph appeared on the front page of the *Times* three times, more than any other person that week. On October 13, when the widow returned to the United States, four stories were devoted to her and her family. Of the many personalities involved, including the hijackers, terrorists, President Reagan, even Leon Klinghoffer himself, the victim's widow received the most prominent coverage.

Preliminary analysis of the second week showed that reports on the family dropped off sharply. Mrs. Klinghoffer secluded herself in her apartment. With the remaining hostages freed and the hijackers in custody, the *Achille Lauro* story was losing its news value.

But when Leon Klinghoffer's body washed ashore in Syria and was returned to the United States, Mrs. Klinghoffer came out of seclusion to receive her husband's body at the airport—and she immediately appeared again in a front-page story and photograph. On the following day, accompanied by New York City's mayor and New York's governor and two U.S. senators, the widow buried her husband—and a photograph and report recorded her slumped shoulders and wavering steps.

General themes of the *Times* reports can also be noted before a closer analysis. The initial anxiety of the daughters provided the theme for the first stories. Anxiety gave way to horror and grief the following day when the daughters received word of the killing. When Mrs. Klinghoffer returned to the United States, story themes centered around her mourning and the eulogizing of her husband. A full chain of sorrow—from anxiety to mourning—was thus reported and portrayed by the *Times*.

This kind of preliminary analysis is helpful to get a general picture of coverage. But to understand the more subtle meanings offered by *Times* reports, individual accounts need to be considered in depth. The language of the *Times* needs to be examined in detail. The following sections thus analyze reports about the victim and his widow and consider those reports from the perspective of myth.

SCENES OF HORROR AND IRONY

News of the *Achille Lauro* hijacking broke on October 8. On October 9, while the drama was still unfolding, the first stories about the Klinghoffers appeared in the *Times*—and the family was placed on the front page. A story by correspondent Sara Rimer was headlined "To Hostage Families, Waiting Back Home Is Also a Nightmare."[6] The report described the two daughters, Lisa and Ilsa, as they "waited for news at their parents' apartment in Greenwich Village."

At this point, oddly, the *scene* was more important to the *Times* than the family. The Klinghoffers were just two of 400 hostages, many of them New Yorkers. The *Times* was simply following good, standard journalistic practice: focusing on individuals to represent what was happening to many people, and developing a local, hometown angle. The Klinghoffer home was selected by the *Times* as a local setting to represent the anxiety and consternation of hostage relatives. In retrospect, the choice of scenes was truly remarkable. Events unfolded, of course, to charge this choice of scene with drama and irony.

The *Times* reported that the daughters had waited in the apartment, with relatives of other hostages, "all through the night Monday and all day Tuesday," while friends had "gathered around the television and answered the constantly ringing telephone." The daughters were particularly worried about their father, who had suffered a stroke several years earlier. They "tried to comfort each other" with family jokes: "I can just picture Mommy telling Leon, 'Wait till we get back, they're not going to believe this,'" Ilsa told Lisa. The report ended with a hopeful quote and a last look at the scene:

> At the Klinghoffers' apartment, the telephone rang again and again as children of the members of the group bolstered each other.
>
> Ilsa's fiance, 33-year-old Paul Dworin, stayed close throughout the day. "They're OK," he said. "They're OK I just know it."[7]

"CHEERS, THEN HEARTBREAK"

The next day's newspaper reported the death of Leon Klinghoffer. A front-page story datelined from the Mediterranean described the surrender of the hijackers and the discovery of the killing. The Klinghoffer family was the exclusive focus of a second front-page story, "Cheers, Then Heartbreak at Apartment on 10th Street."[8] Agonizing and highly dramatic, the account detailed how the family learned of the murder.

The original purpose of the reporter was again simply to pursue a local scene. Presumably, after being used to represent the anxiety of hostage relatives, the Klinghoffer family was going to illustrate their joy and relief. The world—and the family—had not yet learned of Klinghoffer's death.

Sara Rimer thus recorded a scene of anticipation and celebration in the parents' apartment. Daughters, friends, and relatives were lifting champagne glasses, "about to toast their parents' deliverance." Then the phone rang and Ilsa's fiancé answered it.

As if through a zoom lens, focus on the wide scene sharpened to become, instead, a tight close-up on the daughters. Lisa and Ilsa, the report noted, "did not at first notice how quiet he became." He put the phone down. He told the women their father might be dead. "Their screams, heartbreaking after so much jubilation, filled the living room where their friends and relatives looked at each other in horror and disbelief."

The story was purposefully and skillfully manipulated. It appeared to be only a reprise of the traditional journalistic form: the dramatization of international events by a local scene. But then the daughters—and the readers—participated in a terrible irony.

The dramatic skill of the reporter and editors must be noted, as well as the good news sense or "good fortune" that placed Sara Rimer in the apartment. It is quite remarkable that the Klinghoffer home had been chosen as a dramatic instrument by the *Times before* the death of the father. The hometown angle became, literally overnight, an international story of the victim and widow.

ENTER THE WIDOW

The next day, October 11, the international news spotlight shone brightly on the Klinghoffers. No longer just one of many awaiting the resolution of the *Achille Lauro* hijacking, the grief-stricken family had been catapulted into global prominence. Almost immediately, the spotlight found the widow. For the remainder of *Times* reporting, coverage was dominated by a clear and constant focus on Marilyn Klinghoffer.

On the front page of October 11, the process began: A photograph from Port Said, Egypt, showed Marilyn Klinghoffer being escorted from the *Achille Lauro*. She was a picture of tragedy. Her chin rested on her chest. Her eyes were sunk in dark circles. Her hair was wind-blown and wild. In contrast to her mournful expression, she wore a bright, floral, low-necked dress, a sad reminder of her holiday cruise.

The accompanying front-page story, by E. J. Dionne Jr., also in Port Said, offered "a vivid account" of the killing of Leon Klinghoffer gathered from interviews with passengers. Yet even at the end of this account, the focus shifted to Mrs. Klinghoffer. The story recounted "the most moving scene" when the widow came ashore.

She was wearing a white flower print dress and was utterly downcast. She barely raised her eyes to look at the mob of reporters and cameramen who pushed and shoved their way around her. Finally, Mrs. Klinghoffer, looking disraught [*sic*], looked up and said "Get away."[9]

A most moving scene? Authorities eventually had to take Mrs. Klinghoffer back to the ship—back to the site of her husband's murder—to escape the media mob on shore.

VICTIM AS HERO: DEATH AS SACRIFICE

Another story on the same day introduced an important theme that would mark *Times* coverage thereafter. The widow and family were used to depict the victim within a drama of heroic sacrifice. The victim was portrayed not as a sufferer of ill fortune but as a hero. His death was depicted not as tragedy but as sacrifice.

Entitled "Wife Calls Victim of Hijackers a Hero," the story began with the words of the widow: "'Your father was a hero,' Marilyn Klinghoffer told her two daughters yesterday."[10] The account, again written by Sara Rimer, was partially devoted to the widow's "first telephone call home," as related by Lisa Klinghoffer's husband. But after giving details of the call, the report explored and extended the widow's characterization of her husband as a hero.

Leon Klinghoffer was described by the report as a "determined man," who had recently fought hard to recover from a stroke. The son-in-law called him "a devoted husband, a loving father and a good friend." A friend said, "He was an unbelievably gentle man." A neighbor said, "He always smiled and he'd say hello." And a niece testified, "All he talked about was family and love."

An important transformation was taking place in these words. Starting with the reactions of the widow and her family, *Times* coverage began to develop a portrait of the heroic victim. Not a portrait of dashing deeds or spectacular action, the depiction offered by the *Times* called forth the heroism of everyday life—life given, now literally, for others. Drawing upon the power of the family's grief, the *Times* placed the tragic death of the victim within a mythic story of sacrifice.

Reports on the following day, October 12, continued the portrayal of the heroic victim sacrificed. In a long story, "Aged Victim, Portrayed as

Helpless, Is Recalled as a Strong, Happy Man," Sara Rimer was again on the scene in the living room of the Klinghoffer apartment.[11] The widow was on her way back to the United States and relatives had gathered in the home.

They "looked at photographs of him and his wife Marilyn and the children, and they laughed at small memories." The report noted that on a coffee table in the middle of the room was a wedding photograph of the widow, "a beautiful dark-haired young woman in a traditional wedding gown." Absent from the scene, on her way home to the United States, the widow still was placed early in the story at center stage.

With this scene set, the report then offered a heroic retelling of the victim's life, beginning with an almost archetypal introduction for U.S. heroes: "He struggled all of his life . . . to overcome his humble beginnings on the Lower East Side." More testimony was given about his character. "He was a contented, happy man," his mother-in-law said. "He loved his friends and family." Daughter Lisa recalled her father's fondness for simple pleasures, such as a television show: "'He was addicted to *Dynasty*,' Lisa said. 'Joan Collins—wow!'"

The report offered its own testimony. "Everyone in the family went to Leon for advice," Rimer wrote, and added, "The entire family speaks of the courage with which Mr. Klinghoffer overcame two strokes several years ago."

Significant support was offered for the portrayal of the victim as hero. President Reagan, the story noted, had telephoned the daughters. He told them that "their father was an American of whom everyone could be proud." No reason was given why Leon Klinghoffer should inspire pride, rather than, for example, sorrow. But the president's words added an important dimension to the report. They confirmed that the portrayal of Leon Klinghoffer as a heroic victim was not just a characterization of the story, but was a depiction acknowledged in U.S. public life.

THE WIDOW AT CENTER STAGE

On Sunday, October 13, *Times* coverage of the Klinghoffers climaxed with four stories, each centered around one compelling drama: The widow had returned home. A large, front-page photograph of Mrs. Klinghoffer arriving at Newark International Airport provided a graphic centerpiece for the stories. She was dressed in black. Her eyes were sunk in dark circles. She clutched the hand of a friend.

One front-page story, by Robert D. McFadden, described the scene.[12] "Clad in black, staring straight ahead with a look of despair in her eyes," Mrs. Klinghoffer was escorted to a limousine by two U.S. senators and a congressman, in a reception befitting the widow of a hero.

Though Mrs. Klinghoffer had returned with other hostages from the cruise ship, her singular social status as the widow was affirmed by all. Only she was singled out by the *Times*—and by Washington officials.

Inside the paper, a story by George James pointedly separated the returning hostages from Mrs. Klinghoffer. The others wore "cheerful pastel-colored cruise clothes"; the widow "wore a black shawl and black slacks." The others were united with relatives in a large, gay room, filled with people; Mrs. Klinghoffer met her daughters in a private room. "In one room was jubilation, in the other grief."[13]

Two other reports that day focused on the widow. Both involved a telephone call from President Reagan to the widow, the president's second call to the family. The first account, by Sara Rimer, who apparently remained in close contact with the family, used the phone conversation between the president and the widow to depict the widow's love for her husband and her rage at his killers.[14]

Her stirring words were recounted. "These people don't deserve to live. They are despicable," Mrs. Klinghoffer told the president. "No," he replied. The widow told the president she faced the hijackers in a police lineup in Italy and said she "spit in their faces." The president answered, "You did. Oh God bless you."

The story then turned to others to portray the strength and presence of the widow. Family members said that "they were not just reassured, but awed, by the sight of her," and Ilsa's fiancé said, "She's the bravest woman I've ever met." The story finished with its emphasis squarely on widow and victim: "With Marilyn Klinghoffer home, the mourning of Leon Klinghoffer could now begin."

The second account was a transcript of the conversation between the president and the widow, "as taken down by the Klinghoffer family and provided to the *New York Times*."[15] An interesting point for broader considerations of privacy: The family willingly contributed to the public aspect of the widow's grief. Recording and providing the transcript, holding press conferences, allowing access to *Times* reporters—all these acts reflected acknowledgment or acceptance by the family of the public nature of the family's loss.

With five straight days of reports about the victim and his widow, culminating with four stories in the Sunday paper, the first week of *Times* coverage provided a complex and highly dramatic portrayal. In the first days, a traditional journalistic device of using a local scene to depict world events was transformed into an intimate, intense account of personal tragedy.

It was compelling reporting. But the power of the stories was used for more than the depiction of grief. Through detailed reporting of scenes manifesting the love, anger, and pain of the widow, through the inclusion of powerful public officials who contributed to the portrayal, the *Times* dramatically depicted Leon Klinghoffer within a public drama of a heroic victim sacrificed.

"HE WILL LIVE IN HIS NATION'S MEMORY"

In the next week, *Times* coverage of the Klinghoffers dropped sharply. Even when the body of Leon Klinghoffer was found and identified, the family was not questioned or even mentioned. Portrayals of Klinghoffer as a heroic victim could be seen, however, in the selection and placement of two photographs. On October 17, a photograph of Klinghoffer's coffin, carried by Syrian soldiers, appeared on the front page. The prominence given to the photograph and the involvement of the military suggested that the victim was of international stature.

On the following day, a photograph of the Klinghoffers' daughters was printed. The women, continuing to maintain their public profile, held a press conference "announcing establishment of a fund to combat international terrorism in memory of Leon Klinghoffer."

On October 20, Leon Klinghoffer's body was returned to the United States. The widow received the body at Kennedy Airport, and the *Times* made its clearest statement yet of the symbolic stature attained by the victim and his widow. Accompanied by a three-column, front-page photograph of the widow standing beside the flag-covered coffin, the *Times* story by Eric Pace explicitly cited Klinghoffer as a national symbol:

> While his widow wept, the mortal remains of Leon Klinghoffer were ceremoniously returned to his native city yesterday, and his memory was hailed by President Reagan and New York legislators as a symbol of innocence and goodness in a harsh world.[16]

Within that one sentence, the symbolic sacrifice was succinctly stated. The sentence, indeed the story, began with its focus on the widow: "While his widow wept." Before the president, before Leon Klinghoffer, the widow was placed on the stage.

Other details in the lead contributed to the heroic portrayal. "Mortal remains" suggests that the victim has other, *immortal* remains. The phrase might refer to everlasting life or perhaps to the victim's life in the nation's memory, interpretations appropriate for a national hero. References to the president, New York legislators, and a ceremonious return also showed the victim's national stature. Finally, the victim was specifically hailed, by officials and by the report, as a symbol of innocence and goodness.

After the lead, the story further developed the themes of innocence and heroism. From remarks by Senator Daniel Patrick Moynihan, the reporter selected these quotes: Klinghoffer was "a symbol of righteousness in a world filled with evil and cruelty," and the victim "will live in his nation's memory always." A statement from President Reagan was mentioned with these lines quoted: "May Leon Klinghoffer's memory be a blessing to the world."

Along with heroic characterizations of the victim, the report also offered, through seven lengthy paragraphs, minute details about the widow's grief. "In dark glasses and a dark suit," she watched "impassively at first." Soon she "lifted her glasses and dabbed at her eyes." She "approached the coffin, put her hands to her lips and touched it." When the coffin was placed in the hearse, she "put her handkerchief to her face again." She "wiped tears from her eyes again and again." She was embraced and kissed by the officials, and it "was then that she turned away and her body briefly sagged." Then, "escorted to a limousine, Mrs. Klinghoffer slumped bleak-faced in the rear seat."[17]

On the following day, the *Times* furnished more details of the widow's grief and the victim's heroic status. It followed the widow to the graveyard. The headline made clear the story's theme: "Klinghoffer Eulogized as Public and Private Hero." And the story again referred directly to the victim's symbolic stature: "From a father, husband and small-appliance manufacturer who lived his 69 years for the most part in relative obscurity, Mr. Klinghoffer has been transformed into an international hero and political symbol."[18]

The report noted that New York City's mayor, and the State of New York's governor, and two U.S. senators were in attendance, and that condolences had come from former Israeli prime minister Menachem Begin.

From the many eulogies, the *Times* selected Ilsa's statement for one of its closing paragraphs: "The world knows you now as a hero," Ilsa said. "But you were always a hero to us."

With this report, fittingly filed by Sara Rimer, who had begun the paper's reporting on the family, two weeks of *Times* coverage of the victim and widow came to an end. As the newspaper itself noted, a once unknown man had been transformed—especially in the pages of the *Times*—into an international hero and political symbol. Through its stories on Leon Klinghoffer and his widow, the *Times* offered portrayals of a victim, a virtuous, heroic man who symbolized innocence and righteousness and whose death was to be etched upon the national memory.

What was the meaning of all this? How did news coverage of a hijacking lead to talk of heroic victims and symbolic sacrifice? Myth can provide some of the answers. Like myth, *Times* stories on Leon Klinghoffer can be seen as symbolic dramas that attempted to explain and give meaning to events. Like myth, the stories can be seen as wrestling with some of the deepest questions of human existence: What is the meaning of human life? How should we live while knowing that death may come, literally, at any moment?

RECONCILING HUMAN EXISTENCE

One of myth's important social roles is to reconcile people to the seeming randomness of human existence. All our careful plans, all our most cherished dreams can be shattered by an instance of coincidence: a car out of control, a sniper's bullet, a flash of lightning, a terrorist strike. Life is lived always in the presence of death.

Myth must take on tasks too great for human logic and rationality. It must balance opposites—or as Eliade wrote, "the apposition of contraries," the *"coincidentia oppositorum."* Myth has the difficult task of reconciling people to life that shows itself by turns benevolent and terrible, creative and destructive, infinite and brutally finite, Eliade wrote. He added that "myth reveals more profoundly than any rational experience ever could, the actual structure of the divinity, which transcends all attributes and reconciles all contraries."[19]

To do this well, such myths are told over and over—sometimes as the same story, sometimes in different forms—so that the lesson is not forgotten. Myths "reveal 'nature' better and more intimately than any empirical or rational experience and observation could," Eliade wrote, "and it is to maintain and renew that revelation that the myth must be constantly celebrated and repeated."[20]

Though the news does not tell the story of Leon Klinghoffer over and over, the news does reenact again and again the story of *the Victim*. Names and places change but the story remains essentially the same: an innocent victim—guilty only of coincidence, bad timing, the unfortunate fate of being in the wrong place at the wrong time—is somehow killed in a hijacking, airline crash, fire, robbery, flood, or explosion. Then, through the words of the widow or others left behind, the news elevates and transforms the victim into a hero, a person whose life story is gathered and told, whose passing is marked and mourned.

We know these victims are not really heroes, in the usual sense of that word, unless they have died while doing some heroic deed. Yet the portrayals of victims as heroes seem appropriate and somehow comforting. In their attempts to give meaning to the death of an innocent person, to somehow explain lives lost to fire and floods, news stories turn death into sacrifice and victims into heroes. Myth has been doing that for centuries.

THE SACRIFICE OF THE VICTIM

The death of the victim and the transformation of the victim into hero is a myth found in cultures around the world. In Christian cultures, of course, the victim often finds expression in Jesus Christ. Jung was particularly interested in the symbolic power of Christ's story. According to Jung, the story of Christ—hero and victim—is of central importance because the victim "is a symbol of the self."[21] We see ourselves, we place ourselves, into stories of victims.

The thought is echoed by other writers. Another of Jung's disciples, Erich Neumann, in his classic book *The Origins and History of Consciousness*, stated that the heroic victim is "the exemplar of individuality."[22] The literary and social critic Kenneth Burke acknowledged something similar in his own writings. He sees the hero as a "personally fit victim."[23]

In the *Times*, Leon Klinghoffer is certainly portrayed as an innocent, heroic victim. He "struggled all of his life . . . to overcome his humble beginnings." In life, he was an "unbelievably gentle man," and "all he talked about was family and love." In death, he was "an international hero" and "an American of whom everyone could be proud." He was a "symbol of innocence and goodness in a harsh world" and a "symbol of righteousness in a world filled with evil and cruelty." His memory will "be a blessing to the world."

The idea of the victim as "the self" might offer particular insights into *Times* coverage, especially the intense, minute, dramatic depictions. Perhaps every bit of grounding, every detail that situated the victim as a real person in a specific time and place, better served to represent an individual who then could serve as an "exemplar of the self."

And so the stories detailed Leon Klinghoffer's humble beginnings, his job selling appliances, his marriage, his battle to overcome strokes, his fondness for *Dynasty* and Joan Collins. And so the stories examined each movement of the widow's grief: the handkerchief to the eye, the hand to the lip and then to the coffin, the sag of her body, and the slump of her shoulders.

Crucial, private moments were laid bare to the public, such as word of the death, the return of the body, and the burial of the man. No detail was too small, even the simple and sad expressions of human misery: a daughter's tears dropping onto a photo album, the widow's hand touched to the flag-draped coffin, or the halting eulogy of a friend.

"The nature of the hero is as manifold as the agonizing situations of real life," Neumann wrote. "But always he is compelled to sacrifice normal living in whatever form it may touch him, whether it be mother, father, child, homeland, sweetheart, brother or friend."[24]

As a reader, I recognize some of the details provided by stories of Leon Klinghoffer's life. I can relate to the roles he played: father, husband, friend. If Eliade, Neumann, Jung, and others are correct, I recognize myself, perhaps not quite consciously, in these details. The victim represents the self—myself.[25]

MYSELF AND MY WIDOW

This approach to the *Times* reports can be taken, somewhat tentatively, one intriguing step further. It's a step, though, that might add more to our understanding of news stories about victims. If the sacrificed hero represents myself, then the news allows me, the individual reader, the privileged—and positively rare—opportunity to attend my own death.

The age-old question can be addressed: What will it be like when I die? In a sense, through the myth of the heroic victim and the symbol of the self, I can view *my* own passing, see the effect of *my* death, hear testimony about the value of *my* life.

I see my family and friends gather in sorrow. I listen as they mourn my passing. I follow them to the graveyard. I am curious—Who showed up? Clergy, senators, even the president testify to my worth. I hear I am a symbol of righteousness, all right, a blessing to the world.

Mostly, I focus on my widow. I watch her every move. I see her sorrow as she touches my coffin, dabs at her eyes, and stumbles away. Her grief testifies to my worth. Even in the face of the meaningless of life that must end in death—symbolized so well by my meaningless, senseless death—I can see, after all, that my life had meaning.

"THE BATTLE OF THE GIANTS"

Faced with giving meaning to the murder of Leon Klinghoffer, faced with giving meaning to life in the face of death, the *Times* reports, surely unconsciously, drew from the power of an age-old myth. Perhaps only myth was capable of balancing the eternal opposition—what Freud called "the battle of the giants."

> And now, I think the meaning of the evolution of civilization is no longer obscure to us. It must present the struggle between Eros and Death, between the instinct of life and the instinct of destruction, as it works itself out in the human species. This struggle is what all life essentially consists of, and the evolution of civilization may be simply described as the struggle for life of the human species.[26]

Life and death did struggle in the *Times* reports. Invoking the great myth of the victim, the news reports answered the negation of terrorism. Terrorism offered negation and death; the news reports offered affirmation and life. Terrorism said the self was meaningless; the news reports of the victim's widow cried in reply: *the self has meaning.*

NEWS, VICTIMS, AND TERRORISM

Understanding *Times* coverage of Leon Klinghoffer in this way allows me first to offer some tentative conclusions about the specific subject at hand:

news coverage of terrorism. This study, of course, is small in scope and exploratory in approach. But possible implications can at least be considered.

One possible conclusion: News coverage does aid and support the goals of the terrorist. Terrorism is an act of communication from the terrorist to an audience, which might be an individual, nation, or the whole world. The terrorist victim is the primary symbol in the communication: Terrorists actually want the victim to symbolically represent the audience. Offering up the myth of the Victim, news reports—especially by the *Times*, the State Scribe—invite intense identification of the individual reader with the terrorist victim, thus helping the terrorist.

The terror—as opposed to disgust over the slaughter or grief over the loss—resides in a personal, primarily unconscious understanding that the victim is a symbol of the self: It could have been me. As I noted, often only fate or timing places the victim in the terrorists' path. Myth in news stories thus helps establish the link between victim and audience. Myth says the sacrificed victim could have been myself. Myth, as news, provides some of the terror of terrorism.

Public officials aid the terrorists in similar ways. As we saw in the death of Leon Klinghoffer, the involvement of the president, senators, and other officials with the tragedy of Marilyn Klinghoffer helped create the mythic, heroic victim. Public officials too support the symbolism of the terrorist.

However, public officials may not have been mere pawns reacting to terrorist manipulation. Without wishing to appear too cynical, I must note that another possible conclusion may be that mythic portrayals of terrorist victims offer benefits to politicians. For example, by publicly calling Leon Klinghoffer a national hero, the president and New York politicians were provided access to a huge national and international stage and involved themselves sympathetically in the emotional drama surrounding the grief of Marilyn Klinghoffer. Some political gain might have been realized from embracing the widow on a public stage.

Other possible conclusions of mythic news portrayals of heroic victims: Policymakers can perhaps more easily gain public support for measures of prevention and reprisal. For example, after the *Achille Lauro* hijacking, the federal government later placed restrictions on travel by U.S. citizens to areas of the Middle East. The restrictions recognized the symbolism of terrorism—each U.S. citizen was a possible victim, a symbol of the nation, for terrorists.

Mythic images in the news might also help public officials create a compelling climate for revenge. An attack against an individual citizen—if it is recognized by the State Scribe, other news outlets, politicians, and the public as an attack against the nation—can be avenged. For example, on April 14, 1986, U.S. air and naval forces bombed Libya. In a speech that night, President Reagan said the attack was a direct response to terrorism against U.S. citizens:

> I warned Colonel Khadafy that we would hold his regime accountable for any new terrorist attacks launched against American citizens. When our citizens are abused or attacked anywhere in the world on the direct orders of a hostile regime, we will respond so long as I'm in this Oval Office.

Mythic news portrayals of terrorist victims can help create or sustain passions that allow such retaliation against terrorism.

THE CONSOLATION OF VICTIMS

Broader conclusions can at least be considered, particularly in relation to news coverage of victims, which has become a heated issue in our times. Critics of the news—including some journalists—see news reports of victims as lurid violations of ethics and decency. They charge that the news tramples upon the privacy of victims in attempts to offer sensational, melodramatic stories, or in one potent phrase, "a pornography of grief."[27]

Understanding news coverage in terms of myth, however, brings a different and much larger perspective. The myth of the victim's death, the philosophers tell us, is an important social tale. Humans need to hear, need to tell, that story. Logic will not explain the sudden death of a victim. Rationality will not comfort those left behind. As Eliade said, myth—perhaps only myth—is capable of reconciling humans to such fate.

By recounting the story of the victim, by elevating the victim into a hero through the great grief of those left behind, the news plays a role that reaches back deeply into the long relationship between myth and humankind. It offers some reconciliation and consolation with the ultimate fate of all life: death.

Leon Klinghoffer, the *Times* tells us, lived a worthy life. Leon Klinghoffer lived heroically through simple, everyday acts. Though he was wrenched away from us too soon, Leon Klinghoffer will live always in the hearts of those who love him. And so, the news tell us, will we.

Telling myths, we see once again, is a crucial part of being human. We tell myths about things that are most important to us. We tell myths to define evil and good, to pass on the memory of what we believe and what we cannot believe. We tell myths to give meaning to the meaningless and to explain that which cannot be explained.

In explaining the murder of a 69-year-old man in a wheelchair, in reporting great tragedy and loss, the news takes on the role, consciously or unconsciously, of myth. In turning to stories about victims, editors and reporters draw from timeless dramas that attempt to reconcile people to the fate of human existence. In the face of chaos, order is established. In the face of death, life is affirmed. In the face of tragedy, news becomes myth.

Chapter 4

The Scapegoat

The Killing of Huey Newton and Degrading Political Radicals

Social revolutionary, Mercedes owner, killer, protector, illiterate, doctor of philosophy—Huey Newton had a host of public roles. Born in Louisiana in 1942, named after Huey Long, populist governor of the state, Newton was the youngest of seven children. Within a year, the family moved to Oakland, California. By his own testimony, Newton was a student of the street and graduated illiterate from high school.[1]

Soon after, however, he taught himself to read and enrolled in Oakland's Merritt College during the ferment of the mid-1960s. His interest was radical black politics, specifically those of Malcolm X. He embraced the doctrine of black self-defense preached by Malcolm X: "It doesn't mean that I advocate violence, but at the same time I am not against using violence in self defense. I don't even call it violence when it's self defense; I call it intelligence."[2]

Through coursework, Newton met Bobby Seale. Concerned with police mistreatment of blacks in Oakland, Newton and Seale formed the Black Panther Party for Self Defense in 1966. They flipped a coin; Seale won the right to be president and Newton became minister of defense. The Black Panthers patrolled behind police, photographing arrests of blacks. They put out a newspaper—the first issue explored the killing of an Oakland black man by a police officer.

The Black Panthers first reached the national stage in May 1967 when well-armed members marched in Sacramento, the capital of California, to protest restrictions on carrying arms. In the charged context of violence between blacks and police at that time, the message of the armed Black Panthers was electrifying. Newton's blistering critique of police oppression was given nationwide play.

Trouble kept Newton in the national spotlight. In 1967, he and a friend were stopped by Oakland police. In a struggle, an officer was killed. Newton, critically wounded, was charged with his murder. His impassioned defense inside and outside the courtroom won him admirers in ghettoes, on college campuses, and within select social circles. The relationship between the Panthers and liberal New York socialites was satirized in a popular book by Tom Wolfe, *Radical Chic and Mau-Mauing the Flak Catchers*.[3]

"Free Huey" became an anthem of the late 1960s. After a long trial, Newton was convicted of the lesser charge of voluntary manslaughter. Even this conviction was overturned on appeal; after two subsequent mistrials charges were eventually dropped.[4]

Newton and the Panthers remained in the national spotlight. But they resisted easy categorization. They were committed to the black community. They organized voting drives, free health clinics, breakfast programs for children, an accredited elementary school, a clothing outlet, and a bus service for relatives visiting prison inmates. Panther chapters were opened nationwide.

Yet violence followed the Panthers. At least 15 were killed in confrontations with police. It was later revealed that J. Edgar Hoover personally had overseen COINTELPRO, a program of FBI harassment of the Panthers and other radical groups.[5] Newton himself was shadowed by violence. In 1974 he was accused of murdering a 17-year-old prostitute. He fled the United States and took asylum in Cuba. After three years in exile, he returned to stand trial. The jury deadlocked. Charges were dropped. Soon after, in the early 1980s, torn by death, trials, and dissension, the original Panthers disbanded.

Newton pressed on. The violence and confrontations seemed to fade into the past. He returned to college. In 1980, the once-illiterate high school graduate earned a doctorate in an interdisciplinary program, the history of consciousness, at the University of California at Santa Cruz. His dissertation was entitled *War against the Panthers: A Study of Repression in America.* He worked on a book and movie scripts.

Then, in the early morning of August 22, 1989, Newton was shot and killed on a West Oakland street known as a site for drug deals. He was 47. The next day, Tyrone Robinson, 25, a member of an Oakland drug gang, was arrested and charged with murder. He was later convicted of the killing.

Newton's death was front-page news, and provided an opportunity for the press to review 20 years of black politics. Thus it was an occasion for analysis and assessment. Assessing Newton would be no easy task. He was radical, violent, charismatic, revolutionary. He gave civil rights a compelling urgency and served a pivotal role on the U.S. scene in the 1960s and 1970s.

My interest in coverage of Newton's death began with two stories printed in the *New York Times.* I distinctly remember my surprise. I noticed immediately how the front-page story, and an accompanying obituary, almost maliciously degraded and demeaned Newton and his work. I didn't have strong feelings about Newton. During the turbulence of the 1960s, I was still fairly young and much more concerned about the scores of New York Yankee games. But my surprise at *Times* coverage of Newton's death was so strong that I rummaged through the library the following day, looking at how other newspapers had handled Newton's killing. The results of that rummaging led me to another eternal story.

THE SCAPEGOAT: DELEGITIMIZING DISSENT

If news is only a dispassionate observer and reporter of political events, coverage of radical groups such as the Black Panthers should be interesting but relatively straightforward. The political protest should provide some debatable issues for a story. The passion should contribute some provocative emotion. The conflict should make for dramatic narratives. Radical thinkers should make for thoughtful news.

If news is myth, however, coverage of radical groups should be much more combustible and complex. These groups deviate greatly from the social consensus. And myth is inextricably involved with affirming and defending social consensus. As Eliade noted, myth hails societal origins, celebrates social values, and extols exemplary models. In doing so, myth can have dark consequences for those who deviate.[6]

Societies can tolerate, even encourage, a certain amount of disagreement. But those disagreements usually are kept within fairly narrow confines. Those disagreements usually are not permitted to question basic values, let alone the very structure of the society. Myth offers order but also demands order, recounts beliefs but also restricts beliefs, confirms tradition but also conforms tradition. In support of social order, myth offers stories that delegitimize dissent and stigmatize dissenters.[7]

Often myth does so through the Scapegoat. Exemplary models can be "bad" as well as "good." Through the Scapegoat, myth can "make an example" of those who disagree too vigorously with the social order.

The Scapegoat has origins in the quite natural practice of transferring a physical load to another's shoulders, usually a beast of burden, such as a mule or an ox. Rituals developed in which bodily and mental ailments and burdens could also be transferred to another individual, animal, or object. Eventually, these practices developed into potent rituals and myths whose centerpiece is the transference of evil. The misfortunes and faults of society are transferred to an individual or sacrificial animal (like a goat) who is then driven, literally or symbolically, out of the society, cleansing and purifying those left behind. As opposed to the Hero, the Scapegoat is portrayed as embodying the sins of society. Myths degrade and demean the Scapegoat in stories that define sin and dramatize its punishment.

Sir James George Frazer, one of the foremost scholars of Scapegoat myths, saw them as "public attempts to expel the accumulated ills of a whole community."[8] In his multivolume *The Golden Bough*, Frazer devoted an entire book to variations of the Scapegoat myth across human societies. For example, Frazer writes:

> In Siam, it used to be the custom on one day of the year to single out a woman broken down by debauchery, and carry her on a litter through all the streets to the music of drums and hautboys. The mob insulted her and pelted her with dirt; and after having carried her through the whole city, they threw her on a dunghill or a hedge of thorns outside the ramparts, forbidding her ever to enter the walls again.[9]

The accompanying drama made clear that the woman drew with her the evil spirits and malign influences of the city. In Athens, Rome, Mexico City, and many other cities, societies imprisoned potential scapegoats, at the public expense, who were later used to purify the city in times of plagues, droughts, or famines.[10]

Modern societies, though they might deny the term, also employ scapegoats. Jews, blacks, communists, women, and numerous others have been cast as embodiments of evil in some societies. In whatever society they appear, stories demean the scapegoats and call out for their expulsion from the social scene. Kenneth Burke, the literary and social critic, sees the process as crucial to social order and asks "whether human societies could possibly cohere without symbolic victims which the individual members of the group share in common."[11]

CASE STUDY: HUEY NEWTON AND THE NEWS

An excellent opportunity for exploring news stories involving the Scapegoat myth was offered by Huey Newton's death in August 1989. The central question is: How did the *Times* and other newspapers portray Newton and his work? To what extent did the news, like myth, degrade and denounce the challenge to social order?

Certainly, Newton was an enormously complex figure who could have been depicted in many ways. Some stories could have portrayed the excesses of his challenge to social order. Other stories might have emphasized his heroic, almost cult-like status among many African Americans. Still other stories might have highlighted his battles against poverty, racism, and other social ills that continue to confront the black community. His public career spanned two tumultuous decades and his international reputation was forged as much from his passionate defense of black power and radical politics as from his notorious confrontations with police.[12] How was Newton portrayed?

This chapter has a much tighter focus than others in the book. Rather than decades of coverage and hundreds of stories, this study keeps its focus exclusively on stories of Newton's death. The focus allows us the full benefits of a rich, textual analysis in which each word and quotation can be considered in depth. It also allows a large comparison with other newspapers. It will be interesting to see if newspapers shared a common portrayal.

I selected 11 other newspapers for some geographical diversity as well as their elite quality and influence: the *Atlanta Constitution, Houston Post, Kansas City Times, Los Angeles Times, San Francisco Chronicle, St. Louis Post-Dispatch,* (Oakland) *Tribune, Tulsa World, USA Today, Wall*

Street Journal, and *Washington Post*. I studied issues from the dates August 22 and 23, 1989, the days following Newton's killing.

NEWS, RACE, AND RADICAL POLITICS

Though the focus is on Newton and the Black Panthers, the issues are broader. This study looks at how the news, like myth, enacts public dramas of the Scapegoat that isolate and marginalize those who challenge social order. As we saw in earlier chapters, coverage of mainstream politics seems integral to the press's First Amendment role. The news serves as the eyes and ears of the public, observing and reporting actions of elected officials. However, coverage of politics outside the mainstream, from the political right and left, can be troublesome. Radical groups may protest deep-seated and fundamental social values. They may attack legal authority. They may resist the courts and challenge the fairness of the judicial system. They may criticize the established order, including the news. They may challenge widely held cultural and political beliefs. Sometimes the challenge turns into conflict and the conflict turns violent.

Coverage of radical politics thus raises difficult issues. Social institutions—including the news—might be under attack. Publishers, editors, and reporters, no different from most people who grow up in a society, often share most of society's cultural and political beliefs. How do newspapers respond to people who challenge fundamental beliefs?

Some writers already have looked at this issue. They harshly criticize news coverage of radical politics. They argue that news coverage seeks to delegitimize and disarm perceived threats to social order. They find that although journalists themselves are often seen as politically liberal in their beliefs, the news *media* are a conservative ideological force. News media serve, in this view, as "agents of social control" who preserve "the status quo by providing unsympathetic coverage to those whose behavior threatens it."[13]

When radical politics also involve race, writers say, the news can have an even more difficult time. Critics long have argued that the news media miss or ignore matters of race because of the overwhelming white face of the nation's newsrooms.[14] Others argue that the news performs a more damaging role. They say that the news media, when they do report on race, foster stereotypes and predominantly offer negative images, such as the portrayal of young black males as criminals and drug users.[15]

Black political leaders in particular attract negative coverage, critics say. The news degrades black activists and situates moderate black leaders on more "legitimate" middle ground.[16] From coverage of Malcolm X to that of the Black Panthers, of Louis Farrakhan, and of Al Sharpton, stories of black leaders who espouse controversial views reflect a troubled relationship among the news, race, and politics. The question becomes: How does the *Times*, and more broadly the news, handle such challenges? Myth may provide at least part of the answer.

STILL FRONT-PAGE NEWS

Some preliminary results: Even two decades after the 1960s, Huey Newton was still news. Of the dozen newspapers I studied, 10, including the *Times*, carried the story of his death on the front page, a testimony to Newton's enduring status. The two other papers, the *Washington Post* and *USA Today*, noted the death on the front page but placed the actual story inside.

Because Newton's death was a sudden, unexpected event and Oakland is not a city where most U.S. newspapers maintain bureaus, many newspapers did not have their own reporters on the scene. Thus, for their lead accounts, seven of the newspapers relied upon some combination of Associated Press (AP) and other wire service reports. Most of these papers, however, supplemented the lead report with staff sidebars or obituaries—another testimony to Newton's status. Five of the papers, the *San Francisco Chronicle*, the Oakland *Tribune*, the *Los Angeles Times*, the *Washington Post*, and *USA Today*, had reporters in Oakland and used accounts attributed solely to their own staffs.

Though the *New York Times* does not often place wire service stories on its front page, preferring to rely on its own staff, Newton's death caught the *Times* too without a correspondent in Oakland. The *Times* chose to run an AP story. The article was placed on the front page. It "jumped," that is, continued, inside, on the obituary page, alongside a second, staff-written obituary. The inside package spread across the whole top half of a page.

It is important to note that newspapers can and do freely edit and adapt AP stories—deleting whole sections, adding material from their own reporters, changing language, and rearranging paragraphs. For example, unlike any other newspaper, the *Times* almost immediately inserted in its front-page AP story the information that Newton had recently earned a PhD. This relatively inconsequential information was placed rather jarringly in the third paragraph, amid a description of Newton's killing. The reason? The *Times* style is to use honorific titles, such as Mr., Mrs., Miss, or Dr., and the *Times* refers to people with PhDs as "Dr." And so the paper, in the third paragraph, was providing explanation on why it was going to refer to "Dr. Newton" throughout its coverage.

The *Times*'s own piece, written by Dennis Hevesi in New York, was entitled "Huey Newton Symbolized the Rising Black Anger of a Generation."[17] The article was accompanied by a small, one-column head-and-shoulder photograph of a bearded, bemused Newton, taken a year before, and a larger two-column photograph from 1967 of Newton in a beret with a rifle at his shoulder.

A DRAMA OF DEGRADATION

My close reading found that the two *Times* pieces—the adapted AP report and the staff obituary—portrayed Newton as a scapegoat in a drama of degradation. The lead report was not a simple account of his killing. The obituary was not a mere reflection on his life and times. The two stories, particularly taken together, offered a drama that used the occasion of Newton's death to recite his sins and demean his life.

How was the myth of the Scapegoat accomplished? As the following sections show, three primary themes could be seen in the stories:

1. The *Times* stories disavowed Newton's life through the use of ironic details and characterizations.
2. They invalidated his significance by depicting him in incongruous, almost humiliating circumstances.
3. They repudiated his accomplishments by focusing largely on his criminal record, portraying him as if he was noteworthy only for a life of crime and violence.

The comparison with other newspapers was particularly interesting. The following sections will also show, with a few exceptions examined closely, that all 12 newspapers employed identical themes in their coverage of Newton's death. All 12 newspapers depicted Newton in terms that degraded and demeaned his life and work.

This does not mean that newspapers or reporters consciously or vindictively degraded Newton. The intent of individual papers or writers cannot really be addressed. Writers—in journalism, drama, fiction, or letters—are often unaware of the forces that shape their work. Intent is not at issue. The meaning of news language is at issue.

The argument here is that larger social and political forces were at work: the influence of social order and eternal stories. As myth, the news—an integral member of the established order—offered stories that rejected Newton's lifelong questioning of that order. Faced with assessing the radical politics of the Panther leader, the *Times* and other newspapers turned to an archetypal story—the Scapegoat—and told it in modern terms. The news abused Newton's politics and affirmed the authority of the status quo. The following sections closely examine the language of the stories, isolate and discuss each of the themes, and show how the news diminished Newton's life and death.

DISAVOWAL THROUGH IRONY

The *Times*'s front-page story on August 23, 1989 began:

> Huey P. Newton, the co-founder of the Black Panther Party and a leader of a generation of blacks in the 1960's, was shot to death early today in the neighborhood where he began his organizing.[18]

The jumphead—the headline on page A15 where the story continued, or "jumped"—said, "Huey Newton Found Shot to Death in Part of City Where He Began."

The *place* of death surely was getting emphasized here, and it's fair to ask why. A preliminary observation can be made. By linking Newton's work and death to the same site, the story seemed to be suggesting a kind of irony. It was saying something like, "Isn't it ironic that he was killed in the same place where he began his work?"

Certainly the *Times*'s use of irony should not surprise close readers of the news. Some media critics have argued that irony is the main journalistic approach to writing, a convention that structures much journalism.[19] Even if that argument is accepted, however, it is still important to ask: Why this *particular* irony? How was irony being employed in this *particular* story?

One reading of this irony: The *Times* language implied that nothing was changed by Newton's work. The *Times* was immediately starting the process of diminishing Newton's life. Shot dead on the same streets where he cofounded the Panthers, he could not even better his home neighborhood, the language suggested.

My acute focus on the language of the headlines and the lead might seem peculiar. It may seem to be making too much of a small detail. Maybe those words didn't mean anything. But language always *means* something. And when the language of other newspapers was considered, my study found that those papers also chose to give the death site prominence. This is more than coincidence.

For example, a *Kansas City Times* headline read, "Black Panthers Leader Dies on Turf Where Work Began."[20] Likewise, *USA Today* reported that he died "violently Tuesday morning on the mean streets of Oakland, Calif., two blocks from the one-time headquarters of the Black Panthers movement he co-founded."[21] The *Atlanta Constitution* reported that he was "shot to death in the same troubled neighborhood where 23 years ago he co-founded the militant Black Panther Party to protect blacks from police violence."[22]

The California papers also used the site ironically, almost vindictively. The words in the following newspaper leads bear scrutiny. The Oakland *Tribune* said, "Black Panther Party co-founder Huey P. Newton, *who at one time preached power through guns*, was found shot to death early yesterday on a West Oakland sidewalk not far from the birthplace of the radical group" (emphasis added).[23] The *San Francisco Chronicle* said he was shot "in the West Oakland neighborhood *where he was accused of gunning down a police officer 22 years ago*" (emphasis added).[24]

The newspapers were doing more than implying that Newton could not even save his own neighborhood. The irony here was more troubling. The language suggested that Newton received his just desserts, a kind of ironic justice. Newton "at one time preached power through guns" and he was shot to death. He was killed in the same neighborhood "where he was accused of gunning down a police officer."

The irony has the feel of consummation and completion, as if some terrible circle had come round. The language—all of which appeared in the headlines or leads, one of the ways in which newspapers help guide and structure reading—implied that Newton got just what he deserved. And indeed, the *Chronicle* prominently quoted on the front page a source who voiced, in a deadening cliché, that very sentiment: "He who lives by the sword dies by the sword."[25]

The *Times* was more tempered than these newspapers in its approach to Newton. But the *Times* did share with other newspapers the use of irony to disavow and diminish the importance of Newton's life even as they made him front-page news.

INVALIDATION BY INCONGRUITY

The second paragraph of the *Times* stated: "His body was found lying in a pool of blood." The third paragraph noted that Newton "was shot several times, including at least once in the head."[26]

Those few words might be understood as a mere description of the murder scene. But regular readers of newspapers know that stories do not always provide these kinds of details. In their many accounts of murder and mayhem, in stories of drive-by shootings or killings during robberies, newspapers do not often focus on the state of the body, *how* the victim was shot or the amount of blood. After all, many scenes of violent death, from car accidents to shootings, result in "pools of blood." Reporters just don't include that detail.

According to newspaper tradition and convention, this language *does* appear in stories of gangland killings, or "mob hits." The implication of such language? These violent people met a violent end. The news implies: "Look what these people do to one another."

Using such language to describe the death of Newton made a subtle connection between the killing of Newton and the murder of a mobster. The connection was made stronger by the inclusion of a quote taken from a California district attorney. He called Newton "nothing but a gangster." Thus, a second and complementary theme: *Times* coverage devalued and invalidated Newton's significance with a prominent, gory description of Newton's body, using language usually employed in mob slayings.

And the *Times* added a touch of incongruity, a detail that made the entire scene seem strange and surreal. As I noted already, the *Times* placed Newton's PhD in the midst of the bloody description. The third paragraph thus read:

> Dr. Newton, who earned a Ph.D. from the University of California at Santa Cruz in 1980, was shot several times, including at least once in the head, said Officer Terry Foley of the Oakland Police Department.

All this degradation and devaluation was accomplished immediately—in the first three paragraphs. A reader did not have a chance to see

Newton in any other way. Does this acute attention again look too closely at the *Times* words? Turning to the other newspapers, the study found that they also highlighted bloody details of Newton's demise. The *Los Angeles Times* said he was "shot three times in the head."[27] *USA Today* said he was "found with three bullet wounds in his head."[28] The Oakland *Tribune* said he was "shot at least twice at point-blank range in the head and face."[29] The *Washington Post* added that he was found "face up and fully clothed."[30]

Like the *New York Times*, many newspapers also reported—probably unnecessarily, since they had noted he was shot three times in the head— that Newton was found in the archetypal "pool of blood." The *Atlanta Constitution* said Newton was found "lying in a pool of blood."[31] The *St. Louis Post-Dispatch* noted that he was "found sprawled on his back in a pool of blood."[32] The Oakland *Tribune* called it "a spreading pool of blood,"[33] while the *San Francisco Chronicle* increased the fluid description to a "river of blood."[34]

Other newspapers offered more invalidation through incongruity. They created an incongruous contrast between the once-genteel neighborhood where Newton was shot and the ugliness of Newton's demise. Stories prominently included small but intriguing neighborhood descriptions. The *San Francisco Chronicle* and the *St. Louis Post-Dispatch* noted in their second paragraphs that Newton was found in front of "two Victorian style houses."[35] The *Washington Post* went further, stating that Newton was found in front of "a small, faded blue-and-white Victorian house in West Oakland. Large trees line the street, and a rose bush is in bloom."[36]

What was the possible reason for such "pretty" references to the neighborhood and Newton's body? One reading is that the contrast suggested the intolerable incongruity of Newton's death: What kind of man finds such a sordid end on a street once so grand? The description implicated Newton, complementing the strategy of the leads: Newton's work was in vain, the reports implied, he could not make even this tranquil setting safe. The *Washington Post* article stated this theme explicitly. Newton died, the *Post* said, "in a neighborhood as depressed and beaten down by violence as the Oakland streets that *he and his Panther colleagues once promised to make safer for young black children*" (emphasis added).[37]

The theme was enhanced by other neighborhood descriptions. The *New York Times* article said that Newton died "on a street in a rundown Oakland neighborhood where residents say they fear they are losing the fight against drug dealing and poverty."[38] The *Wall Street Journal* called it a "drug-infested neighborhood."[39] The *Los Angeles Times* termed it a "drug-plagued area."[40] Combined with the leads' irony, the words made plain: The streets where Newton began his work, once a stately, splendid site, were a deadly place. Newton's work had little effect.

In sum, the details of the neighborhood—combined with the bloody details of his death—render an unmistakable portrayal. Shot three times in the face and head, face-up and fully clothed, in a pool of blood, on the dark streets of a once-grand neighborhood he once promised to save, Newton is the picture of debasement and disgrace.

REPUDIATION THROUGH CITATION

The lead paragraphs of the *Times* obituary by Dennis Hevesi at first hinted at another portrayal. They suggested the social and political complexity of Newton's life. The piece began:

> With the most vivid image of him a poster—the Black Panther defense minister poised on a throne-like rattan chair, a spear in one hand, a rifle in the other—it would be easy to see Huey Newton living and dying by the gun.
>
> A fuller picture is more complex.[41]

And in a few paragraphs that follow, Hevesi did attempt to capture some of that complexity. The story noted that Newton was illiterate when he graduated from high school and that he taught himself to read and eventually earned a PhD. "Streetwise to Book Smart," the first subhead read.

Newton's place in the history of the 1960s was also noted. The story quoted Bobby Seale, the cofounder of the Black Panthers, who said, "I'm rather shocked at him dying this way. It's a profound piece of history he and I represent. He and I should have lived to be old militant senior citizens."

But the "fuller picture" of Newton eventually turned out to be not so full. Hevesi followed those few paragraphs with more than 20 paragraphs of inflammatory accusations, recitations of criminal charges, and damning quotations against the Panthers and Newton.

The *Times* story of Newton's life, from birth to death, became a police record. Newton's biography was reduced to a recitation of accusations, police charges, trial dates, convictions, and appeals. Almost three-fourths of the obituary recited Newton's trouble with the law. For example, an early part of the story noted Newton's creation of the Panthers. Rather than look at the complex work of the Panthers, the obituary regurgitated a long disproved charge that the group was "controlled" by the Communist Party and then followed this with some damning quotes:

> In California, the State Senate subcommittee on un-American activities said the Black Panthers were controlled by the Communist Party of the United States to "serve as shock troops on the front line of the revolution."
>
> J. Edgar Hoover, the Director of the Federal Bureau of Investigation, described the Panthers as a "black extremist organization" consisting of "hoodlum-type revolutionaries."
>
> And in 1974, Thomas Orloff, the deputy district attorney for Alameda County who prosecuted Dr. Newton on numerous charges, called him "a man who lived by violence" and "nothing but a gangster."

The four remaining subheads after "Streetwise to Book Smart" indicated the direction of the *Times* piece:

"Called Hoodlums by Hoover"
"'Trigger Point in My Life'"
"Officer Dead, Newton Charged"
"Continual Scrapes with Law"

A third theme in *Times* coverage thus repudiated Newton's work by dismissing his accomplishments and portraying his life through a one-dimensional focus on lawbreaking and violence. With disparaging comments by law enforcement sources and citations of the criminal record, the *Times* piled on detail after detail of Newton's troubles with authorities—from school suspensions to murder charges—and turned Newton's obituary into a police "rap sheet."

Surely there was some justification for including these details. Newton's life was marked by violence and his police record was long. But Newton's struggles with police took place in a rich and troubled context that included urban strife, police oppression, intense debates over civil rights tactics, and especially an FBI program of harassment that specifically targeted Newton and the Panthers. Stripped of context and interpretation, the complex of violence that characterized Newton's life was over-simplified into an emphatic indictment of him.[42]

Once again, the same theme could be observed in the other newspapers. Stories were dominated by critical quotations from law enforcement authorities. And they too gave over most of their space to citations of the criminal record.

For example, some accounts gave four to six paragraphs to the negative comments of Orloff, whose office had failed on a number of occasions to convict Newton. Newton and the Panthers had frustrated, embarrassed, and humiliated Orloff. He was hardly an objective source for comments on Newton's life. Yet, in various stories, Orloff was the primary source. He called Newton "a thug," "a man who lived by violence and outside the law," and, again, "nothing but a gangster."[43]

The *San Francisco Chronicle* placed Orloff's comments prominently in the third paragraph of its lead story: "I must say I am not surprised he ended up meeting a violent death because violence was so much a part of his life. As they say: 'He who lives by the sword dies by the sword.'"[44]

Likewise, in the Oakland *Tribune* an unidentified Oakland police sergeant said Newton "finally got what he deserved. It's really a shame they made a martyr out of him. He died like the thug he was."[45] These highly charged repudiations of Newton's life greatly outnumbered the few favorable comments.

Other language also disparaged Newton. *USA Today* suggested that Newton deceived his followers. The paper said, "in the early '70s, Newton and the Panthers pulled in donations from the 'radical chic,' but one, at least, felt he had been 'suckered' by 'the black hero of the left.'"[46] The *Washington Post* too suggested that Newton was a fraud. The paper offered this description of Newton's court appearances: "Newton, working toward a doctorate in the History of Consciousness program at the University of California at Santa Cruz, *tried to portray himself* as an intelligent academician being persecuted for political reasons" (emphasis added).[47]

As in the *Times*, this negative language was complemented and supported by long recitations of Newton's criminal record. One-third of some reports was devoted solely to past charges, with little distinction made between *charges* and *convictions*. No attempt was made to place the arrests in the context of political confrontations between Panthers and the police.

The *Houston Post* began this section: "Newton, like other Panther leaders, accumulated a long criminal record, and was tried five times in two slayings."[48] The *Atlanta Constitution* changed this last statistic misleadingly to "five counts of murder."[49] A *San Francisco Chronicle* report—"Troubled Life of Huey Newton"—was a chronology of court dates from October 22, 1966 to August 22, 1989.[50]

Critical commentary and criminal records are standard news fare. But, in Newton's case, the sources of criticism, the amount of space given to charges, and the context of overall coverage supported the portrayal of a man of violence who accomplished little and got the end he deserved. The stories effected a repudiation of Newton's accomplishments and a reduction of his life to court dates and a criminal record.

EXCEPTION AND CONVENTION

Exceptions to this overwhelmingly negative portrayal were found. Though they were few, the exceptions help point out the degradation offered by the *Times* and other newspapers. And they suggest some reporting angles that might have been pursued.

In the hours after Newton's killing, people in Oakland responded in remarkable fashion. The death site—used so ironically against Newton in newspaper leads—became a kind of shrine. This has become a somewhat macabre tradition more recently, with flowers piled on sidewalks or outside apartment buildings. But at the time of Newton's killing, the tradition had not yet been established. And this was no ordinary shrine of flowers placed along the sidewalk. Notes of thanks to Newton were attached to some bouquets. One note said, "Huey, thanks for all you tried to do. We won't let the children forget." Banners were draped on a fence. People gathered and stayed. Candles and incense were burned. Videotapes of Newton's speeches were played. Stories were told. People remained into the following night, grieving Newton's death and celebrating his life.[51]

It was a scene totally at odds with newspaper portrayals of Newton as a failure, fraud, and thug. It was a scene unreported by the *Times* and every newspaper outside of California.

Even the California newspapers, with their saturation coverage, found little room for the mourning in Oakland. For example, the *San Francisco Chronicle* carried only an AP photograph of a man crouched in front of flowers at the scene.[52] The Oakland *Tribune* provided quotations from local people at the gathering whose lives had been touched by Newton. But the paper dismissed those who gathered in devotion, saying they were on "a somewhat ghoulish pilgrimage."[53]

Only the *Los Angeles Times* departed from the antagonistic portrait of Newton to report the devotion on the street and allow a more complex picture of Newton to emerge.[54] In the middle of its lead account, the paper reported the clusters of people visiting the scene, the bouquets, the banners, the videotapes. It included the AP photo of the man crouched in front of flowers.[55] And the paper reported a morbid, memorable image that appeared in no other paper:

> One elderly man who declined to give his name spent several minutes using a white plastic-foam coffee cup to scoop up blood that had pooled in a gutter. When he had filled a plastic juice container, he left.
> "Huey was very special, very special," he said while walking off to catch a bus back to his East Oakland home. "You don't find too many black men like Huey."
> "That blood is highly symbolic," said Ojo Pede, 38, a Nigerian exchange student who had watched the old man. Pede, who said he had come down from Berkeley for a personal vigil, did not elaborate.[56]

But even this signal scene received no follow-up. The depth of feeling suggested, the meaning of Huey Newton for people of color in Oakland, was touched upon but then dropped. Indeed, the scene was immediately followed in the report by conventional paragraphs on the time and cause of death as reported by a police spokesman. Yet, for a few paragraphs, a hint of a different approach had been raised.

One possible explanation can be rejected: Perhaps reporters did not have time to file such portrayals of Newton? But deadline pressures do not explain the omission of the vigil scene. Newton was shot in the early morning of August 22, too late for stories in that day's morning papers, even on the West Coast. Stories did not run around the country until the following day. Reporters thus were filing their accounts throughout the day, as the devotions were taking place. Nor can it be said that the memorial—dramatic and spontaneous—lacked news value. Rather, the conclusion of this study will suggest that homage and devotion to Newton simply did not fit with the mythic portrayal of the Scapegoat and the degradation of one who dissented from the social consensus.

ONE DEGRADING APPROACH

To sum up the analysis thus far: A close reading of the *Times*—and a follow-up study of 11 other newspapers—has shown that three themes combined to offer one degrading approach to the death of Huey Newton. Through irony, the reports disavowed the importance of his life. Through incongruity, the reports built descriptive contrasts that emphasized the sordidness of his demise. Through citation of his criminal record, the reports portrayed him as a cheap thug and a gangster. Newspapers omitted sources and events that might refute or balance this portrayal. They depicted Newton's death in terms that demeaned and devalued his life and work.

Many other approaches might have been taken. One approach already has been suggested. News reports could have focused on Newton's stature and role in the black neighborhoods of Oakland. Too, the news could have retained its focus on Newton's trouble with the law but placed these troubles within a drama of a rogue outlaw confronting the system. Yet another approach might have been to see Newton as an embodiment of the struggle against racism, poverty, and drugs. All these approaches could have been employed without violating news values or sacrificing dramatic interest. But only one approach was pursued by all the newspapers.

There was no need for news strategies that portrayed Newton as a hero. There was no question that Newton lived a life strung taut by violence. But that violence and its meaning were not to be captured in some dry recitation of court appearances and quotes from a frustrated district attorney. Newton and violence were part of a context of racism, police persecution, civil rights strategy, and revolution, and the tension between law and authority, books and streets, words and guns. Newton was a worthy, compelling subject for the news. But because he strained against societal preconceptions and journalistic conventions of political protest, he was strategically and emphatically vilified. How are we to explain this unanimous degradation?

IDEOLOGY AND THE NEWS

Some writers might explain this vilifying news coverage solely in terms of entrenched social and political beliefs—that is, ideology. A professor of media and society, Todd Gitlin, has stated that an important task of a society's dominant ideology is to define—but also to define away—radical opposition. The news media, Gitlin argues, often take on this task of "defining away" the opposition.[57] In these terms, the life and work of Huey Newton were "defined away" by demeaning stories offered at his death.

To the dominant social ideology of the United States, Huey Newton was—perhaps still is—a threat. He embodied a willingness to confront, an embrace of the radical and the extreme. He articulated the rage and aspirations of a huge underclass. He represented a sustained challenge to an inadequate social structure. He antagonized authority, redressed grievances, questioned the legitimacy of cops and courts and laws. He was a pain. He would not go away. Even with his death, he would not go away.

From this perspective, as leading ideological institutions, as "agents of social control," newspapers could not let such opposition go without comment.[58] In the news, the rich, troubled life of Huey Newton was presented as a desultory cliché: "He who lives by the sword dies by the sword." The meaning of his life and its tremendous and troubling connections to persistent plagues of poverty, drugs, racial barriers, and oppression were politically crushed beneath the dead weight of the cliché and its ironclad irony.

RACE AND THE NEWS

Other writers might attribute degrading coverage of Newton to race. It is difficult to judge the extent to which the devaluations in the news were tied to Newton's race. Certainly, white activists, as Gitlin has shown, have also met with derogation. White right-wing radicals are also demeaned.[59] Yet writers who have studied the Panthers make clear the early and persistent racism in the news.

"The distortions about the Panthers to which white America has been subjected have appeared everywhere in the media," wrote Gene Marine in his book on the group, "not merely in the 'good' and conscientious newspapers." The news, he added, "can hardly be expected to seek out subtleties about black men with guns."[60]

Gilbert Moore, a black reporter for *Life*, wrote that the "myth" of the fearsome black man "was picked up and perpetuated by a nearsighted press which could not see past Huey's bandoliers. White readers could readily believe the mass circulation of half-truths."[61]

The black writer James Baldwin echoed the sentiment years before Newton's death:

Huey Newton is one of the most important people to have been produced by the American chaos. His fate is very important. And not one person in white America, if they read the mass media, knows anything about Huey, what produced him or what produced the Black Panther Party.[62]

SCAPEGOATS: ALL THOSE WHO DISSENT?

Ideology and race offer important ways of understanding news reporting on Huey Newton. Myth, though, presents a larger view. Surely news stories on Newton did much more than simply report his death. They suggested, in fact, that Newton's demise was in some way the logical, just result of a life lived outside of and opposed to the social consensus. The irony of the leads, the contrasting neighborhood descriptions, the emphasis on his criminal record, the choice of sources—all combined to structure a portrayal that found in Newton's death justice and retribution. His radical ways brought to Newton, the reports suggested, a deserved fate. The news was clearly offering an enactment of dramatically satisfying sanctions against one who would challenge the social consensus. News was providing a scapegoat.

From this perspective, the stories in the *Times* and other newspapers were doing what myth has always done. As we have seen, "which myth gets told" often is related to social order. Myth upholds and affirms accepted and assumed societal values. Sometimes myth does so by making an example of one who rejects or neglects those values.

The Scapegoat is a particularly effective archetypal model. Not only does the Scapegoat myth ridicule and degrade the individual. The myth "explains away" the faults, problems, or issues raised by the individual. And the myth serves as a warning to those who might take a similar path.

In the case of Huey Newton, news depicted the degradation of a scapegoat who chose to challenge the established order. The death of Newton exposed some especially sensitive "fault" lines in U.S. society. Racial politics and radical politics raise unresolved issues that cut to the core of social order. Does the United States have equality for all individuals? Are equal opportunities provided for personal, social, and political fulfillment? Is there fair and just distribution of wealth and power? News coverage of Huey Newton suggests that social order imposes limits on how those questions can be raised and pursued.

Though other papers participated in the overwhelming degradation of Newton, the *Times* bears special attention. As the United States's leading newspaper, the *Times* has particular influence. As the national paper of record, the *Times* leaves an imprint for the future. As State Scribe, the *Times* must be carefully watched for the ways it might degrade and demean those who threaten the state.

Yet, as we have seen, the *Times*, more than most news organizations, seems to embody the status quo. Some reasons: The *Times* in particular relies upon government and official sources for much of its reporting. The *Times* in particular is structured around an internal mission that claims to record impassively the views of these sources. The *Times* in particular is a large and still growing institution that has thrived within the dominant economic and political system. And the *Times* in particular draws many of its reporters from a privileged social and cultural elite who also have prospered within the current system. For all these reasons, the *Times* may have special trouble reporting on challenges to established social order.

The issue thus remains larger than Huey Newton and the Black Panthers. Many groups dissent from society's accepted thinking. From the political left and right, groups protest against various social issues, including the capitalist state, the welfare state, taxes, nuclear power, the power of the federal government, abortion, guns, and gun control. To the extent these groups depart radically from society's beliefs, to the extent they protest vigorously from society's conventions, to the extent they threaten social order, these groups may expect to be isolated and degraded by the news through the myth of the Scapegoat.

Chapter 5

The Hero

Mark McGwire and
"Godding Up" U.S. Celebrities

For much of the 1998 baseball season, Mark McGwire captured the attention of the nation. The St. Louis Cardinal's first baseman was pursuing one of baseball's long-standing marks: the single-season home run record of 61, set by New York Yankee Roger Maris in 1961. Maris, in turn, had surpassed the 1927 record of 60 home runs set by the Yankees's Babe Ruth.

McGwire and Chicago Cubs outfielder Sammy Sosa, from the Dominican Republic, pursued the record throughout the summer. News reports daily—and then almost hourly—followed the quest. And on September 8, in front of a national television audience, the Maris family, and baseball luminaries, McGwire broke the record. The *New York Times* published this story:

> From the time he began playing baseball as an 8-year-old in Claremont, Calif., Mark McGwire has been a reluctant home run hitter and a reluctant hero. McGwire wanted to be a pitcher, not a hitter, and he remained on the

mound until college. He has always wanted to avoid being the primary focus in a team sport.

But no matter how reluctant McGwire is to be the slugger in the spotlight, his thunderous swings produce the sort of prodigious home runs that have turned him into a larger-than-life figure. Every fan loves watching baseballs rocket out of stadiums, so every fan has reveled in McGwire's prowess as he has slipped into his crouch, uncoiled and crushed another pitch. Especially this season.

McGwire's captivating run to history culminated last night when he belted his 62d homer to eclipse Roger Maris's hallowed 37-year-old record for the most in one season. McGwire, whose reluctance abated as he glided toward this moment,broke the record in the St. Louis Cardinals' 145th game. He instantly became the most successful home run hitter for one season and a modern baseball hero.[1]

THE HERO MYTH

The Hero may be humanity's most enduring archetype and the basis for its most pervasive myth.[2] Every society likely has dramatized and personified its core values and ideals in stories of a hero. The Hero, Eliade noted, embraces one of the chief characteristics of myth, "the creation of exemplary models for a whole society." He went on: "In this, moreover, we recognise a very general human tendency; namely, to hold up one life-history as a paradigm and turn a historical personage into an archetype."[3] Myth, as we've seen, "supplies models for human behavior and, by that very fact, gives meaning and value to life."[4]

The Hero myth, like many archetypal stories, often takes similar forms from age to age. The Hero is born into humble circumstance. The Hero initiates a quest or journey. The Hero faces battles or trials, and wins a decisive victory. The Hero returns triumphant. The pattern, in more or less detail, can be found throughout mythology.[5]

Though often the story pattern is similar, the nature of the Hero changes from society to society and from era to era.[6] The nature of the Hero shapes—and is shaped by—society. The Hero can reveal much about society. Heroes serve as exemplary models, as Eliade emphasized, for qualities that an individual society prizes, such as modesty, hard work, courage, virtue, wisdom, or loyalty. "A hero can be poet, prophet, king, priest or what you will, according to the kind of world he finds himself born into," wrote Thomas Carlyle.[7] In this vein, heroes can indeed have "a thousand faces," as Joseph Campbell stressed.[8] They can be warriors or pacifists, leaders or rebels, saints or sinners, rocket scientists, rock musicians, or sports stars.

Sports have been inextricably entwined with the Hero myth. Sports provide fine raw material for the myth. They offer drama and conflict. They often are performed on a public stage. They evoke binary oppositions, which are often found at the heart of myth, such as winning and losing, success and failure. They recur, often daily, allowing myths to be retold as myths must be. For these reasons, myths have celebrated sports heroes since the time of the ancient Greeks.[9]

Like other myths, stories of the sports hero illustrate social values and stake out the boundaries of social order. Sports banquet speakers often extol the values learned from sport, such as teamwork and perseverance. But other social values can be more subtle. For example, some societies may celebrate a sports hero who displays brute force and power, aggression, or an overwhelming desire to succeed. Other societies may hold up heroes who show compassion and concern for others as they triumph. Some societies may embrace fierce individualism. Others may endorse teamwork and sacrifice. In all societies, some values are celebrated, some are degraded. Some behaviors are lauded, some are demeaned. In portrayals of right and wrong, good and evil, success and failure, myths of the sports hero reflect and reaffirm core values and beliefs.

THE MODERN HERO: NO HERO?

Modern society, perhaps unsurprisingly, has developed a particularly ambivalent relationship with the Hero myth. Modern society suggests that heroes are creations needed by "less advanced" societies. "We have become self-conscious about our admiration for all models of human greatness," historian Daniel Boorstin wrote. "We know that somehow they were not what they seem. They simply illustrate the laws of social illusion."[10] Boorstin argued that our mass-mediated society has transformed heroes into celebrities, human pseudoevents who can be created, packaged, marketed. Once created and consumed, these false heroes are degraded and discarded.

Boorstin was not alone. Campbell too felt that modern society was a hostile place for heroes. Writing of "The Hero Today," he said, "the democratic ideal of the self-determining individual, the invention of the power-driven machine, and the development of the scientific method of research, have so transformed human life that the long-inherited, timeless universe of symbols has collapsed."[11] In our time, the Hero has apparently become a celebrity—no hero at all.

The decline of the modern hero most often is attributed to mass media. The massive coverage of social life given by newspapers, magazines, television, cable, talk radio, and now the Internet has helped transform and degrade the hero. Innumerable figures now receive the coverage and consideration that previous societies bestowed on only a select few. The individual hero has been replaced by a multitude.

Walter Ong has studied oral societies in which information is passed and stored through human speech and memory. Heroes in these societies must literally be memorable—a few, select, larger-than-life individuals.

> The figures around whom knowledge is made to cluster, those about whom stories are told or sung, must be made into conspicuous personages, foci of common attention, individuals embodying open public concerns, as written laws would later be matters of open public concern. In other words, the figures around whom knowledge is made to cluster must be heroes, culturally "large" or "heavy" figures like Odysseus, or Achilles or Oedipus. Such figures are essential for oral culture in order to anchor the float of detail which literate cultures fix in script. These figures, moreover, cannot be too numerous or attention will be dissipated and focus blurred.[12]

Modern mass media have created an opposite situation. Mass media, publishing online or on-air 24 hours a day, have an insatiable need for well-known figures capable of attracting and holding audiences. The mass media restlessly churn through such figures, filling much airtime but producing few heroes. Stories on the late Princess Diana and John F. Kennedy Jr. were quickly followed, even when they were alive, by stories on Michael Jordan, Oprah Winfrey, and others. As Boorstin said, "The titanic figure is now only one of thousands."[13] How could a hero stand out?

The mass media also discourage the creation of heroes in other ways. Today's public learns too much information about celebrities' lives. The celebrity is not placed on a pedestal or viewed from afar. Media inexhaustibly report on salary, weight, diet, relationships, family, and traffic tickets. The celebrity is not an exalted, respected personage but someone as familiar as family. Information, though, is not knowledge. Ironically, with excessive information, people *know* celebrities not at all and can come to resent the figure and the process.

Such familiarity breeds contempt. Mass media coverage has also been characterized by sensational and negative reporting. Writers of other eras often overlooked negative news about politicians, sports stars, and Hollywood figures. Modern media seem to revel in negative news. Talk radio, for example, is often an outlet for vilification, a forum for bitterness and bile directed at others. The relationship between some celebrities and the press now often is notable for its hostility.

Sports heroes in particular have not fared well in our modern era. Boorstin counted sports heroes among the superficial creations of a celebrity culture, persons known for being well known, whose "chief claim to fame is their fame itself."[14] Others too have argued that the modern sports hero is a "pseudohero." In *American Heroes in a Media Age*, Susan Drucker looked closely at sports heroes. She wrote:

> What we see evolving from our dependence on the new relationships forged with celebrities is a shift from the traditional notion of the hero as a transcendent character dominating events through great deeds to a more ordinary but highly talented and well-publicized person who reflects our desire to escape ordinariness and gain some recognition in an impersonal, technological world. . . . On the surface professional sports seem to offer a natural source for heroes, but on closer examination they offered celebrated sports figures shaped, fashioned, and marketed as heroic.[15]

The historian Allen Guttmann sees the modern sports hero as a secular replacement for a once-sacred figure. "When we can no longer distinguish the sacred from the profane or even the good from the bad, we content ourselves with minute discriminations between the batting average of the .308 hitter and the .307 hitter. Once the gods have vanished from Mount Olympus or from Dante's paradise, we can no longer run to appease them or to save our souls, but we can set a new record. It is a uniquely modern form of immortality."[16]

MARK McGWIRE: CELEBRITY AS HERO?

Yet in 1998 the news suggested that the traditional myth of the Hero might still be alive. News reports seemed willing to embrace Mark McGwire as a modern hero. His pursuit of the record was framed as a hallowed quest. His background and biography were recounted in reverential tones. His strength was hailed. His feats were lauded. His work ethic was praised. He was seen as an embodiment of important social values, such as hard work, persistence in the face of adversity, sacrifice, modesty, and maintaining a proper balance between work and family. His success was treated as a highly respected accomplishment, one with significance for the larger society.

But coverage of McGwire seemed torn between the traditional and the modern. As McGwire chased the home-run record, news media offered the superabundance of celebrity coverage that characterizes modern society. Some of this reporting yielded the microscopic, probing coverage that reduces and degrades the sports figure. Seemingly every aspect of McGwire's life was opened to inspection, including his childhood, failed marriage, therapy, diet, workout routine, and relationship with his former wife and their son. Media raised questions about McGwire's use of performance-enhancing drugs. They raised questions of race, comparing the attention paid to McGwire with the lesser attention given his rival from the Dominican Republic, Sammy Sosa. They even raised questions about their own reporting, dwelling on the saturation coverage, media ethics, and the relationship between sport figures and the press.

Can McGwire, although surely a creation of American celebrity culture, also be understood as a modern, mythic Hero? Did the news recount the classic story? This chapter looks closely at reporting on McGwire from the perspective of the Hero myth. It looks at the ways in which McGwire was portrayed in the *Times*. It looks for the structure and form of the heroic pattern: the birth into humble circumstance, the quest, the battles or trials, the decisive victory, the triumphant return. It looks for the modern variations of the age-old story. How did the *Times* reconcile the traditional myth and modern society's suspicion of heroes? Finally, it looks at the beliefs and values celebrated or denigrated. Heroes dramatize social values and help chart the boundaries of social order. In what ways might stories of this baseball player and his home runs contribute to social order?

The period of interest extended from February 25, 1998, when Major League Baseball players headed into spring training, to October 25, 1998, as the *Times* and other media finally put the 1998 baseball season to rest after the World Series. During that period, the *Times* published 582 stories that made reference to McGwire. Some "stories" were no more than one-line summaries of game results. Others were long, front-page features. I studied all of them to understand how a modern news medium might transform the accomplishments of a sports figure into myth.

Of immediate interest was celebrity status and its impact on the telling of the myth. As we will see, all of the elements of the Hero myth could be found in *Times* reporting, yet the story did not unfold in the usual fashion. The myth usually begins with the birth and humble beginnings of the Hero. Then, the myth relates the Hero's quest.

Times coverage did not follow this pattern. McGwire was already a celebrity, *well known*, as Boorstin stressed, as an athlete who had hit 58 home runs, three short of the record, the year before. *Times* 1998 coverage began with the quest. McGwire arrived at spring training with his journey set out before him. He undertook the quest and faced the trials of the season. Then, as the year progressed and it became clear that McGwire had a real chance of breaking the record, the reporting looked more closely at his birth and background. Other parts of the strong narrative structure then followed: for example, the decisive victory, the triumphant return. The sections below follow this modern restructuring and look in detail at the myth of the Hero in the *New York Times*.

THE QUEST
A Venerated Record

The first stories on McGwire in the *Times* placed him immediately in the context of a quest. In a February season preview, the *Times* said that McGwire and Seattle's Ken Griffey "are the princes in hottest pursuit of Roger Maris's home run record of 61."[17] Another preview took up the theme: "Except for ardent fans, though, Cardinals watchers will focus on Mark McGwire and his attempt to surpass the 58 home runs he hit last year."[18] Even the editorial page anticipated the quest. In its own preview of the baseball season, an editorial predicted that "somebody may finally eclipse Roger Maris's 37-year-old record of 61 home runs in a single season. Our money is on Mark McGwire of the St. Louis Cardinals."[19] Interestingly, stories early and explicitly used the word "quest," thereby directly invoking the myth. For example, one story discussed McGwire's "quest for one of baseball's most historic records."[20] Another looked at the "player and his quest."[21]

The opening words of opening-day coverage began with the quest: "One down, 60 to go. Mark McGwire started the season with a bang, hitting a grand slam in the fifth inning off Ramon Martinez and leading St. Louis over visiting Los Angeles." The article stated that McGwire was "expected to challenge Roger Maris's home-run record of 61 in this expansion year."[22]

The quest was also immediately portrayed as a highly prized goal with societal import. "McGwire is in pursuit of the single-season home run record, perhaps the most significant record in American sports," one *Times* story said.[23] Another stated, "It is for the most heralded record in American sports."[24] Still another called it "perhaps the most famous benchmark in sports."[25] An editorial said, "the prize is the most venerated record in American sports."[26]

And the quest, the *Times* said, had societal significance beyond sports.

> We are reminded of the collective hold that baseball and Babe Ruth and Roger Maris have on us. The games drag on incessantly; the non-leaders dither; but we always know what Nos. 60 and 61 and 62 signify—power and reflexes, the ball soaring through the stratosphere, the slugger gaping at his wondrous act, the gabber in the booth chanting, "Going, going, gone."
>
> We know. It is in our collective genes. The home run is still America's great signature sporting feat.[27]

Another report said, "No other sport has seen anything like it; in fact, no other sport seems to have a record that can equal the home run mark for glamour, notoriety and its unyielding grip on the American consciousness."[28]

Almost daily, the *Times* followed the quest, reporting on McGwire's successes and failures throughout the season. And around the country, the *Times* noted, the nation too followed the quest. Numerous stories reported that attendance rose at ballparks when McGwire and the Cardinals came to town. McGwire, the *Times* reminded, was a hero. A reporter spoke with a fan, John Moranville, who arrived early for batting practice. "To me, McGwire has brought back a lot of interest in baseball," he said. "I was a fan of the Cardinals with Stan Musial and Red Schoendienst. Back then, baseball was everything to kids. Now, I don't think it's everything. McGwire is bringing that back. Kids need heroes. He's a hero."[29]

Trials

The Hero's quest, of course, cannot proceed without struggle and strife. The *Times* followed the trials McGwire faced. Some of the tests were the usual ups and downs of a baseball season. The *Times* dutifully chronicled the strikeouts and pop-ups.

A dejected Mark McGwire emerged from the showers at Busch Stadium with a blue towel wrapped around his waist, another wrapped around his neck, and a forlorn look on his face. The muscular giant who is chasing Roger Maris's 37-year-old record of 61 homers in a season had a dismal game tonight, striking out three times against the Mets while the Cardinals lost, 4–2.[30]

Modern heroes, however, endure modern pressures. Much of McGwire's struggle—and much *Times* coverage—concerned news coverage itself. "McGwire is showing signs of being a bit overwhelmed by the home-run hysteria that so far is only threatening to consume him everywhere he travels," the paper said. "He popped nine homers at practice, then said, 'I felt like a caged lion, and I didn't like it.'" But, the story continued, "Life in the fish bowl goes on. And until McGwire proves otherwise, both Roger Maris's burden as well as his record remain immense."[31] Another *Times* story reported the media pressure: "Unfortunately for McGwire, his quest for one of baseball's most historic records is still a major story."[32] A similar story acknowledged that the attention focused on a "player and his quest can make his life miserable. It did that to Maris in 1961, and even McGwire had shown signs of strain in recent weeks as he struggled to add to his total."[33]

News coverage brought other modern pressures to the quest, the *Times* showed. On August 10, deep into the season, Sammy Sosa hit his 45th and 46th homers to tie McGwire and raise the very real possibility that the former, rather than the latter, would break the record. The *Times* and other news media seemed then to recognize that Sosa had been relatively ignored in comparison to McGwire.

Suddenly McGwire found himself in the swirl of a controversy. The *Times* wondered if McGwire had been the beneficiary of coverage slanted by racism. News reporting looked back at news reporting and found that stories had indeed favored McGwire. McGwire could not be faulted for the coverage, but he was forced to address the issue. One headline asked, "He's Chasing Record, Too, But Where Is Sosa-Mania?"[34] Another story began: "Sammy Sosa Also-Ran."[35]

"It's always McGwire, McGwire, McGwire; there's too much McGwire," complained Charles Rosario, who works at an electronics store in Washington Heights. "I think it's because McGwire is American, and white, and Sosa is a Dominican, and black. Americans want to see McGwire break the record."[36]

As if in response, McGwire and Sosa apparently formed a bond to defuse the controversy and competition. And the *Times* seemed willing to transform the competition between them into a shared quest. Sosa was often quoted saying of McGwire, "He's the man."[37] When the Cardinals and Cubs played one another, the *Times* reported, "Sosa reiterated he is rooting for McGwire, and McGwire said Sosa's chance to break Roger Maris' record of 61 is as good as his." The story relayed this scene:

> As McGwire was lying in the grass, stretching and waiting for batting practice, a playful Sosa approached him, followed by a horde of TV cameras. McGwire did his best imitation of Sosa's salute, in which he takes two fingers and blows kisses just before thumping his heart before jumping to his feet. The two then embraced.[38]

The *Times* also showed another modern trial produced by news coverage. In late August, an AP reporter, standing with dozens of journalists in front of McGwire's open locker, noticed a bottle with the word "androstenedione"—a legal, over-the-counter drug banned in some sports but not in baseball. For example, Randy Barnes, the 1996 Olympic shot-put gold medalist, was banned from his sport for life because he used androstenedione.[39] "Andro," as it is often called, has been compared to anabolic steroids. It is a testosterone-producing substance that builds muscles and helps recovery from injury. McGwire said he had used it for more than a year, along with the more common creatine, a muscle-building nutritional supplement.

The AP ran a story on McGwire's use of andro and other media followed suit. The reporting caused immediate controversy. *Times* coverage depicted the implications for this hero and his quest. One columnist wrote, "Here, suddenly, comes the potentially myth-debunking news that Popeye supplements his spinach with a testosterone-producing pill."[40]

Some *Times* reporters defended the hero. They emphasized that andro could not directly affect a player's ability to hit home runs—a complicated feat involving much more than muscle mass. They felt that the drug should not taint the quest. "In past years," a reporter wrote, "some of the game's best players were said to have played their careers on amphetamines. So no bluenose asterisk, please, for a McGwire home run record."[41] Some went further and compared the drug to pasta or steak.

> Reckless or harmless, athletes have always sought an edge. Steak, for example, was once considered the best pre-game meal. Now it is dispar-

aged, in favor of pasta. Ty Cobb eschewed both in favor of sharpening his spikes.

The bottom line on Mark David McGwire, however, is that he is legitimately the most astonishing home run hitter the world has known since George Herman Ruth ambled to the plate.[42]

But other *Times* writers were not so sure. Other *Times* stories noted that for years McGwire often missed many games due to injury, yet during 1998 he was almost injury-free. "Of course we would all like to believe that Paul Bunyan has no chemical charge," a columnist wrote. "So how do we deal with an issue that has been dutifully avoided as McGwire mounted his home run assault with a body that vaguely resembles the one he once had?" He added, "This is baseball, not a sport we visit every few years, and this home run quest is one that reaches deep into our childhood souls."[43]

Another wrote, "The long, grueling home run chase has been tainted by the revelation that its front-runner has been using performance-enhancing drugs." The writer wondered why others didn't think so. "We're giving McGwire standing ovations, but I wonder what we're celebrating: the work of a hero or the spectacle of a hero fashioning his own destruction—for our pleasure."[44] A letter to the editor recognized some implications of media coverage for the modern hero: "I long for the time when heroes were heroes, though I'm not sure if the heroes were really more pure or only seemed that way because the public didn't have the chance to dwell on their flaws."[45]

HUMBLE BIRTH AND SOCIAL VALUES

McGwire endured these trials and continued to chase the record. As the season progressed, *Times* reports began to look more closely at McGwire. These reports, however, were not investigative in nature. They were not aimed at "digging up dirt." Instead, the coverage attempted to supply the first part of the Hero myth: narrating his birth and telling the story of his emergence.

In many myths, the story here seeks to "explain" the Hero. It identifies the social values embodied by the Hero. It supplies a model. It points to the lessons to be learned from this exemplary figure. How did the Hero rise from humble background to glorious heights? In reporting of McGwire, the *Times* explicitly proclaimed that this particular hero embodied hard work and persistence. These were the "approved" values illustrated by McGwire. Implicitly and indirectly, however, the *Times* suggested that other values were present. Brute force and almost monster-like power also marked this hero.

Willing to Work

The approved social values were made clear. For example, one report traced the progress of the California-born dentist's son from high school pitcher to Major League Baseball elite. "Nobody visualized McGwire as a great hitter when he was in high school," the report said. But, a coach noted, McGwire "was willing to work." Later the report said, "In time, and with work, McGwire became a star hitter in college and was drafted 10th over all by Oakland in 1984. Three years later he hit 49 home runs in his first season for the Athletics—11 more than any rookie had ever hit."

But making it to the Major League was only part of the hero's emergence. "McGwire continued to hit home runs," the *Times* said, "but his average plummeted from year to year, from .289 to .260 to .231, and in 1991, he batted .201. He had that big hole in his swing, at his hands, and he struck out about once in every three times at bat." His eyesight was partially at fault. He eventually corrected the problem with contact lenses.

Still, the struggles continued. "As soon as he addressed his vision trouble, McGwire started sustaining injuries, primarily to his left heel," the *Times* said. He played only intermittently during the 1993–1994 seasons. "He said he considered quitting and becoming a police officer, but he thought about his father, John, a dentist, who contracted polio at seven. "He never had a chance to play sports when he was a kid," McGwire once explained. "When I think of my father, it makes my injuries seem so minuscule." And so McGwire kept working. "The next thing you know, they're talking about my name along with Babe Ruth, Roger Maris, Mickey Mantle. It's overwhelming."[46]

The *Times* returned to the story after McGwire broke the record. One long feature story began with an almost archetypal, journalistic lead: "Mark David McGwire, born Oct. 1, 1963, was the second oldest in a sports-oriented family of five boys whose cul-de-sac was a field for all seasons."[47] How did McGwire rise to such heroic heights from his common, cul-de-sac background? Again, hard work, was the answer.

> Listen to the people who watched McGwire develop from a robust teenager who played golf and soccer before baseball, and they inevitably dis-

cuss his work habits. Although his tantalizing story sometimes seems pre-destined—he homered in his first at-bat for the Claremont Little League Athletics—McGwire did not wake up as a 17-year-old with a 90-mile-an-hour fastball and a mighty uppercut.

Tom Carroll, who coached McGwire at Damien High School in La Verne, Calif., has a vision of him that swims in his mind. It is McGwire on the field or in the dugout with his red hair drenched, his face sweating. That is how McGwire always looked to Carroll: working or poised to work.

"Mark was not afraid to work," Carroll said. "God gave him talent, but he worked hard, and that set him apart. God gives everyone talents. Mark did something with his."[48]

Through hard work and persistence, the *Times* said, McGwire was able to endure a later litany of modern problems. "Like everyone, McGwire has had his share of problems. He underwent therapy for four years because, he said, he was an emotional wreck after his baseball struggles in 1991. He faltered as a husband, was divorced after four years of marriage and has said he wishes he could do it all over."[49] And the *Times* noted that McGwire worked hard to keep a close relationship with his 10-year-old son, Matthew McGwire, who served as a batboy for part of the summer of 1998 when he visited from San Diego. Hard work, *Times* said, produced this hero.

Power and Force

Though some stories emphasized his hard work, other *Times* stories more subtly affirmed that McGwire was marked for greatness by force and power. Many descriptions, employing traditional sportswriting hyperbole, emphasized his strength, his "6 feet 5 inches and 250 pounds, his biceps and quadriceps straining the fabric of his uniform."[50] His force was seen as superhuman, almost monster-like. One story called him "the massive 34-year-old first baseman."[51] Another said, "Tonight, in the shadow of the Gateway Arch, the big man will flex muscles as broad as the river that flows past."[52] Another called him "this 6-foot-5-inch, 250-pound Godzilla with a bat."[53]

Numerous stories compared him to other myth-like figures of great force, such as Paul Bunyan, Atlas, and Hercules. One story called him "the Bunyanesque slugger."[54] Another said he was "a red-headed Paul Bunyan."[55] Another report talked about McGwire "smashing the ball with his Paul Bunyan swing."[56] Still another referred to his "Atlas-like shoulders."[57] A report noted "the demands that he continue to be Herculean."[58] As one report said,

> It is McGwire, Paul Bunyan with a bat, 6 feet 5 inches of power bulging in his massive forearms and shoulders, who not only transfixes fans and players alike but also sweeps them along in the belief—the hope—that he will make a successful assault on Roger Maris's single-season home run record of 61.[59]

Though the *Times* sought to depict McGwire as a model of hard work, he also emerged as a model of brute force and power.

THE TRIUMPH
The Quest Realized

On September 5, the first stage of the quest was completed. McGwire broke Ruth's record. In its front-page story, accompanied by a photograph, the *Times* celebrated the quest and placed McGwire in the pantheon of baseball heroes: "First there was Babe Ruth, then Roger Maris, now Mark McGwire."[60]

Two days later, on September 7, against the Chicago Cubs and Sammy Sosa, McGwire tied Maris. Another front-page story and photograph carried the news.[61] Coverage of the triumph brought together previous themes of history and family: "It was a priceless slice of history, because of what McGwire accomplished—tying Roger Maris's single-season home run record—and because it was fraught with the disparate feelings of an epic event and a family picnic."

> His father was here. His mother was in the next seat. His son was waiting for him. It could have been a dream, but it was not. It was as real as McGwire's storybook season, which continued to unreel like a movie, one that would star Kevin Costner or Robert Redford. McGwire's son did not arrive from California until 30 minutes before the game, and yesterday was also the 61st birthday of McGwire's father. Is there such a thing as fate? The McGwire family thinks so.[62]

McGwire was also shown to be a generous, compassionate conqueror. Numerous articles mentioned his acknowledgment of the Maris family: "McGwire, so focused on family, did not forget the family of the man he will be linked with forever. Once he returned to the dugout, he pointed to the heavens, pointed to his heart to let the Marises know their father was with him and blew them a kiss."[63]

The competition with Sosa, and its racial implications, was also raised and resolved in the moment of triumph. One story said, "In the last couple of weeks, it has been impossible to miss that McGwire, a very large, white dentist's son from California, has been simpatico with Sosa, a compact, dark-skinned man from the Dominican Republic, and vice versa." The story called them "the two amigos."[64]

On September 8, the final stage of the quest was realized. McGwire broke Maris's record. Again, many of the previous themes were encompassed, including power, Paul Bunyan, family, hard work, and his relationship with Sosa. The lead announced: "Mark McGwire, the St. Louis Cardinals' Paul Bunyan with a bat, made the most out of the least tonight, setting Major League Baseball's home run record by hitting his 62d and shortest home run of the season."[65]

> McGwire has earned his success by working through a mid- career slump and injuries and also personal doubts, brought on by a failed marriage. (Last night he thanked "my great ex-wife and her husband, for getting my son here.") He has openly discussed how he sought therapy, and has been a model father, as well as volunteering in the battle against child abuse. In this year of long home runs and adoring fans and constant media attention, McGwire has seemed to grow into his role, embracing Sammy Sosa in a friendly duel that has only good vibrations.[66]

The *Times* lauded McGwire as "a modern baseball hero."[67] The editorial pages too joined in the acclamation. An editorial proclaimed that "this was a joyful moment to be savored and celebrated, by McGwire and by anyone who loves sports and baseball in particular."[68]

Exemplary Model for Society

The extended coverage suggested that McGwire's successful quest had large, societal lessons. Thomas Friedman, who usually writes about international affairs on the op-ed page, found a civics lesson in the McGwire story. He said:

> What was so striking about McGwire was how a man with a rocky past grew to understand that breaking this record made him a role model, like

it or not, and therefore imposed upon him a special obligation to both his historic predecessors—namely Babe Ruth and Roger Maris—but also to the fans. And because he brought out the best in himself, in both words and deeds—honoring the Maris family, signing endless autographs and giving endless interviews—he has brought out the best in the fans as well. . . .

No, in their own way, this poor Dominican street kid named Sammy and the well-to-do dentist's son from Southern California named Mac are giving the country the civics lesson it needs most—reminding us that a democratic society is not just about the letter of laws, but about the spirit of laws. It is not just about rules, but about norms. It is not just about legalistic job descriptions, but about role models. It is not just about the entitlements of "me" and "now," but about the obligations to those who came before and those who will come after.[69]

Other reports too suggested that the quest had broad, though unde-fined, social meaning. "Before the game, McGwire said that he was only beginning to understand what his and Sosa's pursuit of the record had meant to the country and maybe to the world."[70] Another report echoed the sentiment: "So it has struck McGwire that this pursuit is not about the number, but about the impact this race has had on the nation."[71]

One report summed up the success of this hero: "At last, a modern star moved past the black-and-white ghosts of the past to wrest away base-ball's most prestigious record. Today's era now has its own bona-fide hero, one that has joined the towering figures of old."[72]

THE RETURN: NO JOYFUL
HOMECOMING FOR THE MODERN HERO

Often in myth, the Hero's return is a triumphal celebration. The return of the modern hero, the *Times* showed, is not always a joyful homecoming. The media spotlight does not turn off. Modern heroes, the *Times* demon-strated, get no respite from the crush of media coverage. For the modern hero, the quest ends only when the media says it ends. In the aftermath of the euphoric coverage given to the record, the *Times* showed McGwire still dogged by troubling issues raised throughout the quest. He continued to be questioned about andro. His private life was still discussed. In the last weeks of the season, Sosa again tied McGwire and the subject of ra-cial favoritism was raised again.[73]

Times coverage showed McGwire—his quest finished—struggling still under the strain. "Maybe it's the claustrophobia in Mark McGwire that has turned him into a man who seems to be desperately searching for an air pocket as everything closes in on him: the season, Sammy Sosa, the news media, zealous fans, everything," an article said. "Once tucked in the Cardinals' clubhouse, he is hardly seen and barely heard, choosing to hang out in the back rooms instead of facing a crush of questions."[74]

Only when the season ended, and McGwire finished with 70 home runs, did the media bring McGwire's quest—and his trials—to a close. One last time, the *Times* embraced the hero and the quest as a social salve. It called McGwire "the larger-than-life superstar who has imbedded himself in the hearts of St. Louis fans and captivated the rest of the country with his performance and his demeanor."[75] An editorial concluded:

> Mark McGwire's prodigious home-run production this year has been just the right tonic to resuscitate baseball as the national pastime and to divert a public weary of scandal and global crises. The sight of this gentle, earnest giant handling the pressure of the home-run chase with grace and humility has made an entire nation feel better about itself.[76]

MODERN HEROES AND MODERN VALUES

The ways in which the *Times* combined the traditional heroic pattern and the modern celebrification of the Hero can tell much about our society and its journalism. The Hero is an exemplary figure who embodies social ideals. *Times* coverage of McGwire directly and indirectly depicted him in the context of social values that laid out the boundaries of social order.

The *Times* directly identified some values that McGwire represented. Hard work and persistence were consistent themes. McGwire rose to stardom from his suburban cul-de-sac because of hard work, the *Times* reported. He overcame early difficulties in the big leagues because of "his work habits," the *Times* said. "God gave him talent," as his coach said, "but he worked hard, and that set him apart. God gives everyone talents. Mark did something with his."[77]

McGwire was also portrayed as compassionate and kind. He was a "gentle, earnest giant," the *Times* said. He treated the Maris family with care. He contributed money to child abuse foundations. He developed a bond with Sosa. He had worked hard to forge relationships with his son, his ex-wife, and her husband. McGwire "brought out the best in the fans as well," the *Times* said.[78]

The summer of 1998 was dominated by news of President Bill Clinton's affair with Monica Lewinsky and subsequent Washington political machinations. The boundaries of social order had been very messily transgressed. McGwire was depicted as an antidote for "a public weary of scandal and global crises" who "made an entire nation feel better about itself."[79] He was, in some sense, offered as a substitute for a presidential model flawed by immorality. The national pastime was again soothing the nation. McGwire, the *Times* said, reminds us "that a democratic society is not just about the letter of laws, but about the spirit of laws."[80]

Read carefully, however, the McGwire coverage can also yield other values, perhaps not so readily celebrated. The *Times* and other news media made much of the revelation that McGwire used the drug androstenedione. McGwire's use of the drug can be interpreted in a number of ways. One implication is that McGwire had found a legal loophole and exploited an edge to increase his chances of success. As the *Times* pointed out, McGwire was ingesting a drug banned in other sports, though it was not banned by baseball. McGwire can also be understood as willing to risk future health problems for current success. The *Times* noted that possible side effects of the drug were unknown but might include sterility or cancer. McGwire thus was shown as willing to take those risks. The stress on success—and the willingness to exploit an edge or to exploit one's body— are values that lie just below the surface of *Times* coverage.

Another intriguing social value offered by the *Times* in coverage of McGwire was power. McGwire, the *Times* showed, embodied brute strength and force. Numerous *Times* stories emphasized his measurements, "6 feet 5 inches and 250 pounds, his biceps and quadriceps straining the fabric of his uniform."[81] He was "this 6-foot-5-inch, 250-pound Godzilla with a bat."[82] He was compared to other figures of great strength, such as Paul Bunyan, Atlas, and Hercules. This emphasis on power often characterizes news coverage of sports. And, many researchers have noted, portrayals of power are closely linked to definitions of masculinity and gender roles in society.

Media scholar Nick Trujillo argues that in sports news, "power itself is masculinized as strength, force, control, toughness, and domination" and that "sports media reinforce a traditional sense of masculinity when they emphasize the power of the male athlete."[83] Don Sabo and Sue Curry Jansen find that "representations of men and masculinity in sports media contribute to the social reproduction of cultural values." They see "sports media as an important primer for gender socialization in contemporary times."[84]

Times coverage of McGwire can be seen in these terms. McGwire's success was largely attributed to the fact that he was a strong and powerful man who overwhelmed the opposition with brute force. Coverage mentioned only in passing the tremendous hand–eye coordination needed to strike a baseball solidly. Undoubtedly, *Times* reporting depicted McGwire in a traditional framework of masculinity, a framework that has long marginalized women and structured social values and roles.

Race also played a part in *Times* coverage. Sports is often seen as one area of modern social life where racial inequalities are lessened. Blacks are overly represented in major U.S. sports, though not in coaching and management positions. And studies have found that media representations of black athletes show heightened sensitivity compared to previous times and seldom rely upon negative representations or overt stereotypes.[85]

Nevertheless, in the quest for the Major League home-run record, the "most significant," the "most heralded," the "most venerated" record in U.S. sports, the white man received season-long coverage as a national hero and the black man did not. It was not until Sammy Sosa tied and briefly passed McGwire that the *Times* and other news media recognized the implications of their coverage. Though the *Times* then acknowledged the racial bias in 1998 coverage and the questions that it raised, the preference given to McGwire is a sobering reminder of the unsettled issue of race in the contemporary United States, even as it celebrates its heroes and the national pastime.

"GODDING UP THOSE BALLPLAYERS"

Times coverage of Mark McGwire suggests, then, that modern society still has the capacity to produce heroes, that heroes still embody social values, and that sports still have the ability to supply society with these heroes and myths. Like the Greeks and the Romans, we still look to the huge stadiums and public arenas for stories to enthrall, instruct, and inspire. Sportswriters themselves have long understood the process. The late Red Smith of the *New York Times*, often acclaimed as the dean of sportswriters, recognized and defended the myth making—the "godding up" of ballplayers:

If we've made heroes out of them, and we have, then we must also lay a whole set of false values at the doorsteps of historians and biographers. Not only has the athlete been blown up larger than life, but so have the politicians and celebrities in all fields, including rock singers and movie stars.

When you go through Westminster Abbey you'll find that excepting for that little Poets' Corner almost all of the statues and memorials are to killers. To generals and admirals who won battles, whose speciality was human slaughter. I don't think they're such glorious heroes.

I've tried not to exaggerate the glory of athletes. I'd rather, if I could, preserve a sense of proportion, to write about them as excellent ball-players, first-rate players. But I'm sure I have contributed to false val-ues—as Stanley Woodward said, "Godding up those ballplayers."[86]

Tom Boswell, long-time writer for the *Washington Post*, has written, "Great athletes have, without knowing it or wanting it, been put in some-thing akin to the position of mythic or religious characters in other cultures in other times. That is to say, they have taken on a symbolic quality. For them, no doubt, this is a mixed blessing—a kind of celebrity squared."[87]

MYTH, CELEBRITY, AND THE HERO TODAY

The relationship between humanity and the Hero myth has been the sub-ject of study for centuries. Perhaps we will never completely understand or appreciate the impact and influence of the myth on human existence. The Hero seems to speak directly to individual endeavor and accomplish-ment. The Hero encourages individuals. Yet the Hero also embodies cru-cial social values. The Hero shows that hard work or kindness or sacrifice or study will bring success. The Hero ennobles society.

Modern society, however, seems to have lost its belief in the encour-aging, elevating powers of the Hero. Boorstin, Campbell, and others ar-gued that the glorious, exalted, heroic figure has been replaced by a mod-ern multitude of superficial celebrities with no claim to fame except fame itself. Even Eliade, who recognized the enduring power of myth in soci-ety, struggled with "the mythicization of public figures through the mass media, the transformation of a personality into an exemplary image."[88]

Times coverage of Mark McGwire, however, indicates that the classic myth can sometimes be reconciled with the modern celebration of celeb-rity—and that the reconciliation can provide intriguing insights into society and its news. Clearly, McGwire was portrayed as a thoroughly modern celebrity. Coverage emphasized that he was a superstar of high order, known worldwide, performing daily in the media spotlight, being paid prodigious sums, and enduring the scrutiny of scribes into many corners of his life.

Yet the structure of the Hero myth—the eternal story—can be found. The story is simply retooled for modern audiences. The celebrity/hero already was well known; his story thus began with the quest. And the story finished not with the triumphal completion of the quest but with the season-ending cessation of the media spotlight.

Times coverage thus shows how the Hero myth can be maintained in today's world: Modern society must find its heroes in modern times and tell their stories in modern ways. Contemporary life, the source of the confusion, must also be the source of contemporary heroes. Though today's hero may seem pale in comparison to Hercules, Achilles, or Samson, the Hero must be drawn from the society in which the myth is told. It's a conclusion that Campbell too affirmed. The Hero myth, he found, must be framed in contemporary terms:

> Obviously, this work cannot be wrought by turning back, or away, from what has been accomplished by the modern revolution; for the problem is nothing if not that of rendering the modern world spiritually significant— or rather (phrasing the same principle the other way round) nothing if not that of making it possible for men and women to come to full human maturity through the conditions of contemporary life.[89]

For today's world, the myth of the Hero must be related within a structure that includes celebrity and the omnipresent news media. *Celebrity status is not a deterrent to the Hero myth today. It is a prerequisite.* To achieve mythic heights, to become an exemplary social model, the Hero must achieve celebrity status. Unsung heroes can still be found among us as firefighters, teachers, social workers, crossing guards, explorers, and myriad others. But *unsung heroes* are literally that: unsung, uncelebrated, unnoted. *Times* reporting of McGwire makes clear that to achieve mythic status today, the Hero must be cast in mass-mediated stories that inform and instruct society. The Hero must be made well known by the news. This "well knownness" is also a criterion for mythic status.

Yet we know that the news media bring us multitudinous stories of well-known figures. Our lives are clotted with celebrities striving simply to remain well known. How do we recognize the hero? How do we hear the myth above the din? *Times* reporting of McGwire indicates that here we must rely upon the power of the ancient and the archetypal. The myth of the Hero has endured since humans first told stories. The cycle and structure—the model and paradigm—still must be found today. We must find the story of a humble birth, a background of normalcy. The Hero must be one of us. Yet from this humble background, the Hero must emerge marked by and driven by a quest. This quest must have social value and significance. It must be fraught with adversity and struggle. The Hero must triumph and return home or die in the attempt. The myth, wherever it has been told, has retained this structure and today's myth must do the same.

As we have seen, *Times* coverage found in Mark McGwire the modern retelling of the classic Hero myth. The *Times* offered the heroic pattern. Though the yellowed sports pages may seem an unlikely relative of *The Iliad*, the *Times* did indeed offer readers a retelling of the ancient myth that long has made sense of the world for the world.

Other scholars have found their way to similar conclusions. Leah R. Vande Berg reviewed previous studies of sports heroes and concluded that "in contradiction to Boorstin's claim that there is a single new mold of heroes—empty celebritydom—that there are now several heroic molds."[90] In a study of news coverage of pitcher Nolan Ryan, Vande Berg and Nick Trujillo found that "true American heroes still can be found in contemporary society. However, the heroes of today can never be like the heroes of yesterday. Today's heroes must, by definition, also be celebrities."[91]

In contemporary society, then, old and new come together. The myth of the Hero needs a commingling of the ancient and the modern, the archetypal and the culturally specific. Celebrity status must be combined with exemplary status. The mass media narrative must be reconciled with the timeless story structure of myth. And when this happens, the news brings us heroes—from cinema and sports, from Hollywood and Washington, from the inner city and small towns. The list of U.S. celebrities "godded up" as heroes can, in fact, seem limitless: astronauts like John Glenn and Christa McAuliffe, actors and actresses like Jimmy Stewart and Jodie Foster, religious figures like Billy Graham and Jesse Jackson, television hosts like Oprah Winfrey and Johnny Carson, business leaders like Bill Gates and Lee Iacocca, perhaps even journalists like Walter Cronkite and Katie Couric.

Times reporting on McGwire, then, is of interest not simply as a re-telling of the Hero myth, but as a modern, socially specific, retelling of the Hero myth that shows how U.S. celebrities can become U.S. heroes. Human societies have long been educated, enthralled, and ennobled by stories of achievement and accomplishment. Cynical, skeptical, saturated with celebrities, distracted by contemporary concerns, we can still hear those eternal stories in our news.

Chapter 6

The Good Mother

Mother Teresa and the
Human Interest Story

Mother Teresa was one of the compelling figures of the twentieth century. For decades she worked unheralded in the slums of Calcutta, offering food, shelter, and care to the poor, sick, and dying. She went on to establish hospices around the world and won the Nobel Prize for Peace in 1979. Her death in September 1997, only days after the death of Princess Diana, provoked international mourning. News media around the world waxed philosophical about the twinned passings of these two very different cultural icons. Years after her death, Mother Teresa's name is still invoked as a symbol of compassion. Reports from the Vatican indicate that the formal process of declaring her a saint has already begun.[1]

Mother Teresa, however, was not a simple, one-dimensional figure. Her ways were political as well as spiritual. She aligned herself with the staunchly conservative bloc of Roman Catholicism. She rejected those who wanted to advance the role of women in the church hierarchy. She used the occasion of accepting the Nobel Prize for Peace to decry abortion. She resisted progressive social movements, despite working in the dire poverty of Calcutta. She built a huge, multinational, multimillion-dollar organization, and accepted funds from the dictators of Haiti and Albania as well as from Charles Keating, a key figure in the U.S. savings and loan scandal.

How did the news cover this singular woman? News coverage, of course, was integral to her image and work. Much of the world eventually came to know of Mother Teresa through the news. The spectacular fame of Mother Teresa raises other interesting questions for the news. Before all the global acclaim, Mother Teresa worked for decades in anonymity. She did not "make news" in any conventional sense, except later with her honors and awards. Yet she became an international celebrity. How? And why?

Myth may provide some of the answers. In some ways, Mother Teresa embodied an almost mythic storyline. She was proclaimed by many as a living saint, a symbol of pure goodness. Her very name draws upon the rich archetype of the Good Mother. Insights into news coverage may come from myth. To what extent can myth explain or illuminate news coverage of Mother Teresa? To what extent did myth obscure the social and political controversies surrounding Mother Teresa?

The coverage may have larger implications. News often reports about good people in the community, people who can be understood as symbols of virtue, kindness, or generosity. Can the Good Mother myth bring insights to the study of other news stories?

THE GOOD MOTHER

Central to human experience, the mother figure is a powerful symbol that may exist within every culture.[2] Discussing cross-cultural manifestations of mother images, the anthropologist James Freeman wrote:

> Quite possibly, mother worship reflects or is derived in part from the deep biopsychological bond that infants develop with an adult, usually, but not invariably, the mother. The emotional character of this bond varies widely for different persons, who have different personalities, experience different life situations, and come from different cultures; but infants throughout the world develop attitudes of love, hate, and fear toward those individuals who provide both gratification and frustration of their physical and emotional needs, and who thus appear both nurturant and withholding.[3]

Myths of the mother can take many forms, some directly in conflict. For example, the Terrible Mother appears in many cultures alongside the Madonna, an icon of virginal and blessed innocence. In Jungian psychology, mother archetypes are gathered beneath the Great Mother, which encompasses numerous positive and negative representations invoking birth and death.[4] Mother archetypes can also be highly charged, ideological symbols. They can affirm matriarchal power structures. Conversely, they can proscribe restrictive social roles and idealized cultural images of femininity and gender.

The Good Mother is one of the predominant archetypes in human storytelling. Though the Good Mother has many mythic representations, her common characteristics can be established. The Good Mother is notable first for her maternal qualities. She represents the comfort and protection of the womb and the nest, the crib and the cradle. She nurses, nurtures, and nourishes, as Eliade said, providing a model "to be followed whenever it is a case of *creating* something, or of restoring or regenerating a human being."[5] But the Good Mother can be associated with death as well as with birth. She oversees the passage from this life to the next one. She tends the deathbed and the coffin.[6]

A second characteristic is related to the first: The Good Mother embodies goodness. She represents kindness, gentleness, selflessness, and compassion. The Good Mother sacrifices for others. She gives of herself.

Finally, the Good Mother represents surpassing qualities. "Good," as it modifies "Mother," is an evaluative term. It organizes and classifies. The *Good* Mother implies a polar, oppositional figure, the Terrible Mother, as well as a normal and unremarkable mother. The Good Mother is blessed among women. She is above others. The Good Mother not only serves, she *serves as a model*. She is known and acclaimed for her exceeding goodness. Her special qualities attract others to her.

Communication researchers have found great value in myths of the mother. Various studies I have read use the archetype to explore television drama, contemporary films, Robert Bly's poetry, Western literature, the rhetoric of conservative opposition to the Equal Rights Amendment, and other subjects.[7]

The Good Mother archetype seems especially pertinent to discussions of Mother Teresa. Mother Teresa's public image seemed to be drawn from key characteristics of the archetype. She was a model of nursing and healing, a symbol of kindness and compassion. She was acclaimed as a surpassing model. Yet her almost harsh conservative political and theological views seemingly clashed with the gentleness suggested by the myth. Did the *Times* use the Good Mother archetype in covering Mother Teresa?

MOTHER TERESA IN THE *NEW YORK TIMES*

To take up the question, this study looks at coverage by the *New York Times*. The time period for study is of some importance. Thanks to the imprimatur of the Nobel Prize for Peace she was awarded in 1979, Mother Teresa's name and status became firmly established on the global scene in that year. After 1979, even the casual news reader would recognize the words "Mother Teresa" as a metaphor indicating virtuous behavior. Analyzing later coverage of Mother Teresa thus yields few insights into the news. Reports after 1979 validate and reaffirm her symbolic status.

Thus the most interesting time period for studies of news on Mother Teresa is before 1980. Analyzing coverage in the decades leading up to her Nobel Prize offers insights into the evolution of her symbolic status and the possible emergence of the archetype. This study thus takes up *Times* reporting from 1950, when Sister Teresa first established her order in Calcutta, to 1980, just after Mother Teresa won the Nobel Prize. It studies every *Times* story, photograph, and commentary on Mother Teresa in those three decades.[8] To provide background and context for such an examination, the following section offers a brief biographical summary of the woman known as Mother Teresa.

AGNES GONXHA BOJAXHIU

Mother Teresa has joined an interesting array of cultural figures—including popes, John Wayne, Bob Dylan, Marilyn Monroe, Madonna, and many others—who have achieved status and fame with names they gave to themselves. Born in 1910, in the city of Skopje, in the region later known as Yugoslavia, Agnes Gonxha Bojaxhiu was the daughter of an Albanian grocer and his wife. She grew up immersed in the Roman Catholic faith. At 18 years old, she sailed to Ireland to join the Institute of the Blessed Virgin Mary—more commonly known as the Sisters of Loreto—an order dedicated to missionary work and teaching. Following tradition, she took on a new name. Her book, *A Simple Path*, says she chose

"Teresa" after Saint Theresa of Lisieux, known as the Little Flower of Jesus.[9]

As Sister Teresa, less than two months after her arrival in Ireland, she was assigned to India, where for the next 20 years she taught the daughters of the affluent citizens of Calcutta. Her convent was located not far from the incredible slums of that city. She studied nursing and began to minister to the sick and dying. In 1948, she obtained permission from the church and Calcutta authorities to move from her convent into the slum. In 1950, she founded her own order in the city, an order that offered a combination of health care, food, education, and religion.

As Mother Teresa, she became a citizen of India. She decided that the nuns of the Order of the Missionaries of Charity would wear Indian saris as their habits. She opened centers to serve the poor and sick. She ministered to lepers and untouchables.

Her work attracted increasing positive attention and support from within the church. She received awards from the Vatican and was heralded in the church press. She soon found sustained international attention outside the church. In 1969, Malcolm Muggeridge narrated a long BBC documentary, *Something Beautiful for God*, that led to increased coverage of Mother Teresa around the globe. Mother Teresa added fundraising to her duties, lobbying governments and individuals for support. Her order grew to more than 1,000 nuns with close to 100 centers. In the 1970s, she was nominated year after year for the Nobel Prize for Peace. In 1979 she won the prize, attracting more people to and more support for her order.

In the 1990s, she was slowed by illness and age. She was hospitalized for long intervals. Her order, which now runs hundreds of centers, staffed by more than 4,000 nuns and tens of thousands of lay workers, named a successor in March 1997. She died on September 5, 1997.

Mother Teresa did not escape political scrutiny and criticism. Her stance against contraception and family planning, in a land grappling with overpopulation, earned her enmity and abuse. Other critics suggested that Mother Teresa's fame was a product of Western racism: Of the many people who work with the destitute of India, the Western press beatified a white, Western, Catholic nun. One publication called her "a disaster for India."[10]

Christopher Hitchens of the *Nation* carried on a long campaign against what he called "the cult" of Mother Teresa. He called her a "dangerous, sinister person."[11] He argued that her opposition to birth control was ruinous for India. He pointed out her association with wealthy but disreputable benefactors. He suggested that she used her funds not to help the poor of India but to increase the size and influence of her order.[12]

Hitchens saved particular scorn for news coverage of Mother Teresa. He savaged "the astonishing, abject credulity of the media in the face of the M. T. fraud."[13] In interviews, he charged the news media with laziness and suggested that Mother Teresa was simply an easy symbol and a "handy metaphor" for virtue.[14] In his later columns, he prepared readers for "the tsunami of bullshit that will break over them when 'Mother' gives up the ghost."[15] On the day of her death, he wrote a critical column entitled "Saint of the Rich."[16]

Hitchens acknowledged that his antipathy for Mother Teresa derived in part from his aggressive atheism. But his critique of news coverage was suggestive. In the context of this study, the issue is framed broadly. Rather than critique the news for laziness and pliant coverage, this study is interested in pursuing the possibility that deeper forces guided such coverage. It asks whether reporting on Mother Teresa, specifically in this case in the *New York Times*, was shaped by an eternal story, one of myth's fundamental figures: the Good Mother.

EIGHTEEN YEARS WITHOUT COVERAGE

Here is an intriguing, preliminary finding: For the first 18 years of her work—from 1950 to 1968—the *Times* published no stories about Mother Teresa. In retrospect, the lack of stories is somewhat surprising. India was the focus of much *Times* coverage in the 1950s and 1960s. In the framework of the cold war, which long structured *Times* foreign correspondence, the new Indian democracy was seen as a fragile system, one threatened by communism. For example, a 1957 story in the Sunday magazine looked back at "India's Great Adventure, Ten Years Later." It portrayed India as struggling against the communist threat as well as "the danger of Chinese infiltration."[17] The country seemed to be a requisite foreign post for future *Times* leaders; bylines from India included A. M. Rosenthal and Joseph Lelyveld.

Calcutta in particular received much coverage. Its immense poverty left the city vulnerable to communism, the *Times* reported. For example, one report was headlined "Reds Still Strong in Calcutta Despite China Border Dispute."[18] Another announced: "Calcutta a City of Frustrations; Hordes Existing in Hovels—Educated Find No Jobs and Turn Communist."[19]

Mother Teresa appeared in none of this coverage throughout the 1950s and much of the 1960s. The conventions of the *Times*'s foreign coverage were firmly established. *Times* correspondents relied for sources almost exclusively upon top government officials in foreign capitals. Reporters would support or counter these sources with their own observations or with brief quotations from people on the streets. The writing had its own style and stance: The expert correspondent was filing informed observations in a report from abroad.

Even in the mid-1960s, as the *Times* incorporated more feature stories on ordinary citizens into its foreign correspondence, Mother Teresa made no appearance. For example, the *Times* gave extensive coverage to a 1964 trip by Pope Paul VI to an ecumenical conference in India. While in India, the pope met with Mother Teresa but the *Times* did not mention her. A 1967 story on the destitute homeless of Calcutta—a topic firmly linked in later times to Mother Teresa—had no reference to her.[20]

Finally, on April 13, 1968, Mother Teresa was introduced to readers of the *Times*.[21] "A Calcutta Nun Softens Death for the Poor," by Joseph Lelyveld, ran on page A2.[22] It was a midsized feature, about 19 column inches, accompanied by a 4-inch-deep, 3-column-wide photograph of Mother Teresa. In retrospect, the date itself deserves consideration. The story was published 11 years before the worldwide attention prompted by Mother Teresa's Nobel Prize. Though religious publications and Indian newspapers, such as the *Statesman*, had been writing about her work for years, many observers cite Muggeridge's 1969 BBC documentary as the turning point in international press coverage.[23] Thus, in the context of Western news media, the *Times* found Mother Teresa earlier than most.

But the story appeared 18 years after Mother Teresa had begun her order and four years after the Roman Catholic Church, including Pope Paul VI, had begun singling her out for her life's work. The *Times* surely did not "discover" Mother Teresa.

THE GOOD MOTHER IN THE *TIMES*

From 1968 to 1980, the *Times* offered consistent coverage of Mother Teresa: 33 articles, columns, and photographs were published in those 12 years. Analysis of the *Times* stories showed that the coverage indeed can be understood in mythic terms. The *Times* offered a detailed depiction of the three distinct but related characteristics that make up the Good Mother.

Mother Teresa was offered as a maternal figure. She was praised for her great kindness and compassion. And she was portrayed as a surpassing model, a symbol for humankind. The following sections make clear the myth in the *Times* and explore its implications.

A Maternal Figure

Mother Teresa was often portrayed as a maternal model by the *Times*. In some ways, the portrayal was unlikely. Mother Teresa was, after all, an unmarried, childless, Roman Catholic nun. But the *Times* emphasized her maternal qualities and her relationship with children.

For example, photographs depicted her maternally. The very first photograph of Mother Teresa in the *Times*, accompanying the April 1968 profile, offered the nun, clothed in white sari and robes, facing the camera with a full nursery of children behind her. The caption read: "Mother Teresa, the good Samaritan of Calcutta, talks with a visitor at her nursery."[24] A story on the 1973 monsoon season in India was anchored by a large two-column photograph of the nun, with baby in arms, "caring for a youngster in her refuge in Calcutta."[25] A December 1979 cover story for the Sunday magazine, timed to appear the day before the awarding of the Nobel Prize in Oslo, was illustrated with a close-up photograph of the nun with a baby in arms.[26] Inside, another photograph showed the nun leaning over a young person sprawled on a sidewalk.

Stories stressed her maternal care for the sick and the dying. The 1968 article described a tour of her order's institutions. After a brief mention of a crowded nursery, the story quoted its subject: "The nun, who wears a white cotton sari, remarked: 'This is life. Now we will see the dying.' The words came briskly, without a trace of melodrama." The story moved next to a "Home for Dying Destitutes." It stated, "There is only one criterion for admission. The patients must be so far gone" that the overcrowded hospitals turn them away. However, the story said, "Mother Teresa never turns any away, even when she can offer nothing more than a chance to die with a little dignity and peace. 'The worst thing is to be unwanted,' she says."[27]

The report on the 1973 monsoon began: "This is the season of death in Calcutta." After describing the monsoon's devastation, the story continued: "It is the season when Mother Theresa's nuns are busiest in their crowded shed where dying derelicts, unwanted in hospitals, are placed on cots and washed and fed and given a final touch of dignity."[28] (A number of *Times* reports through the years misspelled the nun's name as "T*h*eresa.") As the myth suggests, the *Times* portrayed Mother Teresa tending maternally to the cradle and the deathbed.

Goodness and Love

Mother Teresa was often represented in terms of goodness and love. Her missions and actions perhaps made such representations natural. Mother Teresa apparently was a good and loving person. The unrestrained language of the *Times* portrayal, however, and the omission of reference to the social and political controversy surrounding her work, are worthy of our interest and complemented other aspects of the myth.

For example, a 1970 feature story headlined "Friend of the World's Poor" stated that "Mother Teresa's mission of love" included centers around the globe. The story was supported by a two-column, head-and-shoulder photograph of the smiling nun. "Shares the hardships of those she serves," said the caption.[29]

Two days later, on Christmas, the *Times* featured Mother Teresa in an editorial, "From Calcutta with Love." The editorial began: "Pope Paul gave the first Pope John XXIII award this week to a 60-year-old Yugoslav-born nun whose pioneering work among the poor in Calcutta has expanded into 'a universal mission of love.'" It provided details of her ministry and routine and concluded: "Few have the stamina, let alone the faith, to follow Mother Teresa's self-sacrificing example. Yet all have a stake in her universal mission."[30]

Other stories too stressed Mother Teresa's goodness and love. New Delhi bureau chief Michael T. Kaufman recounted a day spent with Mother Teresa. Following the nun to a nursery, the reporter noted that the children are given food, clothing, and "as in all Mother Teresa's facilities, given love."[31] The 1979 Sunday magazine cover story used this subhead: "In the sprawling slums of India, 1979's Nobel Peace Prize winner nurtures the poorest of the poor and envelops them with love." Written in the first person, the cover story depicted Mother Teresa's "world-wide empire of love and charity." As a nonbeliever, Kaufman said, he began the story rejecting the idea that "she is an actual saint and that her achievements can be understood only as true miracles."

However, he was deeply moved, he admitted, by his time with Mother Teresa. In one passage, he wrote: "Her eyes look at me with genuine fondness. I feel she has time for me and cares about me, and not necessarily because of either my business or hers." He continued: "Perhaps it is a trick, but it works, and I know better now what the crippled man had meant when he explained his presence at her darshan by saying that Mother loves him." He found that the source of her success "rests in her own rare character, her strong pure passions and, yes, in her faith in God and love of Jesus." The cover story concluded:

> I had not wanted to write as personally as I have about the woman many in India call simply Mother. It has proved unavoidable. By culture, I am alienated; by choice, a skeptic and by journalistic adaptation, suspicious. For 20 years I have instinctively looked for the warts and wens and clay feet of journalistic subjects. Seldom have I been disappointed—almost never. With Mother it is different. I cannot accept her holiness, but her humaneness is exceptional.[32]

A Surpassing "Model for Us All"

Finally, as the myth suggests, *Times* coverage depicted Mother Teresa as a figure of surpassing qualities, a model for others. For example, on December 23, 1970, Paul Hofmann reported that Mother Teresa was the first winner of the $25,000 Pope John XXIII Peace Prize. His quotation from Pope Paul VI depicted Mother Teresa as a model:

> "We hold up to the admiration of all this intrepid messenger of the love of Christ," the Pope said in praise of Mother Teresa. "We do this so that by her example the number of those who expend themselves for their brethren may grow and that there may be better established in the world the sense of solidarity and human brotherhood."[33]

Two weeks later, the *Times* covered the award ceremony itself. A three-column photograph showed Mother Teresa at the award ceremony with Pope Paul VI. Hofmann's lead emphasized the symbolic status of Mother Teresa: "Pope Paul VI today praised Mother Teresa, the founder and Superior General of the India-based Missionaries of Charity, as a symbol of brotherhood among men."[34]

The *Times* often referred to Mother Teresa in saintly terms. In October 1975, a United Nations-sponsored conference on world religions was held in New York. The story, written by Kenneth A. Briggs, the *Times* religion correspondent, was headlined, "Spiritual Parley Hears 'Living Saint.'" Briggs affirmed Mother Teresa's status. Her appearance on the final day, he said, "symbolized her growing world renown." He also extolled her as a model, writing, "She has been called a 'living saint' and her efforts praised as a rebuke to the modern feeling of personal powerlessness." Briggs also provided this admittedly apocryphal anecdote:

> A story is told of a Hindu priest from the Temple of Kali, in Mother Teresa's neighborhood, who had, like scores of Calcutta's hospital patients, been judged a hopeless case and dismissed from an institution to fend for himself. Grudgingly, he allowed the Missionary Sisters to take him in.
>
> On his death bed, he reportedly said, "For many years I have worshipped the image of Kali. Today for the first time I have seen the face of the divine mother."[35]

Three months later, the *Times* reported on Mother Teresa's appearance in Philadelphia at a Roman Catholic conference. Briggs noted that "the appearance of the diminutive nun, dressed in her conventional white Indian sari with blue border stripes, gripped the audience." He reported her now cult-like status: "Mother Teresa has become the most magnetic figure at the congress. Wherever she goes, crowds follow her, hoping to touch her clothing or hear her speak."[36] One 1979 photograph was captioned: "Because of her compassionate concern for the destitute, Mother Teresa has come to be known as 'the saint of the gutters.'"[37]

Acclamation of Mother Teresa as a model would find its fullest expression in October 1979 when Mother Teresa won the Nobel Peace Prize. The lead story on the award was published on the front page with a two-column photograph. Placed prominently, in the second paragraph, was her modest response to the news: "I am unworthy."[38] A *Times* editorial the following day applauded the choice of Mother Teresa. "A Secular Saint" directly offered Mother Teresa as a model "for us all." It began:

> How typical of Mother Teresa that she should remark, "I am unworthy" when told she had just won the Nobel Peace Prize. Her comment was not a casual expression of blushing modesty, only a re-statement of her lifelong conviction that helping the helpless—indeed, helping those beyond help—is the simple duty of us all.

The editorial recounted the global reach of the Missionaries of Charity and noted, "Even before the Nobel award, its work has received international acclaim, and Mother Teresa, whose radiant, lined face resembles a

Byzantine mosaic, has become a secular saint." It concluded: "She may not have furthered world peace in the conventional sense, but she brought love—and peace—individually to thousands of those the world has forsaken."[39]

For the award ceremony itself, the *Times* relied upon an AP account. The lead called her "Calcutta's Saint of the Gutters' and said she accepted the prize "in the name of the poor, the sick and the unwanted children." The primary depiction was Mother Teresa as a model not just for individuals but for nations. From the presentation of Professor John Sanness, chairman of the Norwegian Nobel Committee, the report chose words calling for emulation of Mother Teresa. It said Sanness "urged that rich nations, in assisting poorer nations, emulate Mother Teresa's spirit and respect for individual human dignity." It quoted Sanness: "All aid given by the rich countries must be given in the spirit of Mother Teresa."[40]

THE GOOD MOTHER: UNDENIABLE INFLUENCE OF STORY

Analysis of *Times* reporting on Mother Teresa was fruitful. On one level, the analysis certainly supported Hitchens's claim that Mother Teresa was the subject of uncritical, laudatory coverage. Some observers and journalists indeed might wince at the plainly reverential reporting and the unrestrained embrace of "Mother" as a "living saint." On another level, the study affirmed the complex social forces at work in news portrayals. Mother Teresa first appeared in the *Times* fully formed as an archetypal figure. Sources and forces outside the *Times*—including the success of Mother Teresa's missionary order, her own clear sense of identity, the sway of the Roman Catholic Church, and others—all seem to have had some influence in shaping the *Times* portrayal from the start.

Yet how and why did Mother Teresa get the kind of coverage she did? Here, the mythic framework is most useful. The analysis showed the undeniable influence of the Good Mother myth in *Times* coverage. The eternal story structured the specific story. Mother Teresa was portrayed in pictures and words as an ideal maternal figure. The first *Times* photograph of her was taken at a nursery. The magazine cover photo and others showed her with a babe in arms. Text too supported her maternity. "With Mother it is different," the *Times* correspondent wrote, "Mother loves him." Another cited the dying words of a Hindu priest: "I have seen the face of the divine mother." And Mother Teresa was not simply portrayed as a mother figure. She was presented as an archetypal mother, a saint. Numerous stories referred to her directly as a saint. She was called a "secular saint," a "living saint," and a "saint of the gutters." She was a model. Heralding her awards and honors, proclaiming her virtue, the *Times* held up Mother Teresa as a model for all people, "for all nations."

Year after year, the theme was presented with little change. Roland Barthes understood the process. As he wrote long ago, "Myths are nothing but this ceaseless, untiring solicitation, this insidious and inflexible demand that all men recognize themselves in this image, *eternal yet bearing a date*, which was built of them one day as if for all time."[41]

CONTROVERSY: OUTSIDE THE MYTH

When the *Times*'s portrayal of Mother Teresa is studied closely, however, it becomes obvious that numerous controversies and questions fell outside the myth. The Good Mother archetype can also be put to good use to consider what the *Times* did not report.

As we have seen, Mother Teresa was not an unproblematic figure. Some observers saw her as a disaster for her adopted country. The horrific conditions in Calcutta seemed to cry out for fundamental social change. Yet Mother Teresa did not work for fundamental change. Her expanding ministry was built for—perhaps built upon?—the victims of the horror. In some ways, then, her ministry could have been interpreted as helping to support the horror. Would Mother Teresa's ministry have existed without the horror? Could those desperate social conditions have continued without a multimillion-dollar organization caring for its victims? Such questions fell outside the *Times*'s portrayal of the Good Mother.

The *Times*'s mythic portrayal of Mother Teresa also remained resolutely outside the contexts of gender, politics, and religion. The Roman Catholic Church has long been embroiled in disputes over the subservient role of women in its hierarchy. In Mother Teresa, the church had an internationally acclaimed woman who unreservedly embraced the church's stance. She bowed to the authority of the church. She accepted her role within its structure. In its portrayal of the Good Mother, the *Times* showed Mother Teresa not only as caring and healing but also as obedient and servile. And the *Times* never placed Mother Teresa in the debate over the role of women in the church.

Similarly, Mother Teresa's stance toward birth control raised questions—but outside *Times* coverage. Many of the dire problems Mother Teresa confronted in India could be linked to overpopulation. Yet she espoused the church's firm opposition to birth control and family planning. She used none of her funds or people to grapple with this root cause of India's misery.

Finally, Mother Teresa could have been considered within deep and troubling questions raised by the postcolonial era, another topic left untouched by the *Times*'s use of the Good Mother myth. The United States and other Western countries have long struggled for a new understanding of people and nations once held as powerless colonies. From Asia to Africa to Central America, Western news media depict and dismiss many of these countries via images of political chaos, natural disasters, famine, pestilence, and social futility. These images can be partially understood as explaining away the vile colonialism of the past and the studied neglect of the present. News portrayals of India have been no exception. And Mother Teresa could have been seen in this context. Who was one of the most famous figures to emerge from India in the postcolonial era? A white woman, from the West, who saved these pathetic people, the stories suggested, from themselves.

The *Times*'s use of the Good Mother myth admitted none of these questions or issues. With its focus on Mother Teresa, the paper failed to probe the *causes* of the immense poverty in whose midst she worked. Without history or context, the stories used the sufferings of millions as a mere backdrop for its laudatory tale. Mother Teresa was depicted unsullied, unblemished, and uncontroversial. Her conservative views were glossed over. Her evangelical work was framed in terms of love. Her wide financial dealings had no place in the symbolic structure. The myth, in this case, delimited and denied, even as it celebrated and extolled.

THE HUMAN INTEREST STORY
AND THE GOOD MOTHER

Can we draw broader conclusions from news coverage of Mother Teresa? Was Mother Teresa so singular a person that we are unable to consider larger lessons about news? This woman, called "Mother" after all, was portrayed by the news through the reverential and comforting myth of the

Good Mother. The portrayal seems so *natural.* Yet as Eliade, Barthes, and others have noted, naturalness is a crucial part of myth's work. The stories of myth are not supposed to be understood as myth; they are supposed to seem real and natural. And the analysis suggests that the Good Mother myth can be detected in many other news stories—not just those about Mother Teresa.

By breaking down *Times* coverage of Mother Teresa, the study shows that components of the reporting are actually quite conventional. Though Mother Teresa was singular and complex, reporting about her was not. The *Times* (1) identified a figure already heralded in her own community; (2) profiled her charitable works; (3) reported her goodness and compassion; and (4) held her up as a model of virtue and character. Similar principles can be found in the news almost every day, in the *human interest story.*

From this perspective, the kind of coverage received by Mother Teresa is a staple of news. Human interest stories appear regularly, drawn from all the varieties of social life: a local doctor who volunteers for relief work overseas; a person who tends to victims of AIDS; a foster parent who for decades provides a home for dozens of youths; a prominent official who dedicates weekends to building houses for the poor; a person who rescues stray animals and finds them homes. Each of these subjects, and many more depicted in human interest stories, can be seen as illustrations of the Good Mother myth in the news.

As Helen Hughes made clear in her classic study *News and the Human Interest Story,* the content of such stories is highly structured and routinized.[42] Its form does not change much. It might focus on the private lives of celebrities. It might focus on pathetic or tragic things that happen to ordinary people. But most often, the human interest story focuses on an ordinary individual who has performed charitable or virtuous service for the community. The story highlights the service, heralds the previously unknown person, and offers a model of goodness. In terms of myth, human interest stories, as in stories of Mother Teresa, draw upon the Good Mother.

It was not always this way. The human interest story is a relatively recent invention that can be traced back to the penny press of the mid-1800s. Previously, as Michael Schudson noted in his history of U.S. news, newspapers focused on commercial and international news and "simply did not report on the lives of ordinary people." But the penny press—local and timely and in need of popular content—"focused on the nearby and the everyday." Soon, Schudson writes, "The penny papers made the 'human interest story' not only an important part of daily journalism but its most characteristic feature."[43] And its subjects were taken not simply from the local community but from around the globe.

IMPLICATIONS OF THE HUMAN INTEREST STORY

The social and political implications of such stories sometimes can be overlooked. Myth, however, raises some interesting questions about the seemingly innocent human interest story. Myth, as we have seen, points to the relationship between exemplary models and social order. Myth upholds some beliefs but degrades others. It celebrates but also excoriates. It affirms but also denies. The human interest story, in its retelling of the Good Mother myth, does likewise. Three important social and political implications of these stories can be considered.

Individuals Can Make a Difference

First, the human interest story and the Good Mother myth affirm the belief that individual action is important to social life. Individuals may, in fact, be politically powerless. Social order may, in fact, be dominated by political parties and special interest groups. But human interest stories offer evidence that individuals *can* make a difference. Just as *Times* stories showed Mother Teresa rising from obscurity to become a model for us all, human interest stories suggest that other individuals can also become models, if they only try.

Others have recognized this link between human interest stories and social order. In *Deciding What's News*, Herbert Gans found that editors and reporters chose subjects for human interest stories "because they expect the audiences to 'identify' with a victim or hero."[44] Murray Edelman argued that "human interest stories are political events because they reinforce the view that individual action is crucial: that biography is the paramount component of historical accounts." He wrote that stories about the heroic actions of otherwise ordinary people "erase structural conditions from notice, even while they divert attention from the rest of the political spectacle."[45]

History Makes No Difference

A related implication: As Edelman suggested, the human interest story often ignores history and social context. Tragic situations and events are depicted as if they happen at random, with no relation to an established social or political order. The stories show little interest in exploring why situations have become so desperate or pathetic. The stories are more interested in the virtuous actions of their subjects. *Times* stories of Mother Teresa, for example, spent little time examining the political or social system that brought millions of people such misery. The people, in fact, appear as props in the drama of the Good Mother. In another study of the human interest story, researchers found:

> There is first a rejection of any attempt to explain events as having a relation to social, economic, or political forces. Instead events are portrayed in terms of the actions and interactions of individuals, strongly governed by luck, fate, and chance, within a given, naturalized world, which merely forms an unchanging background. Real and fundamental structural inequalities and deep-rooted social antagonisms remain masked.[46]

Likewise, identifying the bias of news toward personalization, Lance Bennett noted that news "gives preference to the individual actors and human-interest angles in events while downplaying institutional and political considerations that establish the social contexts for those events."[47]

Social Order Is Confirmed

The Good Mother myth as told in the human interest story also affirms the current social order. Community values are given voice. Shared beliefs are dramatized. In the *Times*, through the myth of the Good Mother, Mother Teresa represented charity, compassion, self-sacrifice, and love. These are universal values offered as a model "to us all."

Similarly, James Curran, Angus Douglas, and Garry Whannel found that human interest stories offer "a community that shares common universal experiences: birth, love, death, accident, illness, and crucially, the experience of consuming." They argued that "this community is further given focus by the stock of commonsense assumptions about the world implicit in human-interest stories, paralleling and complementing the construction and reproduction of consensus that takes place in current-affairs coverage."[48]

Some people might dismiss the human interest story as "soft" news, a bit of everyday fluff that fills the space around "hard" political news. But close study of reporting on Mother Teresa has suggested such stories can have important social and political dimensions. And the human interest stories show us once again how the eternal stories of humankind can be told and retold in the pages of the news.

Chapter 7

The Trickster

Race, the News, and the Rape of Mike Tyson

The rape trial of former heavyweight boxing champion Mike Tyson was one of the more prominent, perhaps notorious, news stories of 1992. A dramatic and sensational spectacle, the trial pitted the celebrity boxer against a contestant in the Miss Black America pageant. It daily offered lurid testimony, legal machinations by prosecuting and defense attorneys, and various ongoing side stories, including a fatal fire at the jurors' hotel and charges that Baptist ministers had attempted to bribe the accuser. After two weeks of testimony and 10 hours of deliberation, the jury found Tyson guilty of rape; he was sentenced to six years in prison.[1]

From the start of the trial, questions were raised about coverage by the *Times* and other news media. Some called the coverage sensational and overblown, comparing the hoopla and hype to reporting on a prize fight. For others, the coverage was inadequate and insensitive to women.

Some bitter letters to the *Times* pointed out that most of the trial stories were written by sportswriters and placed on the sports pages, "next to show-dog pictures," as if rape was just another exotic sport.[2]

Study of coverage of the Tyson trial, however, may evoke other issues. Enmeshed in an incendiary drama in which the African American champion of a sport dominated by African Americans was accused of rape by an African American woman, the Tyson trial news coverage unavoidably became embroiled in racial politics. Studying *Times* coverage thus may yield insights into the press's troubled and troubling reporting on race.

The subtitle for this case study is purposely provocative. The "rape of Mike Tyson" offers two, quite different, meanings. It refers, of course, to the rape for which Tyson was tried and convicted. Yet during and after the trial, some observers charged that Tyson himself was "raped." He was raped, they said, by news coverage that violated, degraded, and debased him with subtle—and not-so-subtle—racist stereotypes. Critics charged that Tyson was portrayed as a half-animal, half-human figure, as a dumb but ferocious creature. The portrayal hearkened back to the days of slavery.

This study looks carefully at *New York Times* depictions of Tyson and compares them with depictions in other newspapers. It questions whether racist stereotypes did indeed shape the reporting. It studies the long entrenchment of racist reporting in the news. And it considers how myth may help us understand such reporting.

I want to anticipate here an objection already raised by some colleagues and friends: Tyson's rape trial seems an unlikely subject for press criticism. Why should we worry about how the news covered "a slob like Tyson?" His crime was revolting. His actions and attitudes toward women—long before the rape conviction—have been unconscionable. In this view, Tyson was found guilty of rape and any disapprobation by the *Times* or other newspapers was richly deserved.

Not a defense of Tyson, this chapter nevertheless will pursue the charge that the *Times*'s response to Tyson was ugly and flawed by its reliance upon racist imagery. Should Tyson be condemned for his crime? Yes. Should Tyson be condemned via degrading depictions? No. I start from the assumption that the news must find other means to depict such sordid lives, means that owe nothing to racist archetypes and images. Indeed, on a larger level, I hope to suggest that the perpetuation of racist stereotypes, particularly in such high-profile cases as Tyson's, can be especially debilitating to a press that struggles daily with its representation of people of color.

THE TRICKSTER MYTH

Some might excuse the press by arguing that the "story" of Mike Tyson came simply from reporting the facts. However, the facts do not explain everything. The facts are that Mike Tyson often lived the "ordinary" life of a celebrity athlete. The facts are that the news stories about Mike Tyson actually seem to have retold the eternal story of the Trickster, the original savage/victim, the archetypal animal/child.

"For centuries, perhaps millennia, and in the widest variety of cultural and religious belief systems, humans have told and retold tales of tricksters," write William Hynes and William Doty.[3] They and their colleagues have found the Trickster throughout the world, in figures such as the African Ananse, the Greek Hermes, the Native American Coyote, and the Asian Horangi. Almost always, the Trickster is driven by physical appetites, lust, and desire. He has no control over his impulses. Paul Radin, with Karl Kerenyi and Carl Jung, produced one of the earliest treatments on the Trickster. Radin too found the Trickster to be a kind of antihero "who is always wandering, who is always hungry, who is not guided by normal conceptions of good or evil, who is either playing tricks on people or having them played on him and who is highly sexed."[4]

The Trickster, as Radin implied, usually serves as an exemplary model in reverse. Hynes and Doty call him a crude and lewd moralist. "The rude mockery, even scatology, present in trickster stories is not simply anti-religious or anti-social criticism," they argue. Rather, the Trickster serves as a model illustrating the necessity of societal rules. Like the Scapegoat archetype, the Trickster archetype shows what happens if the rules laid down by society are not observed.[5] But instead of being punished by society in a culminating, climactic drama, in the manner of the Scapegoat, the Trickster continually shows the need for societal standards as he lives an error-filled life of ruin. The Trickster proceeds from one afflicting happenstance to the next, seemingly always on the edge of self-destruction.

Reporting on Tyson can be partially seen as attempts at moralizing through the Trickster myth. The stories in fact will be shown to pontificate and preach about standards and values. But the reporting runs into trouble because of the mixture of the Trickster myth with representations of race.

RACE AND THE PRESS

Scholars from a variety of disciplines have long charted racist representations in the news. Walter Lippmann's classic discussion of stereotypes remains an excellent starting point. As part of his dissection of the press in *Public Opinion*, Lippmann devoted five chapters to public and press reliance on stereotypes. He argued that the stereotype is a form of perception that "imposes" ways of seeing. "For the most part we do not first see, and then define," he wrote, "we define first and then see." The stereotype "precedes reason" and thus unavoidably shapes the story of the storyteller.[6]

Since Lippmann's times, a large literature on race and the media has affirmed that the news represents African Americans in narrowly defined, stereotypical roles. More than 70 years after Lippmann so carefully traced the problem (if not the solution), scholars continue to find that the news still presents the experiences of people of color—in particular, African Americans—in ways that create and maintain racist stereotypes. Although instances of overt racism now appear to be few, these writers say, close study of the news does suggest that degrading racial portrayals are subtly but firmly entrenched.[7]

Other research has focused specifically on stereotyped portrayals of African American athletes. Perhaps the most visible members of their race, these athletes receive intense press coverage. Some critics have charged that this coverage is marred by racist depictions.[8]

Critics have even suggested that black boxers—in particular black heavyweight champions, such as Jack Johnson, Joe Louis, and Muhammad Ali—have been singled out for stereotyping. The high status of the *heavyweight champion of the world* must be acknowledged. Unlike many other sports, such as baseball, football, and basketball, boxing is exceedingly individualistic. The champion rises or falls alone. And boxing does truly crown a champion of the *world*. Boxers from many nations compete for the heavyweight title in matches held around the globe. The heavyweight champion is often the most recognizable athlete on the planet. Writers charge that the U.S. press has sought to deflate African Americans who attain such status.[9]

MODERN RACISM

Other social science research, especially literature on modern racism, is of interest for this study. Social scientists have found that traditional or "old-fashioned" racism, marked by open bigotry and opposition to equal opportunity, has been replaced by modern racism: a more subtle, less open, antagonism toward blacks.[10]

"Racism, as defined by modern racists, is consistent only with the tenets and practices of old-fashioned racism," such as emphatic support for segregation and acts of open discrimination, writes John McConahay. "Thus, those endorsing the ideology of modern racism do not define their own beliefs and attitudes as racist."[11]

"Old-fashioned" racism is relatively easy to see. For much of U.S. history, many whites accepted slavery and supported discrimination. Black people suffered, these people argued, because blacks were inherently inferior. Blacks were lazy, promiscuous, intellectually unfit, prone to violence. Relations between blacks and whites could be "explained" by the weakness of blacks and the intellectual and moral superiority of whites.

Modern racism is less direct. Assumptions of modern racism might include beliefs that discrimination is a thing of the past; that blacks want too much, too fast; that black demands for opportunity are unfair; and that recent gains by blacks are undeserved. Racial tensions exist today, white people might say, because black people cannot escape their past. They are not destined to succeed as a group. They were bred only to be strong. They do not have the genes to compete intellectually with whites. They dwell too much on the past. They always claim to be victims. They want special preferences because of their past.

Stereotypes are a key aspect of modern racism. Modern racists cluster blacks into a limited number of categories with negative characteristics. Blacks are then understood and talked about only in terms of these stereotypes. The stereotypes thus give expression to beliefs and help confirm and perpetuate those beliefs.

Press stereotypes play a role in modern racism. Though journalists do not see themselves as racist, stereotypes and modern racist beliefs permeate the news. A media scholar, Robert Entman, found that portrayals of blacks on local TV news supported components of modern racism. Blacks—especially young black males—are portrayed largely as criminals. The majority of young black men are not criminals, but they receive little coverage. Local news programs only show the young black men who are criminals.

"Local news implicitly traces the symbolic boundaries of the community," Entman argued, and "in day-to-day news coverage, blacks are largely cast outside those boundaries." Elsewhere, Entman put it plainly. He said that "the typical images of blacks on local TV news may reinforce stereotyping that feeds modern racism."[12]

Even such a brief review of the large literature shows that news portrayal of African Americans remains a significant, even compelling, area for press criticism. In *Black Looks: Race and Representation*, bell hooks puts the question eloquently. She asks, "If we, black people, have learned to cherish hateful images of ourselves, then what process of looking allows us to counter the seduction of images that threatens to dehumanize and colonize?"

Her answer: "Clearly, it is that way of seeing which makes possible an integrity of being that can subvert the power of the colonizing image."[13] Although the issue, as hooks knows, is more complex than renaming or rerepresenting the world, the understanding of racist stereotypes must be an essential topic for any study of news and society. For this study, myth may offer some understanding.

Do news stories promote modern racism? As myth, we have seen, news draws upon eternal stories that defend the status quo, justify the current order. Does such justification and defense extend to matters of racial inequality? As myth, news is charged with resolving large social oppositions. Does news resolve oppositions of race through the subtle degradation of blacks via the Trickster myth? Myth thus offers a way to raise important questions about news reporting on race—such as reporting on Mike Tyson.

BACKGROUND: THE TYSON TRIAL

On July 17, 1991, Tyson arrived in Indianapolis for an appearance at the Miss Black America pageant sponsored by Indiana Black Expo. Although he had lost the heavyweight title the year before in Tokyo, Tyson still retained the high-profile, celebrity stature for such appearances, based on his former domination of boxing, his well-publicized divorce from actress Robin Givens, and his run-ins with the law.

Three days after Tyson's arrival in Indianapolis, police received a call from a pageant contestant, Desiree Washington, who claimed that Tyson had raped her in his hotel room the night before. Through August, a grand jury convened to hear the charges. On September 9, Tyson was indicted. A trial was set for January 1992 in Indianapolis.

For those in Tyson's boxing circle, an immediate concern was the long-awaited bout between Tyson and then-current champion Evander Holyfield. Estimates for revenues from the lucrative pay-per-view screening of the fight topped $50 million. No fight occurred, however. First, Tyson suffered injuries while training, postponing the fight, and then his trial began on January 27.

In Tyson's legal circle, another concern was the William Kennedy Smith trial, a high-profile date-rape case, held shortly before the Tyson trial. Smith had been found not guilty, a verdict that led to widespread and loud protest. Tyson's lawyers suggested that public pressure opposing a second date-rape acquittal would be an important factor in the trial.

Tyson's trial lasted less than three weeks. It was interrupted briefly by a fire in the hotel where the jurors were staying. On February 10, the jury found Tyson guilty of rape. The judge sentenced him to six years in prison. He was led away in handcuffs.

After the conviction, the case continued to make news. Reports of a bribe offered by Baptist ministers to the accuser were investigated. Donald Trump, an acquaintance of Tyson and owner of a casino that sponsors boxing matches, suggested that Tyson should be allowed to donate millions of dollars to rape counseling centers rather than serve time in prison. Tyson's attorneys asked the court to allow Tyson to remain out of prison and on bail while his appeal was heard. The request was denied and Tyson was imprisoned.[14]

THE PRESS AND
THE TYSON TRIAL: PRELIMINARIES

Times reporting of Tyson's trial—and the possible mythic dimensions of that reporting—might be revealed best through a comparison with other newspapers. *Times* reporting took place in the context of daily, intense coverage by other news media that also struggled with the many troublesome issues presented by the trial. For this chapter, then, I decided to study four other prestigious newspapers, selected for their status and influence, as well as some geographical diversity: the *Chicago Tribune*, the *Los Angeles Times*, *USA Today*, and the *Washington Post*. I looked at months of coverage: from July 20, 1991—the day that police were notified of the rape—to April 9, 1992, when Tyson's petition to remain out on bail during appeal was denied and he was imprisoned. All news articles, editorials, and commentaries devoted to the Tyson case were examined.

The first striking fact to emerge from an analysis of the Tyson coverage is its sheer amount. Apparently the combination of the sports celebrity's public persona, the nature of the charges, and the dramatic unfolding of the trial proved irresistible. The *Times* published more than 100 stories in the nine-month period. Together, the five newspapers I examined printed more than 500 stories. Daily coverage was offered by all papers during February 1992, the month of the trial.

Also of some interest was the placement of the stories. The *Times* and the other papers largely covered the trial on the sports pages. Although significant moments of the trial—the indictment, the conviction, and the appeal—achieved front-page status, most news reports on the Tyson case appeared in the sports section. Specifically, of the 568 stories on Tyson, 458 (81 percent) were placed on the sports pages. This figure does not reflect stories that began on the front page and jumped to the sports section, and so coverage in the sports section was actually somewhat greater.

As I noted previously, this decision to cover the Tyson trial on the sports pages was bitterly criticized. Some readers complained that placing a rape trial on the sport pages trivialized and demeaned the crime. At least one reader asked whether newspapers were "suggesting that rape is a kind of sport."[15]

THE RAPE OF MIKE TYSON

Although the amount and placement of coverage is of interest, the primary focus of this study was the nature of the reporting. An important aspect of the coverage that emerged from a comparison of the *Times* with other newspapers was the unanimity and uniformity of portrayals.

Specifically, the many press portrayals of Mike Tyson during his trial actually drew from just two, crude, dehumanizing, and—paradoxically—opposing stereotypes for African Americans: the animal savage and the helpless, hapless victim. Tyson was portrayed either as a crude, sex-obsessed, violent savage who could barely control his animal instincts or as a victim of terrible social circumstances, almost saved from the streets by a kindly overseer, but who finally faltered and fell due to the connivance of others.[16]

Both portraits demean and debase Tyson, depicting him as a weak human being subject either to base instincts or the machinations of others. Both portraits depict a man without self-control or determination—paradoxical lacks for a former world champion. Both portraits were presented large, daily, on the vast scale afforded a high-profile media event. And both portraits contributed to the overall myth of the Trickster. These portraits will be studied in detail below. The study will show how such racially charged stereotypes made their way into stories of the *Times* and other papers. And it will show how such stories contributed to the compelling myth of the Trickster that reflected the oppositions of race at the center of U.S. social life.

THE SAVAGE

The first predominant portrayal of Tyson in the *Times* and other papers depicted him as a savage or decidedly inhuman beast. These stories declared that Tyson was a brute, an animal, unfit for society. The stories "explained" Tyson with a common stereotype: He was just another black animal. Rejecting notions that Tyson's problems were linked to race or his background, this portrayal included lengthy accounts of his previous problems with women and the law, anticipated his punishment by authorities, and savored the possibility of his humiliation, and even his death, in prison.

Labeling "the Animal"

This depiction often was accomplished through direct characterization. News stories labeled Tyson as an animal and beast. One *Times* column was headlined, "The 'Animal' in Mike Tyson." It said that Tyson needed to stop "acting like an animal."[17] A story in the *Chicago Tribune* claimed that none of Tyson's advisers "ever could tame the animal within."[18] A *Los Angeles Times* article quoted a boxing historian who said that Tyson's indictment "reinforces the belief that Mike Tyson is an animal."[19]

Numerous reports noted the accuser's testimony that Tyson had instantly been transformed from a gentleman into an animal. The *Times* quoted her charge that Tyson "changed completely from a sweet, nice person into an animal, like a demon. In seconds."[20] One column on the conviction said, "Sentencing is March 6. The monster has been captured."[21]

Tyson was a danger to society, according to some reports. One *Times* piece said that Tyson "seems to be living out a bad rap album, which might be titled, 'Nasty as He Wants to Be.'"[22] Another *Times* column called him "a dangerous man, filled with anger toward women" and suggested that "it might take a stun gun and a platoon of armed guards and round-the-clock therapists to break through to the chaotic inner world of Mike Tyson."[23]

Jim Murray of the *Los Angeles Times* wrote that "Mike Tyson comes into public focus as a combination Jack the Ripper and Bluebeard."[24] The *Chicago Tribune* stated that "fighters are like attack dogs, trained to be vicious and rewarded for it, but unfit to be around innocent people."[25]

The portrayal was aided and shaped by the controversial defense strategy of Vince Fuller, Tyson's attorney. Fuller portrayed his client as a vulgar, sex-obsessed athlete whose actions were so crude and intentions so obvious in Indianapolis that any woman who ended up with him should have known what she would get.[26]

News reports simply extended this defense position. For example, one *Times* report noted that "the defense in the rape trial took the position that their man was a lecher, a jerk, a grabber, a callous, out-for-one-thing thug."[27] Another article said, "His lawyers sought to portray the former world heavyweight champion as a vile creature."[28] The *Chicago Tribune* wrote, "His own lawyers argued Tyson was so obviously such a rutting beast that anyone who found herself alone with him got what she deserved."[29]

Times writers pilloried the notion of Tyson as role model. Ira Berkow called Tyson "a role model in reverse."[30] Defending boxing, George Vecsey said the sport had "more decent people than ominous slobs like Tyson."[31] Anna Quindlen, the *Times* syndicated columnist, asked, "Why in the world should Mike Tyson, a man who apparently can't pass a ladies room without grabbing the doorknob, be a role model?"[32]

Other papers too took up the theme. The *Chicago Tribune* noted that "Tyson is our savage side, not our role model."[33] *USA Today* commentator DeWayne Wickham wrote, "Any minister who thinks Mike Tyson is a hero probably believes Sodom and Gomorrah got a bad rap, too."[34]

Chronologies as Condemnation

Another part of the portrayal of Tyson as a savage was the inclusion of "chronologies" or "highlights" of Tyson's life, which organized his past problems with the law, emphasizing all his acts of violence. Such "biographies" could be understood as proof for a contention that Tyson was a creature who had lived barely in control of his great strength, a creature who needed to be restrained and imprisoned.

For example, after his conviction, the *Times* printed a 35-item chronology, "The Tyson Years," that began with his professional boxing debut and included entries such as, "May 8: Dents his $183,000 silver Bentley convertible when he sideswipes another car in Lower Manhattan."[35] Minor car accidents do not usually become part of people's biographies in the *Times*. The paper seemed anxious to record each and every possible social infraction.

The *Los Angeles Times* offered a 57-date "Mike Tyson Chronology" that included dates of speeding tickets.[36] A *USA Today* report, "Tracing Major Events of Heavyweight's Life," included the item "Tyson and friend thrown out of a department store."[37] A column in the *Washington Post* began with details of Tyson's legal troubles and concluded, "So, all in all, Tyson's indictment for rape on Monday was not a surprise. What took so long?"[38]

Rejecting Racism as an Excuse

Press portrayals of the savage also rejected protests that Tyson was a victim of racism. A *Times* column asked rhetorically, "Would Tyson be treated differently if he were white?" It answered itself: from the beginning, "Tyson has been treated differently from almost everyone, white or black" and that such treatment "may have let him get away with murder, at least figuratively."[39] The *Chicago Tribune*'s syndicated columnist Mike Royko dismissed the "view by some blacks that Tyson is the victim of some sort of white conspiracy to bring down successful black men."[40]

An editorial in the *Washington Post*, "The Mike Tyson Verdict," took issue with the paper's own reporting:

> The somewhat sympathetic portrait now being painted of Mike Tyson as "an undereducated, financially unsophisticated gladiator who frittered away much of his earnings on high living, legal entanglements and fees to managers and promoters" (as carried in one story yesterday) may be accu-

rate. But it doesn't go far enough. There is no warrant in law or custom that gave Mike Tyson the prerogative of forcing himself upon a woman without her consent.[41]

A column in the *Los Angeles Times* said, "And please, don't blame it on the ghetto. No, not this time. Evander Holyfield grew up in a ghetto, too. And it wasn't him standing before the judge Monday night. It was Michael Gerard Tyson."[42] A commentary in the *Washington Post* from a reporter in France rejected the notion of racism in particularly strong terms:

> I'm sick of Mike Tyson and his sleaze, even 4,200 miles away. . . . I'm sickened by those who want to absolve Tyson of any responsibility for his behavior because he was once impoverished and orphaned. I'm sickened by the people who want to make Tyson the victim of a racist conspiracy even though virtually any black woman who walks within arm's reach of him does so at risk.[43]

Anticipating His Humiliation

Another key aspect of the portrayal of Tyson as a savage was the enactment in the *Times* and other papers of his humiliation and demise. At his conviction and sentencing, reports painted Tyson's discomfort in the greatest detail, as if enjoying the spectacle of his pain. In the *Times*, Dave Anderson noted the judge's repetition of the sentence, "ten years, ten years, ten years," and said that the "three phrases hit him harder than any three punches ever had."[44] Indeed, the *Times* headline seemed to lead readers in a cheer: "10 Years, 10 Years, 10 Years."

The *Chicago Tribune* detailed his wait for the verdict: "Tyson's eyes flitted everywhere. When the jurors came in, they would not look at him. He stood up, grabbing at the tie around his throat. He put his hands to his sides and tried to keep them still, but his fingers fluttered, grabbing at the edges of his gray suit. His eyes stared somewhere into the corners of the room."[45]

E. R. Shipp of the *Times* described Tyson's reaction to the verdict: "After hearing the sentence, Mr. Tyson removed his watch and tie pin and gave them to one of his lawyers. He then briefly embraced Camille Ewald, the woman who helped rear him, before being escorted from the courtroom by sheriff's deputies."[46]

Other papers also offered vivid descriptions that detailed his humiliation. "There was a half-grin frozen on his face, and in a mocking gesture, he rattled the chains on his handcuffs," said the *Chicago Tribune*. "Seconds earlier, police had proved to him how much freedom he'd lost. They pushed him up against a wall, his palms flat against the cinder block. They went through his pockets and he hung his head."[47] The *Washington Post* noted that "he would exchange his suit and tie for the standard prison attire of white T-shirt and blue jeans and would undergo a strip search, de-lousing and a shower before being assigned to a two-man cell."[48]

Supporting these descriptions were front-page photographs in the *Times* and other papers of Tyson in handcuffs, being led away by sheriffs.[49] The *Times* put one photograph of Tyson in handcuffs on the front page and another in the sports section. A photo in the *Washington Post* was mockingly captioned: "In former heavyweight champion Mike Tyson's new entourage there are a lot of people wearing badges."[50]

USA Today founder Al Neuharth expressed satisfaction that "the overgrown brat who literally got away with everything but murder in his native New York ran into the realities of lifestyles in the heartland of the USA."[51]

Perhaps the most disturbing aspect of the portrayal of Tyson as a savage beast was the anticipation by some reports of the punishment and humiliation that Tyson might receive in prison. Reports anticipated his subjugation to authorities, possible brawls and knife fights with other inmates, sexual attacks, the risk of AIDS, even death.

Before his conviction, reports anticipated his demise. George Vecsey in the *Times* said "Tyson is destined for jail or a bullet or a knife or an auto wreck."[52] A *Chicago Tribune* piece titled "Tyson Could Become a Marked Man in Prison" led with the thoughts of an anonymous Indianapolis cab driver. "'I've got a lot of buddies who are prison guards in Indiana, and they said the prisoners can't wait for Mike Tyson to arrive. They're drawing straws. . . . Can you imagine the prestige those guys in prison would have if they could say they whipped Mike Tyson?' said the cabbie."[53]

A Dave Anderson column in the *Times* seemed to take particular pleasure in Tyson's hard fate. "The Humiliation of No. 922335 Mike Tyson" stated that "life for Mike Tyson as a jailhouse celebrity will be hard and humiliating."[54] It then offered a litany of trouble, suggesting, even anticipating, the pain that awaited Tyson, beginning with attacks by prison guards as well as by other prisoners.

Most prisoners will welcome him, but sooner or later somebody will challenge him. The gunslinger syndrome. In every prison there's always somebody who thinks he's the toughest guy on the block, the cell block.

If that somebody is tougher, at least in a prison brawl, he's really the boss of the prisoners now. But even if Mike Tyson is tougher the first time, that somebody might try to get even with a knife or a razor or a gun. Weapons have been known to be smuggled to prisoners, for a price.

Anderson set up the scenario of a prison attack on Tyson and provided an alternate scenario in the event that Tyson won the brawl: vengeance by the knife, razor, or gun of another inmate. He then conjured up the daily humiliations that Tyson would face, including the possibility that Tyson himself would be raped:

> When it's time for Tyson to be assigned to a prison job, look for him to be put behind the kitchen counter wearing a little white jacket. The champ serving other inmates three times a day. Humiliating.
>
> Being constantly counted by the guards is constantly humiliating. Counted in his cell. Counted to and from work or meals. Counted to and from the yard. Counted as much as 20 or 30 times a day. . . .
>
> Homosexual attacks are a fact of prison life, but according to James Scott [an imprisoned boxer], that threat has decreased because of the fear of AIDS. . . .
>
> More than anything else, Mike Tyson must now cope with the loneliness of prison. Especially at night in the solitude of his cell.

The Anderson column in the *Times* exemplifies press portrayals of Tyson as an inhuman beast who finally was getting the punishment he deserved. These reports were almost bitter in their rejection of previous notions of Tyson as a role model and looked forward to his punishment and humiliation.

THE VICTIM

The second primary depiction of Tyson in the *Times* and other newspapers portrayed a victim. Emphasizing the hard poverty of his childhood in Brooklyn, this portrayal recounted his orphaned life on the streets, his lengthy childhood criminal record, and his confinement in an upstate reform school. They seemed to partially absolve Tyson of blame for his troubled life.

These reports placed particular emphasis on Tyson's white surrogate father, Cus D'Amato, an aging boxing trainer who died, the stories suggested, before he finished "building" his young protege. Other reports, while not absolving Tyson of culpability, placed blame for Tyson's fall on a larger system of entitlement that society grants to athletes, and perhaps, even more broadly, on dark wishes and fantasies that people harbored about Tyson.

The depiction of the victim was often founded upon establishing the crippling effects of an impoverished social life. The coverage was indicative, then, of how cultural and political struggles—other than race but accentuated by race—became part of the reporting on Tyson. The reporting also has links to traditional narratives and tales in which lower class people, granted sudden wealth, find they cannot escape their caste or past.

Labeling the Man-Child

Often the depiction of Tyson as victim was done directly by appealing to the difficulties inherent in Tyson's rise from the lowest class of his childhood on the streets to the highest class of celebrity and wealth. A *Times* report noted that Tyson's sentencing "made for a somber end to a story that included his meteoric rise from a harrowing childhood in a broken home and on the streets of one of the nation's most notorious ghettos, Brownsville, Brooklyn."[55] The *Chicago Tribune* said plainly, "The Tyson trial reveals the stories of two victims, one of rape, the other of circumstances."[56]

William Raspberry wrote in the *Washington Post* that "in many ways, Tyson really is a victim—of a bad childhood, of bad advice, of bad choices."[57] Another report in the *Post* said "Tyson is portrayed by members of his entourage as a victim, not a victimizer."[58]

Some accounts argued that Tyson could not escape his past. *USA Today* used a book about Tyson as the basis for a story on the "Boxer as Victim." According to the report, the book showed Tyson as a "pathetic, love-starved man-child worthy of reconsideration. He is a victim, not a victimizer."[59] The *Washington Post* columnist Tom Boswell wrote, "American sports may never offer a sadder story than Tyson's. His childhood was such a nightmare that, at one level, the basic human reaction is to say, 'There but for the grace of God go I.'"[60]

"Dr. Frankenstein and His Monster"

Another part of the portrayal of Tyson as victim found a special tragedy in the death of his trainer Cus D'Amato. Tyson was depicted as an "unfinished" work who may not have strayed had the old white man lived. A *Times* column used the views of Tyson's biographer Jose Torres: "There is one question that does need to be answered, and quickly: Is there anyone out there who can help this kid? Torres thinks that Cus, if he were alive, would pull Tyson out of the Holyfield fight and try to scare him straight."[61]

The *Chicago Tribune* noted that "D'Amato discovered Tyson but died too soon to save him."[62] *Tribune* columnist Clarence Page pointed to D'Amato's influence and asked, "How different might Tyson's life have been if only someone had taken him under wing to rebuild his life, not just his career." He concluded, "When D'Amato died, so did Tyson's beacon and discipline."[63]

Tennis star Arthur Ashe, writing in the *Washington Post*, said, "Tyson has had no authority figure since D'Amato who could look him in the eye and say, 'You ought to be ashamed of yourself.'"[64] Tom Boswell, also in the *Post*, stated that D'Amato "built" Tyson into a teenager and asked, "what if, like Tyson, your role model dies at just the wrong moment and makes the whole ordeal seem like a cosmic joke?"[65] Jim Murray in the *Los Angeles Times* used similar language and said, "D'Amato wanted to remake the person as well as the fighter."[66]

New York Times columnist Robert Lipsyte recognized the implications of the language. He quoted an exchange between himself and Tyson's biographer Torres:

> "Cus D'Amato didn't finish the job. . . . Cus was in such a hurry to make a heavyweight champion that he didn't make a human being. When D'Amato died, Mike was not a finished person."
> "That sounds like Dr. Frankenstein and his monster," I said.
> "Exactly," said Torres.[67]

Caught in Battles of Race and Gender

Some reports suggested that Tyson was the victim of racism. William Rhoden of the *Times* noted that "the prosecution of Tyson also inspired indictments of a racist judicial system, which, statistics prove, gobbles up black and Hispanic men."[68] William Gildea of the *Washington Post* focused on supporters who were convinced Tyson was victimized. Gildea quoted World Boxing Council president Jose Sulaiman about the conviction: "I am starting to think it is true that what certain people here say, that it was a dinner of blacks by white cannibals."[69]

The *Chicago Tribune* too at times depicted Tyson through the eyes of supporters who were convinced the trial was racist. "They said that he had been railroaded, that he was a victim," said one report.[70]

Another part of the portrayal of Tyson as victim was to cast the boxer as just another athlete caught up in a system of male entitlement. The *Times* criticized "the business of conferring hero status on athletes who have not earned it."[71] A lengthy, 4,000-word report in the *Los Angeles Times* suggested aberrant sexual conduct by athletes may be the "result of lifelong coddling" and argued that "what society has fostered is a segment of the population—elite athletes—that has learned from an early age that they are special. Often they form the idea that rules don't apply to them."[72]

Robert Lipsyte, of the *New York Times*, wrote: "This is what it's about. Naked power. What you can get away with because you're a big boy, because too many people are afraid of you and dependent on you and hooked on a system of male entitlement that tolerates, if not encourages, a man forcing his way."[73]

Other reports took up the entanglement of gender and race and tentatively offered the viewpoint of some in the black community that Tyson was a victim of a more subtle battle: a struggle for power between black men and black women. Rhoden of the *Times* noted that the case "exposed the raw nerve of sexism, through various issues surrounding the brutalization of women."[74] *USA Today* stated simply that "men and women, especially in the African-American community, are divided on whether boxer Mike Tyson should have been convicted of rape."[75]

Another *USA Today* commentator, Barbara Reynolds, was more direct. She took up the issue of Tyson's support from ministers and stated that "throughout history, black ministers often have stepped forward to replace whites as oppressors rather than liberators of black women." She also noted that too often "black women echo those traditional views, even against their own self-interest."[76]

A columnist in the *Chicago Tribune* also addressed the gender tensions that the Tyson trial caused for African Americans: "Those issues—protecting a man perceived as a hero for blacks and the strained relationship between black men and women—echo another celebrated case involving an African-American male and female: Clarence Thomas and Anita Hill." He continued: "The cases have stunned the black community like a one–two punch. In both, two points were clear: Vocal segments of the black population took the side of a black male against his black female accuser, and as a result, the woman was vilified."[77]

Clarence Page of the *Tribune* too perceived that Tyson was embroiled in larger tensions between African American men and women. He too noted the vilification of the black woman and called it "the Rasheeda Moore Syndrome," for the woman who took part in the FBI cocaine arrest of District of Columbia mayor Marion Barry. Page wrote: "'The bitch set me up,' moaned Barry. The quote soon appeared on T-shirts that sold briskly outside his trial, adding weight to an old stereotype about the alleged treachery of black women."[78]

The *Washington Post* gave over the front page of its style section to a lengthy report that argued that black women saw Tyson as a victim and had little sympathy for Tyson's female accuser:

> In interviews on two college campuses, and in listener calls to local radio stations, the refrain from a number of young black women has been: She asked for it, she got it, and it's not fair to "cry rape." They may find Tyson's general attitude toward women repugnant—he seems to be well known as the crude propositioner he portrayed himself as during the trial—but there is little sympathy for her.[79]

Others' Fantasies and Fears

Some reflective columns offered the subtle perspective that Tyson was a victim—even a creation—of others' fantasies and fears. For these writers, Tyson had become a highly charged, symbolic character used by writers and audiences in a kind of appalling, yet appealing, horror show of race and menace. The *Times* columnist Lipsyte stated that, with the rape charge, Tyson had managed "to transcend boxing, to join Jack Johnson, Joe Louis and Muhammad Ali as a social as well as a pugilistic symbol."[80] Lipsyte wrote, "suddenly, even as Freddy Kreuger appears in his last 'Nightmare on Elm Street,' Mike Tyson has cracked into our subconscious: He is what we are afraid of, and we created him." A *Los Angeles Times* commentator said:

> We shake our heads, we cluck our tongues, we wag our fingers, we use words like "criminal" and "shameful" and "reprehensible." We are talking about Mike Tyson, but we are missing the point. The point can be found with one glance into the mirror. A sports champion is charged with

rape, and then convicted, and we are simultaneously disgusted and intrigued, appalled and enthralled.[81]

Such reports subtly add to the portrayal of Tyson as a victim of circumstances outside his control. The majority of these reports demean him as they symbolically disempower him. The portrayal surely is complex and torn by numerous cultural and political issues. Yet the reports are founded upon a racially charged, symbolic type: a powerless African American man, helpless because of a combination of his deprived background, his society, the women of his race, and other people's fears.

MIKE TYSON: THE TRICKSTER

On one level, examination of *Times* and other press coverage of the Tyson trial has confirmed that portrayals of the boxer were drawn from degrading, dehumanizing stereotypes. Cast as an animal savage or a hapless dupe, Tyson was debased by press coverage that used his troubles to enact larger stereotyped dramas about him. Despite the intensity of the coverage and the nine-month duration of the judicial and journalistic process, little insight was provided into the boxer and his life. Neither the *Times* nor any of the elite, influential papers studied here offered more than superficial story lines and crude stereotypes. Even those enraged at the cruelty of Tyson's acts must be dismayed at such shallow portrayals.

My findings certainly support those who criticized press coverage of Tyson's trial. The implications in terms of the trial, however, are unclear. With the trial jury sequestered, the influence of coverage on the trial would not appear great, except perhaps from images offered in pretrial coverage.

The uniformity and unanimity of the press portraits, though, certainly are troubling to those concerned about press representations of Tyson and African Americans. How did so many reporters and editors produce and reproduce such similar demeaning portrayals? The influence of eternal stories, especially the Trickster myth, must be acknowledged. Like the Trickster, Tyson was portrayed as an animal barely in control of his strength and wants. Like the Trickster, Tyson was portrayed as a dumb and helpless victim of himself and others. And like the Trickster, Tyson was shown as lewd, cruel, brutal, and stupid, a figure inviting ridicule and inciting fear, a scurrilous figure on a path of senseless and self-imposed suffering. Some Trickster stories show remarkable similarities to news stories about Tyson. For example, in Native American myth, Mink tries to be respectable by blundering and bluffing his way into doomed marriages. Coyote, driven by animal lust, rapes a beautiful girl and endures punishment by the people. Tricksters stumble and crash and, if they're not quite denting $183,000 silver Bentley convertibles, they are barely in control of their ceaseless motion. Almost all Trickster myths depict some punishment meted out to this offender of social mores and laws.

THE TRICKSTER AND NEWS STEREOTYPES

Those who are sensitive to media portrayals of African Americans will not be surprised by these findings. The Trickster myth—especially the two components isolated in Tyson coverage: animal and victim—can be found often in news coverage of African Americans. News portrayals borrow liberally from the Trickster myth in their depictions of welfare mothers, street criminals, crack addicts, teenaged wolf packs, promiscuous athletes, and numerous other stories in which blacks are cast. Take one infamous example: Rodney King, the Los Angeles man whose beating by police was captured on home videotape, often was depicted by the news as animal and victim, another subject for the Trickster myth.

The results of this study thus perhaps are most discouraging in the context of the long body of press criticism that has continued to demonstrate racist stereotypes in the news. More than 70 years after Lippmann's analyses of stereotypes, more than 25 years after the Kerner Commission criticized press portrayals of race, the news still draws upon racist images.

Myth, though, provides another way of looking at the problem. *This study complements the previous literature by pointing out how racist stereotypes are invoked subtly but inexorably by the press within the language, conventions, and narrative forms of myth.* Myth offers highly structured story forms that have existed for centuries. Stereotypes offer socially specific figures and images accepted and assumed by a group. Together, stereotypes in myths are a potent combination whose portrayals resonate with naturalness and familiarity even as they demean and degrade.

News portrayals might have offered varied, complex depictions of Tyson. The man is not a hero, but he is not an animal either. Instead, a complicated, compelling subject was starkly reduced to a few of the most offensive representations of race: Did the black, savage, sex-driven, former heavyweight champion use his animal strength to rape the virginal black princess who naively left herself alone with him? Or did the dumb, innocent, but well-hung black boxer get manipulated again, this time by a promiscuous, black gold digger who had deliberately thrown herself at him only to be hurt by the size of his organ and his crude, rude approach to sex? These were the sparse choices inserted into the modern myth, choices echoed and extended by months of coverage, choices that affirmed delimiting, dehumanizing, and degrading portrayals of African Americans.

Findings from the Tyson trial coverage thus highlight in particular the cruel process of *reduction* that lies at the heart of stereotyping. In fact, the critical tension surrounding the Tyson trial coverage can be conceived not only in terms of offensive representations but also in terms of pitiless reductions. The problem was not only that Tyson was depicted with racist stereotypes—though that was part of it. The problem was that over nine months, five newspapers, and 500 articles, the press confined itself to two depictions, both drawn from a small well of racist stereotypes for African Americans. As journalists and readers consider racism in the press, they need to think about the damages caused not only by what was printed and said but by what was unprinted and unsaid. That is, racism may result from a dearth of types, a lack of complex depictions, a reliance on a few degrading narratives, and an overwhelming paucity of portrayals.

MODERN RACISM IN THE NEWS

If we accept the thesis that members of the press are not overtly racist, yet still produce racist portrayals, then attention must be directed to the language contributing to such portrayals. Specifically, the study's findings of Tyson as Trickster may be seen as an illustration of modern racism in the press.

As we have seen, scholars of modern racism affirm that traditional racism has been transformed. Bigoted terms, support for segregation, and blatant discrimination are no longer openly espoused or condoned. Yet racism remains. Grounded in beliefs that discrimination no longer exists, that the history of segregation casts no shadow today, and that the problems facing the black community can be attributed to individual faults, modern racism offers "explanations" for black life in the post-civil-rights era.

Stereotypes, we've seen, are key to modern racism. Stereotypes help organize negative beliefs about blacks. And the espousal of stereotypes gives expression—safely masked—to those negative beliefs.[82] Press stereotypes are particularly crucial, for they are one of the means, Entman says, by which "mass cultural institutions may promote negative stereotypes that are congruent with modern racism."[83] Consistent with modern racism, however, the media's racial stereotypes are subtle. "Rather than the grossly demeaning distortions of yesterday," Entman argues, "stereotyping of blacks now allows abstraction from and denial of the racial component."[84] Press stereotypes legitimize individual stereotypes. They help organize social beliefs. They provide a way of understanding that can be passed on to the large public.

From this perspective, then, news reports about Tyson can be seen as illustrative of modern racism. Most of the articles cannot be judged individually as explicitly bigoted depictions or as "grossly demeaning distortions." Yet as they reported on Tyson and his troubles, the press reports clearly represented and reproduced racist stereotypes. And these stereotypes attained especial power thanks to the myth of the Trickster.

Some defenders of the *Times* and the press still might want to argue that much of what was said about the boxer was "true." But a careful study of news language rejects that claim. It is important to be clear: Tyson is *not* an animal, beast, or monster. He is not a helpless man-child, passive victim, or symbolic creation. He is a man convicted of a heinous crime. The depictions may appear to have the aura of truth—may appear to explain—precisely because they are narrated in familiar stories and draw from stereotyped categories designed to do just that.

RACIST IMAGES IN THE NEWS: WHY?

But why? *Why* did reporters for the *Times* and other papers—if they are not blatant racists—portray Tyson in terms of such an offensive, destructive myth? Why did the work of black and white reporters show the influence of stereotypes? More broadly, why does the news continue to cast the experience of African Americans in racist imagery?

Though I depart here from the insights provided by my analysis of texts, these questions call out for consideration. Some answers have been put forth in the realm of social psychology. In research on cognitive structures in stereotyping, social scientists suggest that people quite naturally process and store information through the use of categories, or *schemas*.[85] Categorizing others comes easily to humankind. Culture, economics, and politics apparently affect these schemas. Social tensions and economic pressures are brought to bear. Often, a larger, more dominant group categorizes and stigmatizes another group with negative terms.

The U.S. social, cultural, and political matrix has produced generations of racial conflict—and generations of a dominant white group categorizing and stigmatizing African Americans. Journalists likely have not spent much time considering their cognitive categorizing. I know I haven't. But most journalists have been born and raised in U.S. society and they cannot expect that their cognitive categorizing will be free of dominant stigmas and stereotypes.

In an oft-quoted passage, Lippmann wrote, "In the great blooming, buzzing confusion of the outer world we pick out what our culture has already defined for us, and we tend to perceive that which we have picked out in the form stereotyped for us by our culture."[86]

In Lippmann's view, culture and society lead journalists to a system of selection and exclusion. "For when a system of stereotypes is well fixed," Lippmann wrote, "our attention is called to those facts which support it, and diverted from those which contradict it."[87] News stories thus are formed before they are gathered. These story forms take root—as "unquestioned and unnoticed conventions of narration," argues Michael Schudson—and reproduce and perpetuate stereotypes in the news.[88]

The process may well be an unconscious one. As the British researcher Stuart Hall noted in a broader discussion of ideology in broadcast media, ideological distortions do not occur "at the level of the conscious intentions and biases of the broadcaster." He argued instead that "the ideology has 'worked' in such a case because the discourse has spoken itself through him/her."[89] Similarly, Entman suggests, "Because old-fashioned racist images are socially undesirable, stereotypes are now more subtle, and stereotyped thinking is reinforced at levels likely to remain below conscious awareness."[90]

COUNTERING RACIST STEREOTYPES
THROUGH MYTH

As we have seen, one of myth's important roles is to resolve basic oppositions at the heart of human life. Birth and death, the raw and the cooked, winning and losing, good and evil, black and white—much of life is built around polar oppositions. "The sad truth," psychologist Carl Jung noted, "is that man's real life consists of a complex of inexorable opposites."[91]

For Claude Lévi-Strauss, the French anthropologist, the resolution of oppositions is central to myth. "The purpose of myth," he said in a classic statement, "is to provide a logical model capable of overcoming a contradiction." Eliade agreed. "Myth expresses in actions and drama what metaphysics and theology define dialectically," he said. "Heraclitus saw that 'God is day and night, winter and summer, war and peace, satiety and hunger: all opposites are in him.'"[92]

Myth attempts to resolve contradictions—but myth is not always fair or just. Myth justifies and supports the main, dominant society. If a society is founded upon inequality, that society's dominant myths "explain" and support such inequality. For example, if a society denies women the opportunity to work or to participate in politics, myths will be told that justify the exclusion and resolve this opposition between men and women. Myths will portray the weakness of women, the superiority of men.

The Tyson case offered a mass of oppositions: good and evil, man and woman, weak and strong, black and white. But race, in particular, came to dominate discussions. It's not surprising. In U.S. society, race has long posed a basic and unresolved opposition, especially between blacks and whites. With historical roots in slavery, with decades of struggle for civil rights, with racial tensions still charging events every day, relations between black people and white people surely are grounded in opposition. And the dominant society can be expected to hold myths that justify and explain racial tensions.

As myth, as storyteller of the social order, U.S. news attempts to resolve the oppositions of race. It often does so by degrading African Americans. Why have African Americans endured decades of pain? Social order cannot be at fault, news suggests. The blame must lie with *them*.

Yet we have seen that myth is eminently flexible. Myth can sometimes be used to challenge the social order. Can myth confront and counter racism in the news? Though I wander still farther from my textual analysis, some thoughts can be hazarded. Some groups fight racist stereotypes by offering training and sensitivity workshops for journalists. Other groups work to diversify overwhelmingly white newsrooms. These laudable efforts attempt to end stereotyping journalist by journalist. The efforts place their emphasis on the cognitive categorizing of people in the newsroom.

Myth places its emphasis on language. Rather than plumb the depths of the human mind, myth stays on the surface of the printed page. Myth suggests a place to begin is not necessarily with the *mind* of the reporter but with the *words* of the reporter, the language of the news. I assume that most journalists are not emphatic racists. Yet we have acknowledged that journalists, like many in the United States, have been shaped by a society that stereotypes and discriminates. And as public storytellers, journalists give public expression to these stereotypes, placing them into deep-rooted story forms that try to explain and resolve the oppositions presented by race.

At the very least, journalists can be shown the unintended racist ways of their stories. They can be sensitized to language that degrades and demeans. They can be directed toward other language and alternate images. They can be shown different stories that respond to the opposition of race. In this way, myth can be put consciously to use in ways that might counter racism.

It is, of course, too simple. It is only a place to begin. Support, though, is offered by bell hooks, author of *Black Looks: Race and Representation*. She too appeals for a change first in language. She writes that "the issue of race and representation is not just a question of critiquing the *status quo*. It is also about transforming the image, creating alternatives, and asking ourselves questions—about what types of images subvert, pose critical alternatives, and transform our worldviews."[93]

Confronting racism in society and journalism is a formidable, imposing task. Eliminating some racist images in the news will not eliminate racism in the United States. Yet, for reporters, editors, press critics, and readers, a place to begin can be the language, the stories, of the news. Other myths can be told.

Chapter 8

The Other World

Haiti and International News Values

On October 11, 1992, more than 2,000 people gathered in protest outside the *New York Times* building in Manhattan. The object of their protest: the *Times*'s coverage of Haiti, in particular the reporting of Caribbean correspondent Howard French.

The protesters charged that the *Times*'s coverage was weighted heavily against the liberal, progressive president Jean-Bertrand Aristide, who had been overthrown by a September 30, 1991, military coup and was now living in exile in the United States. Haiti, which shares an island with the Dominican Republic just southeast of Cuba, had long been—before Aristide—a friendly site for exploitive U.S. businesses. The protesters charged that Howard French was an instrument of a U.S. foreign policy determined to keep the progressive president in exile in the United States as long as possible.

French's reports from Haiti, they said, relied heavily on sources connected to Haiti's military regime and the wealthy elite who opposed Aristide. And, they charged, French ignored sources with ties to the much larger pro-Aristide rural majority. Aristide himself, the protesters pointed out, had not been interviewed by French since the coup. The *Times*, they

147

said, seemed to be supporting the coup and ignoring a legitimately elected, wrongly deposed leader.

Times editor Max Frankel defended French in a letter to the protesting groups. Two weeks later, however, Aristide was given space to state his case on the *Times* op-ed page, and soon after French published an interview with Aristide.[1]

In the months and years after the coup, as Aristide's exile in the United States dragged on, his supporters continued to find fault with French's coverage of Haiti. They charged that French, following Washington's lead, treated the military coup leaders with deference. Moreover, they said, French and the *Times* contributed to a smear campaign against Aristide, giving prominent coverage to allegations that Aristide had been an egotistical, perhaps mentally unbalanced, leader who encouraged violence and vengeance seeking among his supporters.[2]

In July 1994, perhaps in response to the critical pressure or simply as part of a regular rotation, Larry Rohter, the *Times* Miami bureau chief, assumed the position of Caribbean correspondent, offering a fresh start for *Times* coverage of Haiti.

It was a critical time: Over the next two years, the Clinton administration struggled with the issue of how to restore the democratically elected president to power while also appeasing U.S. and international business interests; a U.S. invasion of Haiti was called off at the last moment; U.S. peacekeeping forces eventually landed in Haiti; Aristide was returned to power; and, after he served out his term, the Haitian people elected a new president.

In the midst of such crucial changes and in the context of the *Times*'s previous coverage, Larry Rohter's reporting merited the closest scrutiny. It's unusual, but not rare, for individual correspondents to attract such critical attention. *Times* reporters in particular attract scrutiny due to the paper's status among national and international officials as well as to its agenda-setting influence on other media.

Traditionally, criticism has been most intense when *Times* reporters vary too much from U.S. foreign policy lines. For example, Walter Duranty, the *Times* Russian correspondent in the 1920s and 1930s, was criticized then, and more recently, as an apologist for Stalin. Huge Stalinist abuses, such as the forced famine that killed millions, were ignored or underplayed.[3] *Times* correspondent David Halberstam, who began covering South Vietnam in 1962, often contradicted optimistic pronouncements from Washington about the strength of South Vietnamese forces and the limited role of U.S. "advisers." President Kennedy himself asked *Times* publisher Arthur Sulzberger about the possibility of transferring Halberstam.[4] In late 1981, Raymond Bonner reported the massacre of hundreds of men, women, and children by United States-backed Salvadoran forces in the village of Mozote. Bonner's reporting was a major embarrassment to the Reagan administration, which was already having trouble promoting public and congressional support for the right-wing Salvadoran government. The White House and conservative forces united to discredit Bonner and his reporting.[5] Weeks later, Bonner received humiliating word from the *Times* that he was being reassigned to a beat in the United States. The incident had a bitter epilogue. In 1993, a United Nations commission confirmed the massacre and provided solid evidence that the Salvadoran and U.S. governments had attempted to cover up the truth. The *Times* reported the U.N. findings with little drama. Its story did not even mention Bonner—who has since rejoined the *Times*.[6]

This chapter too offers in-depth scrutiny of the work of one *Times* reporter but does so in a broader context: an increasingly important theoretical debate over the direction of international news values in a post-cold war world and the ways in which myth might shed light on those values.

A VACUUM OF VALUES

Coverage of Haiti, of course, falls under the heading of international news or foreign correspondence. Such news has long been the subject of scrutiny and critical study. Numerous commentators have noted that the U.S. press has almost always covered international affairs from the perspective of U.S. political interests.[7] The cold war offered the premier model for such coverage, providing basic, enduring, organizing principles for selecting and reporting international events. Reporters and editors covered international events, from Haiti to Vietnam, based on their relevance to the cold war.

Those organizing principles are now obsolete. The United States's archrival, the Soviet Union, has dissolved. Communism is no longer considered a real threat to capitalism. No other nation can match the United States's combined military and economic strength. As press critic Daniel Hallin writes, "The Cold War perspective, which once organized virtually all foreign affairs coverage into an ideological picture supportive of American world hegemony, now no longer does so."[8]

Without the ideological guidance of the cold war perspective, today's journalists operate in a vacuum of values. How can reporters make relevant, to U.S. readers, events in Haiti or East Timor or Ethiopia? James F. Hoge, editor of the journal *Foreign Affairs*, laments that "with the old gauges broken, the press is struggling to understand the new international order of risks and opportunities."[9] Jon Vanden Heuvel makes a similar observation. The media, he notes, "are still struggling to develop a satisfactory new approach to reporting the world." He continues:

> The end of the Cold War has opened new horizons for the American media, but embedded in that wider perspective is the problem of making sense of a world in which change is the only constant. The old criteria for covering foreign affairs on the East–West confrontation model—and many of the old standards of newsworthiness—don't apply in a post-Cold War model.[10]

The press, including the *Times*, has openly acknowledged the controversy and confusion raised by the removal of the cold war framework. In an internal *Times* memo since published, then-foreign editor Bernard Gwertzman reflected on the need for different values. He began:

> To the foreign staff: I thought it might be useful to share some ideas on where we are and where we should be going in our foreign coverage in the post-Cold War environment. What has spurred this memo, of course, is the breakup of the Soviet Union and Gorbachev's resignation at Christmas 1991, which followed so closely upon the collapse of the communist system in Eastern Europe two years earlier. Not only have these developments drastically altered the world's political map, but they have had an inevitable impact on how we as reporters and editors do our jobs.[11]

Gwertzman acknowledged the "remarkable" previous influence of U.S. foreign policy and the nuclear superpower rivalry on reporting. "This competition consciously and subconsciously dominated government policies, affecting newspaper coverage as well," he wrote. "Without this threat of nuclear destruction, there is an obvious need to question some of our assumptions about coverage." While unable or unwilling to offer specific directives concerning news values, Gwertzman made it clear that new thinking was in order:

> We are all professionals and it makes little sense in trying to define for a reporter what is news and what isn't. But it is certainly true that we have

widened our net considerably on what we want to cover and some of the traditional political stories of the past may not resonate as they did before.[12]

TWO MODELS FOR
INTERNATIONAL NEWS VALUES

No dominant framework stands ready to replace the organizing and authorizing powers of the cold war model. In this rudderless context, journalists and academics have proposed alternate frameworks for describing how U.S. news media might cover the world. Two primary models have emerged.

For some theorists, the press stands at an unusual crossroads, one rich with opportunity. With U.S. foreign policy purposeless and with U.S. correspondents forced into reflection about their world role, some scholars see the opportunity for a journalism of global justice. They see the chance for a humane journalism that gives overdue attention to the suffering of people who fell unnoted outside the media's former cold war framework.[13]

Clifford Christians, John Ferre, and Mark Fackler argue that the time is right for a press "nurtured by communitarian ethics," and affirm that "under the notion that justice itself—and not merely haphazard public enlightenment—is a *telos* of the press, the news-media system stands under obligation to tell the stories that justice requires."[14] Some observers have suggested that a change toward humanitarian news values is already under way, that press and television coverage of international tragedies—"the CNN effect"—is driving U.S. foreign policy.[15] James Hoge writes, "Foreign policy-makers speak as if they are bedeviled by the nature of post-Cold War press coverage, often alleging that it is television film footage that dominates agenda-setting."[16]

Other theorists, however, offer a bleaker model. They suggest that the dissolution of the cold war framework has rendered the press, especially the *Times*, even more vulnerable to the United States's foreign policy agenda.[17] Noam Chomsky finds only confirmation of his decades-long struggle to demonstrate that "the major media and other ideological institutions will generally reflect the perspectives and interests of established power."[18] Other scholars see the news media withdrawing from the international scene, ceding foreign affairs to the policymakers. Unwilling to articulate national interests and unable to find a coherent way to organize costly foreign coverage, the press will increasingly focus its attention on domestic matters, these scholars argue, venturing offshore only for the most dramatic disasters or when U.S. foreign policy is already directly in play. News images of the struggle against communism will be replaced, Daniel Hallin fears, by dizzying, unstructured images of a world in conflict, images of disorder, images ultimately of anarchy and chaos, resulting in an overarching "image of 'Fortress America,' an island of civilization in a sea of political barbarism."[19]

MYTH AND INTERNATIONAL NEWS VALUES: THE OTHER WORLD

The two models—of a humane press driving foreign policy and of a servile press dictated to by foreign policy—offer stark, contrasting outlooks on the course of international news values, a course still being shaped as this new century begins. The key question is, What news values will structure U.S. news? Myth, deeply entwined with social values, deepens the question. If news is myth, the focus of discussion is not only news values but the larger values of society. If news is myth, news values will reflect not only professional judgments regarding newsworthiness and importance, but also the prevailing values and beliefs of the larger society. If news is myth, what kinds of stories will be used to portray the new world?

Myth, of course, has a long history of portraying new worlds. Sometimes the Other World represents paradisal beginnings: fabulous gardens of earthly delights, fantastic islands of beauty and wealth, filled with nymphs and songs. Other times the Other World is a forbidding place: the underworld, a land of darkness and chaos, teeming with miserable throngs, the land of the dead or dying. In Greek myth, Orpheus journeyed to Hades to win back his bride, Eurydice. Odysseus embarked on an extended Odyssey that took him to both wonderful and terrible lands. The Babylonian hero Gilgamesh traveled through dark tunnels and dazzling gardens, to worlds of terror and beauty. These are worlds different from "home." These are worlds of the Other.

Joseph Campbell gives a psychological perspective to these myths of the Other World. The myths, Campbell says, are projections of individual fears and desires. "The regions of the unknown (desert, jungle, deep sea, alien land, etc.) are free fields for the projection of unconscious content," he wrote. All the incestuous, patricidal rumblings of the unconscious are "reflected back against the individual and his society in forms suggesting threats of violence and fancied dangerous delight—not only as ogres but also as sirens of mysteriously seductive, nostalgic beauty."[20]

Others see the myths in societal terms. The myths help define a society in relation to other societies. Writing about his own case studies of Greek mythology, the scholar Jean-Pierre Vernant affirmed that myths articulated a distinctive view of the world. "Seen as a whole," he argued, "this system appears to have a fundamental social significance: it expresses how a group of people in particular historical circumstances sees itself, how it defines its conditions of life and its relationship to nature and the supernatural."[21]

Through myths of the Other World, a society reveals much about itself. The paradisal Other World might be a land of milk and honey with no labor or stress. Or the paradisal Other World might be a land of peace and harmony with no fighting or war. The differences in these visions are important. They tell us much about a society. The darker Other World too tells us much. The Other World might be a land of poverty and chaos without structure or rules. Or the darker Other World might be a land of the dead who are punished for their sins in this life. Like all myths, the Other World reveals and confirms social values and beliefs.[22]

BACKGROUND FOR STUDY: HAITI AND LARRY ROHTER

Framed in terms of myth, the debate over news values can take on a larger perspective. Through Rohter's work on Haiti, this chapter explores reporting of the new world in terms of news values and myth—in particular, the myth of the Other World. To ground this analysis, the chapter first offers brief background on recent relations between Haiti and the United States. U.S. actions in Haiti during the 1990s were convoluted and hard to follow. A brief summary of events and a short biographical sketch of Larry Rohter might prove useful before an analysis of reporting is undertaken.

"The Uses of Haiti": The 1990s[23]

In 1986, after the Duvalier family dictatorship had plundered and terrorized Haiti for three decades, demonstrations and dissent finally succeeded in deposing Jean-Claude "Baby Doc" Duvalier. Many Haitians sought a period of *dechoukaj*—an uprooting—of the dictatorial past from their politics and culture. But a military junta, led by General Henri Namphy, who had the support of the United States, seized power.

Popular resistance—which came to be called *lavalas*, a kind of purifying flood or outpouring—increased. It began to coalesce around a Catholic priest, the Reverend Jean-Bertrand Aristide, who had returned to Haiti in 1985 after three years of graduate study in Montreal. Aristide combined liberation theology with a progressive social policy of land reform, higher wages, and the end to military oppression. He attracted broad and intense support among the rural poor and urban youth.

For four more years, Haiti endured political turmoil. Hundreds of people were killed as the military attempted to suppress the resistance. The elections of December 1990 marked a major turning point. Aristide, who by then had been expelled from his order, the Society of Saint Francis de Sales, because of his political activism, agreed to run for president against the United States-backed candidate Marc Bazin. Aristide swept to victory with almost 70 percent of the vote.

U.S. agencies watched the Aristide administration with alarm. Aristide's policies were seen as radical reforms, with numerous repercussions for U.S. business interests. For example, Aristide proposed to raise the minimum daily wage to near $3, almost twice the going wage. The U.S. Agency for International Development, which had spent millions of U.S. tax dollars to promote U.S. business investments in Haiti's low-wage economy, regarded Aristide as a disaster.

Haiti's wealthy elite, who still had huge resources, felt they had little to lose by trying to stop Aristide. On September 29, 1991, Aristide was overthrown by a military coup financed by Haiti's upper class. Tales of U.S. complicity or at least support continue to be told. Aristide was flown to Caracas, Venezuela, and General Raoul Cedras took power.

The Bush administration offered little support to Aristide, despite the fact that he was a democratically elected president voted into office by a large majority. A weak embargo was put into place, but the administration was more interested in restoring a constitutional democracy than in restoring Aristide.

With little U.S. pressure, the coup leaders began a campaign of extermination against Aristide's supporters. Bodies lay in the streets each morning and the death toll rose into the thousands. Many of Aristide's supporters fled Haiti to seek asylum in the United States, but the Bush administration, claiming that the refugees were not fleeing political persecution, instituted a policy of returning them forcibly to Haiti.

Haitian backers of the coup, along with sympathetic U.S. administrators, began a propaganda campaign against Aristide with materials that recently have been denounced as crude and false CIA disinformation.[24] A file of Aristide's alleged human rights abuses was circulated to Congress and reporters. "Aristide's Autocratic Ways Ended Haiti's Embrace of Democracy" was the headline of one *New York Times* story by Howard French. Another rumor was circulated that Aristide was a manic–depressive. In the United States, as we have seen, Aristide's supporters protested such coverage outside the *Times* building.

During the 1992 presidential campaign, Bill Clinton promised to change U.S. policies toward Haiti. After his election, he broke some of those promises. Bowing to pressure from Florida officials who feared an influx of Haitians, in January 1993 Clinton announced that he would maintain Bush's policy of returning refugees to Haiti.[25] Clinton did, however, work at restoring Aristide to power. In March 1993 Clinton actually met with Aristide.

Clinton found that Cedras was unwilling to relinquish power. After a much stiffer embargo was imposed in June 1993, the United States and the Haitian junta reached a tentative agreement. Blanket amnesty would be granted to the military. And Aristide would be returned to power by October 30 in a process monitored by the United Nations.

Months of terror followed as military death squads, especially a paramilitary group known as FRAPH, lashed out at Aristide supporters. In early October, Cedras reneged on the agreement. As the *USS Harlan County* attempted to dock in Port-au-Prince with the participating U.S. forces, it was met by heavily armed gangs. Unwilling to engage in a military battle, the Clinton administration backed off. U.S. forces withdrew, economic sanctions were reimposed, and a new stalemate began.

Throughout 1994, the Clinton administration threatened military action against the coup leaders. The issue caused a rift among the U.S. left, which was divided into those who opposed any U.S. intervention in Haiti and those who wished to see the progressive Aristide restored to his rightful position.[26]

On September 15, Clinton appeared on national television to announce an imminent invasion of Haiti. On September 17, as the invasion neared, a high-profile U.S. delegation made a final attempt at diplomacy with Cedras. The delegation included former president Jimmy Carter, former chairman of the Joint Chiefs of Staff Colin Powell, and chairman of the Senate Armed Services Committee Sam Nunn. Military planes were actually in the air, heading toward Haiti, when a last-minute deal was reached; the planes were recalled. Within weeks, some 16,000 U.S. troops landed unchallenged in Haiti. Aristide was returned to power.

For 16 months, Aristide served out the remainder of his term, ending the oppression by the military and introducing reforms in wages, work, health, and justice. Forbidden by the constitution to succeed himself, he oversaw elections in June 1995. Rene Preval, Aristide's prime minister, was elected president and was inaugurated in February 1996. These were the events facing Larry Rohter, the *Times* Caribbean correspondent.

Larry Rohter

William Lawrence Rohter, known personally and professionally as Larry Rohter, was responsible for reporting the tumult and turmoil within Haiti for the *Times*.[27] Appointed *Times* Caribbean correspondent in July 1994, Rohter had spent much of his life gaining experience in international affairs.

Born in Oak Park, Illinois, in 1950, Rohter studied political science in the School of Foreign Service at Georgetown University, graduating in 1971. He immediately went on to the School of International Affairs and Institute of East Asian Studies at Columbia University, where he received a master's degree in international affairs in 1973. He became fluent in Portuguese and Spanish and learned written and spoken Chinese.

While studying at Columbia, Rohter worked for the New York bureau of Rede Globo, a Brazilian communication company, filing news and entertainment stories. Soon after graduation, he joined the style section of the *Washington Post*, where he specialized in music from 1974 to 1979.

Rohter's work in international reporting began in 1980. He was hired by *Newsweek* as a correspondent in Rio de Janeiro. Then, after a brief stint as Latin American bureau chief, Rohter went to Asia, first as Peking bureau chief and then as Asian regional editor.

In 1984, Rohter joined the *Times* as a metropolitan reporter. He toiled in the New York City and other U.S. city bureaus for three years. In 1987, he was appointed Mexico City bureau chief, serving until 1990. He came back to the United States and in July 1991 took the position of Miami bureau chief, a position that involved some Caribbean reporting. Three years later, in July 1994, he returned full time to international reporting as Caribbean correspondent.

His first report appeared on July 8. Its subject was Haitian refugees.[28] Panamanian president Guillermo Endara announced that he was withdrawing his offer to provide "safe haven" for 10,000 Haitians. With that story, Rohter's reporting on Haiti began.

FOUR THEMES IN HAITI COVERAGE

I studied all of Rohter's bylines from July 1, 1994 to February 29, 1996—a total of 196 stories. Rohter's Caribbean beat took him to Cuba, Panama, Guatemala, Nicaragua, the Bahamas, Colombia, Trinidad, Honduras, and El Salvador. Yet Haiti dominated Rohter's work.

In July 1994, his first month on the beat, he filed stories only from Haiti. Through September, October, and November of 1994, as Aristide reassumed power, Rohter again filed only from Haiti. Indeed, of Rohter's 196 stories, 120 were about Haiti. During periods of intense activity, such as the negotiations between the U.S. delegation and the military junta, and the subsequent landing of U.S. troops, Rohter was filing reports daily, at times even penning two stories a day.

Through in-depth examination of Rohter's reporting, my study identified and analyzed four primary themes that structured the correspondence: (1) the delegitimation of the de facto government, (2) the approbation and then disapprobation of Aristide, (3) the avoidance of U.S.–FRAPH ties, and (4) the degradation of Haitian life. These themes, complex and sometimes contradictory, offer plentiful insights into the changes confronting U.S. news in the post-cold war world and how such news is influenced by myth, particularly the myth of the Other World. Each theme is examined closely in the following sections.

The Delegitimation of the "De Facto" Government

A primary theme in Rohter's early reporting, in the midst of Aristide's exile, was the delegitimation of the military junta that overthrew Aristide. Rohter's correspondence worked in concert with the Clinton's administration's attempt to restore Aristide to power. As detailed below, Rohter effected this theme in numerous ways. He chronicled killings and other acts of violence by the junta. He employed sources who denounced the group. He labeled the junta with terms of illegitimacy. And he reported, with almost satisfying detail, the humiliation of junta members as they were forced into exile.

The delegitimation of the de facto government was first accomplished through accounts of beatings and murders inflicted by its forces. For example, within hours after U.N. human rights monitors were expelled by the junta, the military increased its terror. Rohter highlighted the killings the next day and dismissed the junta's explanations. "Immediately after the rights observers were expelled, a dozen men whose identities remain unknown were killed and secretly buried," Rohter wrote. Government officials described the victims as car thieves, Rohter continued, "but the American Embassy isn't buying the story."[29]

The same week, Rohter quoted an unnamed source who said that "the repression has become ferocious."[30] The *Times* accompanied this story with a photograph of a Haitian policeman whipping people who were standing in line for free food. Soon after, another report led, "Government security forces shot and wounded a critic of military rule on Monday and beat and arrested several other people who were applying for refuge in the United States, witnesses and diplomats said today."[31]

Rohter's reports regularly included critical statements, such as "the military-dominated government has routinely ignored constitutional guarantees, sending soldiers, police and paramilitary groups, for example, to attack or kill political opponents, break up political meetings and search homes."[32]

Rohter also accomplished the delegitimation of the government through his use of sources. As the junta defied U.S. attempts to restore Aristide to power, diplomats and embassy spokesmen served as ready sources to denounce the regime. For example, after the expulsion of the U.N. monitors, Rohter quoted Stanley Schrager, the U.S. embassy spokesman, who called the act "a not unanticipated display of empty bravado on the part of an illegitimate and illegal regime."[33]

On the same subject, he began a "Week in Review" piece by stating that the leaders were "choosing once again to thumb their noses at the United States and its allies." He immediately followed with a quote from U.N. envoy Dante Caputo, who denounced the action as "a provocation," and with a reaction from President Clinton, who said, "We've got to bring an end to this."[34]

As the United States prepared to invade Haiti, U.S. officials postured and threatened in Rohter's *Times* reporting. "'At this point, there is really nothing left to talk about,' one said. 'Either they go on their own or they are thrown out.'"[35]

The delegitimation of the government was also effected by Rohter's use of language. In particular, Rohter challenged the government on how it was to be named. On July 21, 1994, Rohter noted that "last week, the Ministry of Information issued a communique ordering journalists to stop referring to Mr. Jonassaint and his Cabinet as a 'de facto' Government, insisting that it was a 'provisional and constitutional' Government." The order, Rohter noted, "has mostly been ignored."[36] The next week Rohter, perhaps mischievously, began his report: "Haiti's de facto military government began today to organize elections."[37] In the weeks after the government communique, Rohter increased his use of the term "de facto government." Indeed, in just one *Times* story Rohter referred to the "de facto president," the "puppet civilian government," the "compliant rump parliament," and the "de facto government."[38]

Rohter anticipated the U.S. invasion that would remove the military government. In a front-page story, Rohter began:

Haitians are asking foreigners here, especially Americans, many variations on a single question, now that the United Nations has authorized an American-led invasion of this country and economic sanctions are at last fully in place: What are you waiting for? When are you coming? Why aren't you already here?[39]

The departure of the junta, particularly the exile of Cedras, was depicted in degrading terms. Rohter said the departure was "under circumstances that can only be described as humiliating." He went on to describe the humiliation. He first reported that U.S. embassy spokesman Stanley Schrager said that Cedras's departure represented "the end of a sad chapter in the history of this nation." Then, Rohter wrote:

Struggling to maintain his dignity in his farewell remarks, General Cedras made it clear that he did not share that opinion. Ignoring the deafening and often obscene chants of ordinary Haitians who had gathered beyond the American cordon, shouting that he was a murderer and casting aspersions on his ancestry, hygiene and sexual habits, he defended his three years at the head of the Haitian armed forces and warned of impending anarchy.[40]

With such reporting, Rohter's work in the *Times* offered its first theme: the delegitimation of the military government. As Aristide took office, a second theme emerged, one that developed and changed throughout the president's tenure.

The Approbation and Disapprobation of Aristide

Rohter's reporting on Aristide for the *Times* had two distinct phases. In exile and immediately upon his return, Aristide was depicted in heroic terms as the wronged, legitimate ruler of Haiti, who would come back to save his devastated nation. Yet soon after his return, as Aristide resisted U.S. economic and security policies, Rohter's accounts became darker and he began to question Aristide's judgment and approach.

The initial stage of approbation was accomplished through Rohter's portrayal of Aristide as a reasonable and conciliatory presence who would bring peace to Haiti. One of Rohter's early reports focused on a radio message that the exiled Aristide broadcast into Haiti. The lead emphasized that Aristide called for "reconciliation, justice and democracy" in his homeland and that he "forswore revenge against the soldiers who removed him from office." Aristide was depicted in benign terms that even downplayed his possible threats to capitalism: "He also sought to calm businessmen who view him as a radical, saying that he respected the Haitian Constitution and the right to make a profit."[41]

Soon after, Rohter filed a report that lauded the progressive wing of the Catholic Church, particularly the *lavalas* (popular resistance) movement that helped bring Aristide to power. The story painted the movement, seen by some U.S. officials as dangerously radical, in uplifting terms:

> The Rev. Jean-Bertrand Aristide was its most visible symbol and charismatic leader. In his absence, the progressive wing of Haiti's Roman Catholic Church, under constant assault by the state and largely shunned by its own church hierarchy, is fighting an uphill battle to preach the same gospel of social justice and change he espoused.
>
> Known as Ti Legliz, or Little Church, the grass-roots movement has remained one of the few viable centers of resistance to the military-dominated Government that overthrew Father Aristide as President nearly three years ago.[42]

The positive portrayals of Aristide reached their height with stories on his triumphant return from exile. The day before Aristide's return, Rohter filed this lead:

> With the return of the Rev. Jean-Bertrand Aristide, the country's exiled President, just a day away, Haiti was swept by a wave of joyous anticipa-

tion and a sudden burst of energy today as people across the country poured their efforts into preparing a welcome for their leader.[43]

A "Week in Review" essay painted Aristide's return in religious terms. Rohter wrote: "As befits a man of the cloth whose long-suffering followers call him 'ti pwofet,' or the 'little prophet,' his return was celebrated with a fervor that was almost religious in its intensity and as an occasion that offered the promise of deliverance after a generation in the wilderness."[44]

But the disapprobation of Aristide began soon after. Aristide had no intention of completely toeing the U.S. line. U.S. officials were quick to make public their differences with Aristide. Of particular concern, Aristide did not want to retain an army or to privatize some industries—two goals that U.S. policymakers had established for Haiti. Rohter's reporting in the *Times* began to criticize Aristide, though both U.S. proposals ran counter to the *lavalas* movement that Rohter had only recently proclaimed.

The day after Aristide returned to power, Rohter published a front-page story in the *Times* Sunday edition that suggested the president would need to pay heed to the wishes of the United States: "Even after the American troops leave, Father Aristide, who in his earlier, radical days derided the United States as 'the cold country to our north,' will have to contend with the large number of American diplomats, economists and other experts who have come here to help him build democracy."[45] A "Week in Review" essay for the same day said Aristide "must now prove he can speak the pragmatic language of his American patrons."[46]

The retention of the Haitian army was a persistent theme. Aristide's government feared that Americans really wanted a United States-trained and influenced "political counterweight" to the progressive government. Though Rohter pointed out these fears, his reporting was dominated by the official U.S. viewpoint. He consistently gave voice to U.S. officials who called for keeping the army—even when those officials had difficulties explaining why. "Asked recently why a country that has no external enemies needs a standing army, Stanley Schrager, a spokesman for the American Embassy here, said such a force was an essential part of the 'iconography' of nationhood."[47]

Throughout 1995, U.S. officials also struggled to get Aristide to accept the privatization of industry, including the telephone and electric utilities, banks, and the main port. But Aristide feared foreign ownership if his government put such institutions up for sale.

Rohter's reporting embraced the U.S. view of the necessity of privatization: "The issue is crucial because millions of dollars in foreign assistance to Haiti are contingent on the Government's agreeing to and carrying out a comprehensive privatization program." He continued with a threat from an unnamed source: "'These guys will take a major hit' if the privatization program is not put into effect, one diplomat said."[48] Rohter began another story:

> There are just 66,000 telephone lines in all of Haiti, and the government-run telephone company says it does not have the money to install more. The electric company, airport and harbor, also Government-owned and in need of modernization, complain of the same lack of funds.
>
> Selling a share of those and other state enterprises to private investors might appear to offer a promising way out for a poor, nearly bankrupt country.[49]

The disapprobation could also be seen in Rohter's report about Aristide's decision to quit the priesthood in November 1994. The act led to Rohter's reevaluation of Aristide's religious perspective. The *lavalas* movement that Rohter once depicted in uplifting terms was fit into a more negative category, "espousal of a leftist liberation theology," and described more negatively as "a blend of Marxist analysis and Catholic doctrine." Rohter also pointed out that the Salesian order had expelled Aristide "and condemned him as a radical and undisciplined priest."[50] The *lavalas* movement had not changed greatly, but Rohter's interpretation had.

A "Week in Review" essay reworked history as it pursued the "radical" label. "Almost from the day he was ordained in 1982, Haiti's bishops have regarded Father Aristide as a dangerous renegade and leftist radical, a badge he has often worn proudly."[51]

As disagreements intensified between Aristide and U.S. officials, the disapproval in Rohter's *Times* reporting likewise increased. In November 1995, Aristide's cousin was murdered by paramilitary forces. In an impassioned eulogy, Aristide called out for vengeance and also indirectly criticized the United States for slowing Haiti's progress against such violence.

Rohter's reporting was equally impassioned. He labeled the eulogy a "tirade" and his lead, presented on page one, found dramatic, negative consequences in Aristide's words. "With an emotional outburst at the funeral of a slain relative a week ago," Rohter wrote, "President Jean-Bertrand Aristide set off an outbreak of street violence, provoked panic among Haiti's elite and undermined his relations with the United States and other members of the international coalition that restored him to power a year ago."[52]

Even after the election of his successor in February 1996, Rohter questioned Aristide. In a story headlined, "In or Out of Presidency, Aristide Is Still the Issue," Rohter noted that foreign diplomats had been suggesting "only half in jest" that Aristide disappear. "'How about a six-month, round-the-world cruise?' one asked."[53]

In these ways, Rohter's reporting offered a second theme: the approbation and then the disapprobation of Aristide. Related to the portrayals of Aristide were portrayals of the president's sworn enemies, the paramilitary group FRAPH.

The Avoidance of U.S.–FRAPH Ties

FRAPH—the Front for the Advancement and Progress of Haiti—played a crucial role in Haitian affairs. The most feared of the heavily armed paramilitary groups, sometimes called *attaches* because they "attached" themselves to the military, FRAPH was created after the September 1991 coup to suppress opposition to the junta. Its members were descendants—often literally—of the Tontons Macoute, the death squads of the Duvalier dictatorship. They were linked to thousands of killings.

In October 1994, Allan Nairn of the *Nation* broke the story that the leader of FRAPH, Emmanuel (Toto) Constant, was on the CIA payroll, that U.S. officials were well aware of the U.S.–FRAPH relationship, and that U.S. funds were used to support the group.[54]

In that context, Rohter's work on FRAPH for the *Times* can be seen as avoiding the group's real significance. Even after Nairn's reports appeared, Rohter did not substantially probe ties between FRAPH and the United States. Perhaps a result of Rohter's ignorance of the group's origins, deliberate machinations of the State Department, directives from *Times* editors, or all of these things, the *Times* reports misled and misinformed their readers.

It took almost three months for Rohter's reporting even to mention the terrorizing role that FRAPH played in Haitian affairs. His first reference to the group only appeared at the end of a story on September 29,

1994. A crowd of pro-Aristide supporters had been fired upon, Rohter stated, apparently by FRAPH members. A man was killed.[55]

The killing seemed to alert Rohter to FRAPH's dangers. Two days later, he began a series of reports on the group. The reports did chronicle the terror and violence. But in retrospect the reports are most interesting for Rohter's struggle to understand and explain U.S. reluctance to deal with this obvious threat to Haitian society. The possibility that the United States might have been involved with and supporting FRAPH was never raised.

For example, in a page-one story on October 1, 1994, Rohter pointed out how FRAPH was hindering Haiti's democratic movement:

After two days of bloodshed in which armed paramilitary groups attacked demonstrators here, the United States finds its mission to install democracy in Haiti jeopardized by its reluctance to begin disarming the paramilitary gunmen known as attaches. . . . But an American military spokesman today defended the policy of inaction, saying it was up to Haitians to police themselves.[56]

Rohter noted that "many Haitians say they are astonished that the American forces have not yet moved against the attaches, many of whom belong to a group called the Front for the Advancement and Progress of Haiti, or Fraph."

In the same article, Rohter detailed the reasons that U.S. forces should move against FRAPH: the threat to the people, the alarm of other U.N. nations, the increasing violence that might cause an early withdrawal of U.S. troops, and the possible erosion of support among ordinary Haitians.

Rohter used an anonymous "Latin American diplomat" to sum up the argument: "'They have got to disarm these people. They are already paying the political cost of being here, so why not do the job right?'"[57]

On October 4, 1994, Rohter wrote a brief, 400-word profile of FRAPH and fingered Constant as its leader, calling him "a former diplomat" but not mentioning his U.S. ties. Rohter said of FRAPH: "Its gunmen are believed to have been involved in incidents of murder, rape, torture, arson and other crimes on behalf of Haiti's military regime."[58]

In a separate story that same day, Rohter reported that U.S. forces had "finally" moved against FRAPH. "By striking decisively at the headquarters of the most belligerent and feared of those groups, known as Fraph, the American forces that began landing here two weeks ago scored a significant political victory and raised their stock among the populace." But, Rohter noted, the members taken into custody did not include Constant, the leader.[59]

However, the next day, events became more curious. Rohter reported that Constant appeared at a press conference arranged by the U.S. government and said he would lay down his arms and no longer oppose the return of Aristide. The press conference, Rohter said, "was initially announced by the American Embassy, and American Embassy personnel provided the sound system, podium and technical assistance for his first public appearance since the American occupation began."[60]

At the end of the story, an adviser to Aristide questioned why Constant was not arrested. "Constant is the leader of a terrorist organization responsible for the deaths of thousands of people in this country, and one has to ask why the multinational force not only permits him to walk around free but lets him make speeches in front of the National Palace." Despite all these questions, Rohter did not draw the connection for *Times* readers between FRAPH and the United States.

Five days later, in a Sunday "Week in Review" essay, Rohter finally reported what other journalists had already revealed in the weeks before: "Constant, leader of the paramilitary group Fraph, which was responsible for hundreds of government-ordered murders and rapes, had been a paid informer for the C.I.A. and was on its payroll when his group committed some of its worst crimes."[61]

Even after FRAPH was tied to the United States, Rohter did not pursue the connection at length. On October 19, Rohter reported that FRAPH gunmen were still terrorizing the population and that Haitian officials were "quickly growing alarmed at the unwillingness of American troops here to disarm and arrest paramilitary gunmen." Haitian officials were also calling for the arrest of Constant. Rohter noted, however, that after the news conference "orchestrated by the American Embassy," Constant had "promptly dropped out of sight."[62]

It was not until January 1995 that Rohter began to probe the U.S. ties to FRAPH. For many Haitians, Rohter wrote, "the American have turned out to be not saviors of the Haitian people, but rather allies of the paramilitary groups that oppressed Haitians for a generation." But even in this report, Rohter gave voice to U.S. interpretations:

Maj. Regina M. Largent, a spokeswoman for the United States military in Port-au-Prince, said Special Forces units around the country had been told by headquarters that Fraph was "a recognized political organization." Major Largent likened the differences between Fraph and President Aristide's Lavalas movement to those between political parties in the United States.[63]

The curiosities continued. Sometime in early 1985, Constant somehow managed to leave Haiti, obtain a tourist visa to the United States, and disappear, later to surface in New York. U.S. news media, including the *Times*, reported the disappearance in February 1995. In perhaps his most pointed avoidance of the U.S.–FRAPH relationship, Rohter's *Times* account gave over his lead to U.S. officials' protestations of innocence:

> In what American officials describe as an embarrassing but innocent bureaucratic blunder, the leader of Haiti's most notorious paramilitary group was permitted to enter the United States on a tourist visa late last year, and has now dropped out of sight.[64]

With such accounts, Rohter's reporting on Haiti in the *Times* effected a third theme: the avoidance of U.S.–FRAPH ties. A fourth and final theme, the degradation of Haiti, is examined in the next section.

The Degradation of the Nation

A more subtle strategy in Rohter's correspondence was the degradation of Haitian life. In numerous *Times* reports, Rohter offered a portrait of Haiti as a backward society whose religious, political, and social customs rendered it "ungovernable." For example, in an early "Week in Review" piece, Rohter saw Haiti as "a land without a country."[65] He detailed the incredible poverty that plagues the populace and provided a litany of misery: a per capita annual income of $370, the poorest in the Western hemisphere; a life expectancy of 56 years; 70 percent of children malnourished; an illiteracy rate of almost 70 percent.

Yet, according to Rohter and his sources, the most difficult obstacles facing the reconstruction of Haiti "are not material—they are psychological and cultural." Haitians are "distrustful of government" and also harbor a "suspicion of foreigners." Rohter continued:

> In addition, Haiti's political culture has long been characterized by what Roger Gaillard, a leading historian, describes as "an admiration of force, even among educated Haitians." Political disputes are settled not by negotiation, but through the exercise of power, often in crude and brutal

fashion, and respect for democratic procedures and obligations is minimal.

Rohter used other sources to return to the same theme in months ahead. "'Beyond Aristide, there is the more basic question of the governability of the country,' said Suzy Castor, co-director of the Research Training Center for Economic and Social Development." Other unnamed American officials explored Haiti's "200 years of institutional failure."[66] Another Rohter report said:

> Just this month, an American diplomat here pronounced himself perplexed by the "Alice in Wonderland quality" of Haitian politics, where words seem to mean only what their speakers want them to mean. Nor is he the first to feel confused. Citing the phrase coined by a former ambassador, diplomats here routinely counsel new arrivals that in Haiti it is best to believe "nothing you hear and only half of what you see."[67]

The *Times* headlined a story on the July 1995 elections "So Far at Least, Inept Is the Kindest Word for Haitian Democracy." Rohter stated, "It is not easy to determine whether last week's irregularities were the product of deliberate wrongdoing or simply an extraordinary display of incompetence."[68]

Rohter also could not resist exploiting the use of voodoo by Haitians. His writing suggested that Haitians were a backward people marked by their primitive beliefs. Writing about preparations for All Souls' Day, he reported that the mayor "found it necessary to urge residents of the capital to stop stealing bones, which are used in voodoo rituals, from tombs in the cemetery."[69] He reported from one tomb, where "a large crowd had gathered to watch as voodoo practicioners tried to communicate with the dead and the smell of clairin, or Haitian moonshine, permeated the air."

On Christmas Day 1994, Rohter again returned to voodoo in a profile of Haiti. Although he did attempt to explain how Haitian society combines Catholicism and voodoo, he also pursued legends of zombies and the use of voodoo for vengeance. The article was accompanied by a photograph of animal sacrifice—on Christmas![70]

Rohter's sometimes condescending view of Haitian life could be discerned in his choice of sources. U.S. officials, embassy spokesmen, and Latin American diplomats dominate Rohter's work. Even when he is attempting to discuss aspects of Haitian life, Rohter turned to academics in the United States, rather than to the Haitians themselves. Haitian men and women appeared only irregularly in Rohter's work. When they did, the Haitians made token appearances to provide anonymous quotes, such as those provided by "a toothless vendor" and "a middle-aged lawyer in a rumpled blue seersucker suit."[71] The Haitians were not worth being named. In these ways, Rohter's correspondence in the *Times* degraded and demeaned Haiti.

MYTH, NEWS VALUES, AND A NEW WORLD

With the end of the cold war and the beginning of a new century, U.S. news coverage of international affairs finds itself at a crossroads. For previous generations of reporters and editors, the world could be organized and explained in relation to the political, military, economic, and cultural rivalry of two superpowers. News values—the criteria by which the news media select, order, report, and give meaning to events—were structured by this one dominant model, a model that has tumbled with the stones from the Berlin Wall. Today, the questions facing the *Times* and other news organizations include: How is international news to be defined in this new era? What news values will guide the selection and shaping of events?

As we have seen, two models have emerged. One model has embraced the era as a time of promise for journalism. This model valorizes aggressive, progressive news values that promote social justice, and might be called the model of "a new global and human journalism."[72] Other scholars have offered a more pessimistic model, a model of international news dictated by the actions and initiatives of U.S. foreign policy. This model might be described as promoting "Fortress America" in a world of chaos.[73]

This chapter has offered a preliminary assessment of the prospects for each model through a case study: the work of one *Times* correspondent, the reporting of Larry Rohter from Haiti. Analysis of that reporting supports the most cheerless view of post-cold war news values. In the amount of coverage, the nature of the content, and the strategies offered, Rohter's reporting for the *Times* can be seen as working in concert with U.S. foreign policy. Even as that policy shifted course—rejecting the junta, warily restoring Aristide but insisting that he accept U.S. policy—so too did the reporting. Fears that U.S. foreign correspondence would become captive to U.S. foreign policy were realized in Rohter's reports.

To restate the particulars: The influence of U.S. foreign policy can be seen quite readily in the sheer amount of Rohter's Haitian coverage. As the Clinton administration made Haiti one of its first major foreign policy campaigns, Rohter gave over most of his work for almost two years to following Haiti. The Caribbean correspondent of the *Times* over some 20 months filed, for example, five stories from El Salvador, three stories from Colombia, three stories from the Honduras, two stories from Trinidad, and none from the Dominican Republic. From Haiti, as previously noted, Rohter filed 120 stories.

The themes of Rohter's reporting also worked in concert with U.S. policy. Rohter's reporting did not stray far from U.S. policy perspectives. As the United States prepared for an invasion to remove Cedras, U.S. officials postured mightily through Rohter's reporting. Rohter's denunciations of the regime and his chronicling of the junta's repression made a case for U.S. intervention. At the same time, his depictions of Aristide as the rightful leader, whose return would bring peace and reconciliation, also bolstered the U.S. case.

When Aristide and U.S. policy soon began to conflict, Rohter's themes shifted. The uplifting portrayals of Aristide and the *lavalas* movement segued to critical accounts of intransigent ideology and radical leftist politics. As FRAPH continued to terrorize the population and U.S. forces refused to move against them, Rohter's avoidance of the U.S.–FRAPH relationship shielded *Times* readers from the U.S. establishment of a conservative "counterweight" to Aristide's progressive politics. And Rohter's depiction of Haiti as an "ungovernable" place whose people were not "culturally or psychologically" equipped for the demands of democracy captured the patronizing and paternalistic attitudes that have driven U.S. imperialism in the Caribbean for decades.

HAITI AS THE OTHER WORLD

Myth provides another, complementary way to understand Rohter's coverage. Like all reporters, Rohter did not have to create brand-new story forms to report events from Haiti. He, his editors, and his sources consistently drew upon an established narrative—an eternal story—that helped shape coverage even as it explained and justified U.S. policy. In Rohter's reports, we can see the unmistakable structure of the myth of the Other World.

Underlying the reporting of Haiti's political turmoil—turmoil orchestrated often by U.S. policies—is a classic portrayal. Haiti is rendered as a primitive land, filled with danger and chaos, and ruled by death squads and paramilitary patrols who leave the streets littered with corpses. Its helpless people perversely admire bloody shows of force as they engage in animal sacrifice and bone-stealing voodoo rituals, even on Christmas. And they passively remain under the sway of rogue leaders and psychotic priests with no respect for order or reason or privatizing industry. It's a nightmare world.

Rohter provides us with a modern depiction of the Other World, one that also seeks to define our society in relation to other societies. As Vernant argued, myth "expresses how a group of people in particular historical circumstances sees itself."[74] The myth expressed in Rohter's reporting portrays a mighty and superior people descending with fascination and disgust into a primitive place on the globe. The Other World is a world to be feared and perhaps someday avoided. But for now it's a world in desperate need of U.S. guidance and military might.

THE OTHER WORLD IN U.S.
INTERNATIONAL NEWS

The Other World is not a rare portrayal in U.S. news. Close reading of the *Times* and other newspapers shows that reporting of international affairs often relies on the myth of the Other World. In fact, many nations do not appear in U.S. news unless and until they provide stories that allow the myth to be told. From around the world, U.S. reporters and editors apply news values that judge other nations newsworthy when they provides stories of bloody coups, tribal warfare, perverse politics, strange customs, and other tales of the underworld for the U.S. audience back home.

Even a cursory reading of international news shows the influence of the myth of the Other World on news values. We find stories about animal sacrifice in Taiwan; female genital cutting in Africa; the stoning of the devil at Mecca; a thwarted coup in Qatar; Central American drug warlords; a military junta in Sierra Leone; genocide in Rwanda; ethnic cleansing in Kosovo; stolen Aboriginal children in Australia; and many other dark tales. Once again, we can marvel at the durability of myth. A tale told for centuries is told to usher the United States into the twenty-first century.

Modern mythology, Joseph Campbell said, confronts an enormously complex "fact-world that now has to be recognized, appropriated, and as-similated."[75] U.S. society today faces an enormously complex "fact-world," a post-cold war world in which the United States is the lone super-power on the world stage. U.S. international news confronts that world through tales of the Other World. It offers coverage that affirms U.S. supe-riority and other nations' inferiority. It provides scary, fantastic stories of a world beset by anarchy and chaos. It promotes the "image of 'Fortress America,' an island of civilization in a sea of political barbarism."[76] It does all this with a myth as old as Odysseus.

Chapter 9

The Flood

Hurricane Mitch and
News of Disasters

Hurricane Mitch was a particularly devastating storm. Spawned in the Gulf of Mexico in late October 1998, Mitch became a huge hurricane with wind speeds of 180 miles per hour. It was ranked as Category 5, making it one of the top four storms of the century. Then things actually got worse. Rather than moving swiftly over sea and land, the hurricane stalled off the Central American coast. That area suffered deluges of rain and days of misery. Rivers cascaded over their banks. Floodwaters rose to the top of trees. Huge mudslides roared like avalanches down mountainsides, wiping out entire villages. In the span of a week, more than 10,000 people were killed. The Central American floods became one of the top news stories of 1998.

This book began by suggesting that comparisons could be drawn between news coverage of the flood and myths of the Flood. Many societies, from the Choctaw tribe to the Incans, have told themselves tales of the Flood. As I noted previously, the stories are quite similar. People stray from the right path and they are punished by the devastating waters. A select few survive to rebuild and renew society.[1]

The purpose of this chapter is to closely study news coverage of the 1998 Central American disaster in terms of the Flood myth. After briefly looking at research on the Flood myth, I will explore how the myth can provide insights into *New York Times* reporting. Those insights then can be used to take up broader issues. The Flood myth belongs to a larger family of myths that uses calamity and catastrophe to instruct and inform. Likewise, news reports of floods can be seen as part of a larger body of natural disaster stories that include earthquakes, volcanic eruptions, blizzards, and fires, and perhaps even man-made disasters, such as airline crashes and train wrecks. These disaster stories are a staple of news. Similarities between these stories and myths of catastrophe thus allow us to consider again the important subject of news values. Do U.S. journalists make decisions regarding coverage of disastrous events guided by stories as old as humankind?

THE FLOOD

Stith Thompson demonstrated in his multivolume *Motif-Index of Folk-Literature* that the myth of the Flood has appeared across centuries and cultures.[2] Alan Dundes, who edited a book on the subject, argues that "the flood myth is one of the most widely diffused narratives known."[3] Many reasons have been put forth for this wide diffusion. Some writers argue that a real, cataclysmic flood did occur on Earth. Fundamentalist Christians continue to search for Noah's Ark. Others find in Flood myths the human need to explain our origins. They say that humans are mostly water. We are born into the world on the waters of the womb. We need stories that dramatize and explain the life that flows within us. Other scholars find that the Flood myth serves as the ultimate morality tale. They say that humans are warned to mend their ways or the cleansing waters will come to inundate an impure world. Freudian scholars see more fundamental drives at work in the Flood myth. They attribute the prevalence of Flood myths to humans, in every culture and time, dreaming with full bladders.[4]

Though the Flood myth has many interpretations and permutations, some basic characteristics or themes can be established:

1. Flood myths almost always are based on the premise that humankind has sinned or that a particular people have erred or strayed from the path of righteousness.

2. The Flood comes and is total in its devastation. The Flood does not discriminate in choosing its victims or evaluate their fine gradations of evil. Whole populations are destroyed.
3. Humans are helpless against the power of the Flood. The Flood humbles. People struggle futilely.
4. Humankind, once purified, is regenerated and renewed. Some few worthy or fortunate individuals live to rebuild society, solemn and chastened in the wake of the Flood.

The following sections explore whether these characteristics and themes really can be found in the *Times*'s coverage of the 1998 Central American floods. In attempting to describe and explain the disaster, did news stories draw so precisely upon the myth of the Flood?

THE FLOOD MYTH IN THE *NEW YORK TIMES*

To study such questions, I looked at coverage by the *Times* from October 26, 1998, when the first reports on Hurricane Mitch, which spawned the floods, appeared in the *Times*, to December 6, 1998, weeks after the disaster, when the cleanup was under way and the intense coverage waned. I scrutinized every *Times* article, editorial, column, letter, and photograph—some 125 news items in all.

As will be shown in detail below, I found that the myth of the Flood could indeed be found in its entirety in the *Times*'s coverage. All four of the myth's primary themes played a dominant role in *Times* reporting. Humans were shown to have erred and strayed from a right path. The flood came and was complete in its devastation. Human efforts and ingenuity were helpless in the face of the flood. And in the wake of the flood, people began the slow process of rebuilding.

Though the myth unfolded in its entirety, the structure of the story was somewhat different in the *Times*'s coverage. Myths often begin by relating the wrongdoing of the people. This shows why the flood must come. In the *Times*'s coverage, reports of the devastation came first. Then humanity's futility was shown. Next followed reports of survivors found. And then, in the aftermath of the flood, stories looked back and began to consider why the flood had come. Only then did they suggest that the flood had come to those who had erred or strayed. The following sections follow that structure and demonstrate the ways in which the myth of the Flood took modern form in the *New York Times*.

Complete Devastation

A central aspect of the Flood myth is that the flood's devastation is total and complete. Descriptions of the Flood emphasize its enormity. This is not just a serious storm: It is a catastrophe. Entire peoples are washed away. The earth is laid waste. During the first days of the hurricane, even before the full ravaging had occurred, the *Times* offered themes of widespread destruction. On October 28, the hurricane paused off the Honduran coast. Floods washed out roads, downed bridges, overflowed rivers, and killed 32 people. The *Times* had not yet been able to get its own reporter to the scene. So it used an AP report on October 29 that gave its third paragraph to a quotation of ruination: "'The hurricane has destroyed almost everything,' said Mike Brown of Guanaja Island, who was within miles of the eye. 'Few houses have remained standing.'"[5]

The rains continued. Floods caused mudslides that added to the destruction. On November 1, the *Times* used another AP account to report that mudslides had "buried several communities near Nicaragua's northwestern border with Honduras." The mayor told reporters that only 57 of the 2,500 people living in 10 communities at the foot of Caistas Volcano had been accounted for. "It is like a desert littered with buried bodies," he said.[6]

On November 1, the *Times* finally managed to get its own reporter, Larry Rohter, to the scene. The next day, death and destruction became front-page news. "Intense and widespread flooding in the wake of Hurricane Mitch has killed more than a thousand people in Central America, with hundreds more still missing, their villages buried under huge mudslides," Rohter's report began.

His first quotation, in the fourth paragraph, emphasized the devastation. "Some communities were completely destroyed," said Leonora Rivera, a spokeswoman for the Nicaraguan Red Cross. She said that "the number of dead will increase considerably once it stops raining and we can get into isolated areas." General Rodolfo Pacheco, chief of the Honduran Air Force, was quoted at the end of Rohter's story: "This is catastrophe beyond measure. It's incredible. The entire nation is in danger."[7]

The following day, the *Times* devoted much of its front page to the flood. Four of the six columns above the fold were blanketed by a dramatic, 6 x 8-inch color photograph. Taken from an aircraft, with the photographer looking down as if from the heavens, the photograph showed trapped residents on a tiny island of high land surrounded by muddy waters that had risen to the top of the trees. Rohter's report ran on the top right column of the page. The second paragraph stated:

> "There are corpses everywhere—victims of landslides or of the waters," Carlos Flores Facusse, the President of Honduras, said in a grim television address this afternoon that followed a thorough inspection tour of his stunned and beleaguered nation of four million people. "We have before us a panorama of death, desolation and ruin throughout the entire country."[8]

The report directly drew upon mythic references of destruction. It said, "Relief workers and evacuees, who were visibly disturbed over what they had seen, used phrases like a 'vision out of Dante' or 'a deluge of Biblical proportions' to describe the destruction." It concluded with the words of the Honduran president: "The floods and landslides have erased many villages and households from the map, as well as whole neighborhoods of cities," he said. "I ask the international community for human solidarity."[9]

Another front-page report by Rohter emphasized the decimation. "In one way or another, every part of Nicaragua has been devastated by the relentless floods and landslides that followed Hurricane Mitch," the story began. It went on to describe "a realm dominated by destruction and suffering."[10] Two days later, another front-page report continued the theme. The lead paragraph reported:

> Where just a week ago there were fertile fields of corn, beans and peanuts almost ready for harvest, there are now only discolored corpses, swelling grotesquely in the tropical sun. Where the simple thatched houses of peasants have always stood, all that remain are clusters of ripped and shredded clothing and a few scattered kitchen utensils.[11]

Times reports also quoted U.S. officials who attested to the destruction of Honduras and Nicaragua in particular. "'Those two nations have been wiped out,' said J. Brian Atwood, head of the United States Agency for International Development, which is overseeing the Administration's disaster relief effort in Central America."[12] Another source said, "It's total, pure devastation. I've never seen a human drama of that magnitude."[13]

Humanity Humbled

The Flood myth also emphasizes that humans are helpless in the face of the Flood. In society after society, humans come to think that they have advanced beyond nature, that their knowledge, ingenuity, and technology have placed them beyond nature's power to hurt. The Flood sweeps away such hubris. Humanity is humbled. Similarly, even as early *Times* reports emphasized the destruction, they also suggested the capitulation of humankind to nature's forces. One of the first *Times* stories, on October 27, said:

> People fled coastal homes and the Honduran Government sent air force planes to pluck residents off remote Caribbean islands today in the face of the most powerful hurricane in a decade to threaten Central America. Thousands of people abandoned or were evacuated from coastal regions of Belize, Mexico and Cuba.[14]

The *Times* offered numbers to attest to the immense power of the storm. It noted that wind speeds reached 180 miles per hour, that 20 inches of rain could fall in the mountains, and that the storm was listed as Category 5, making it one of the biggest storms of the century. The *Times* also offered more descriptions of panicked humans fleeing towns and resorts:

> The rain and winds snapped trees and sent thousands of people fleeing for higher ground. . . . Most of the population of Belize City fled inland in cars and Government buses. In neighboring Mexico tourists rushed to leave the resorts of Cancun and Cozumel, where the hurricane, Mitch, is expected to hit by the end of the week.[15]

The report was accompanied by a two-column photograph of a crying Guatemalan child, in a bright, frilly dress, being lifted by firefighters from floodwaters. Two days later, a similar image was printed: This photograph showed rescuers pulling a woman from rising waters in LaCeiba, Honduras.[16]

Even the highest officials, stories said, were humbled by the flood's power. One *Times* report stated:

"Not just this country, but all of Central America is cut off," President Arnoldo Aleman of Nicaragua said in a televised address to his nation in which he urged vulnerable citizens to seek shelter on higher ground. His Honduran counterpart, Carlos Flores, found himself trapped in San Pedro Sula, an industrial city of 500,000 people that was cut off from the capital by flooding.[17]

Two weeks after the storm first hit, Rohter interviewed Flores, who said, "In 72 hours we lost what we had built, little by little, in 50 years." Flores added, "In Honduras everything will be measured before and after" the floods.[18]

Witnesses testified to their helplessness. A *Times* story quoted a cleric: "I have seen earthquakes, droughts, two wars, cyclones and tidal waves," said Miguel Cardinal Obando y Bravo, the Roman Catholic archbishop of Managua and the nation's senior religious figure. "But this is undoubtedly the worst thing that I have ever seen."[19]

A rescue worker emphasized the humbling powers of the flood. "'We could hear people buried in the debris imploring us to help them,' said one shaken resident-turned-rescue worker, who would give his name only as Nicolas. 'But there was nothing we could do for them. It was the most impotent I have ever felt in my life.'"[20]

The *Times* often portrayed relief efforts as futile. "Honduran authorities struggled today with meager resources to deal with catastrophic damage from torrential rains and floods," one report began. "Many families have been waiting for days on top of their houses or perching in trees without food or water, the officials said. 'The demand is so great and the equipment we have is so little that we feel impotent,' said the Army Chief of Staff, Gen. Mario Hung Pacheco."[21]

Humanity was left with little more than prayer and beseechment. Rohter ended a "Week in Review" essay with the words of a survivor: "'We've lived through earthquakes, a pair of civil wars, volcanic eruptions, tidal waves and now this, all in the last 25 years,' said Maria Lourdes Rodriguez, a peasant who lives north of here. 'When is God going to take pity on us?'"[22]

Rebuilding in the Wake of Disaster

Though the devastation is complete, though humanity is humbled, the Flood myth ends on notes of rebuilding and regeneration. The Flood waters will be waters of birth as well as waters of death. Survivors emerge, grieving and chastened. In some myths, these survivors were selected prior to the Flood. They were the only good people in the community and the gods have warned them. In other myths, the survivors simply have been granted dispensation by fate or the gods.

The theme can be seen in numerous *Times* reports. One article, "1 House Left in Sea of Mud," began: "Of 164 houses in this northwestern Nicaraguan farming village, only one was standing today in a sea of mud that stretched as far as the eye could see."[23] Another item told the story of Laura Isabel Arriola de Guity, a teacher, who "reportedly drifted on a makeshift raft in the Caribbean for six days before her rescue. Her husband and three children died."[24] Another story began with the myth-like memories of one survivor who saw the earth open before him:

> Selvin Joynarid Perez was standing under the awning of his small house on a bluff overlooking the Choluteca River early Saturday morning, keeping an uneasy watch on the torrential rain and the rising waters below.
>
> Suddenly the earth trembled, he said. He turn to run into the house to wake his wife and 3-year-old daughter. He never made it.
>
> "When I tried to go into the room where my wife and child were sleeping, the earth opened up," he said.[25]

Other reports, too, focused on stunned survivors. Vicente Hernandez, his wife, and brother were away visiting relatives when the flood and mudslides engulfed his village. "'We have been left with nothing but this,' he said, gesturing toward a small plastic bag containing a few items of donated clothing that was attached to the handlebars of the bicycle he was riding. 'Our family has been dispersed, and a great misfortune has fallen upon us.'" The same story ended with the words of another survivor, shocked but ready to move forward. Milton Juarez's farm and livestock were all swept away. "'Everything I had is gone, and all we have been left with is rocks and stone,' he said as he sat on his bedraggled horse and surveyed the destruction here. 'I'm ready to plant, but somebody has to give me seeds. But so far, nobody has come here to help us, nobody.'"[26]

A story of a burial service offered the thoughts of a grandmother, stricken but resigned to go on. "'There were six in that family, and now only one remains, Isaac, the youngest son of my only daughter,' the boy's grandmother, Candida Morales Delgado, said tearfully as the coffin was lowered into the ground. 'We will care for him as best we can because he is all that we have left.'"[27]

More than a month after the storm, the *Times* suggested that survivors had begun the process of rebuilding. In a photo essay for the *New York Times Magazine*, Larry Towell captured the devastation—and the regeneration.

> And yet, the flood waters seem to have washed away something else—a lethargy induced by decades of foreign economic control, along with the humiliation of being used by the Nicaraguan contras in their war against the Sandinistas. Honduras has been energized by the sheer effort to survive as a nation. No matter where I look, I think I've seen the worst. But I am constantly surprised, not just by the destruction, but also by the will of the people to overcome it.[28]

Striking Those Who Have Strayed

A primary characteristic of the Flood myth is that devastation comes to a people who have done wrong. Detailing the wrong—defining the sin—is a crucial and socially specific aspect of the Flood myth. Were people punished for hubris and pride? Did they worship the wrong gods? Did men take wives for themselves, "whomever they chose," as in Genesis? As I noted earlier, myths often begin here. In *Times* coverage, this theme did not emerge until the aftermath of the disaster. Then, stories sought reasons or meanings behind the disaster.

In *Times* reports, the Central American people seemed to be punished for the sins of their nations and governments. Corrupt leaders, petty politics, and backward economies explained the devastation, according to the *Times*. And in a complementary theme, the *Times* suggested, implicitly and explicitly, that such errors would not bedevil U.S. society.

The theme first appeared more than a week into the coverage, on November 5, at the end of a report on survivors returning to destroyed towns. Though the survivors blamed the river, the report raised the idea that devastation had come because officials allowed houses to be built in illegal and unsafe areas.

> Several acknowledged that the houses that had rumbled down the bluff had been illegally built in a zone where construction is prohibited.
>
> "The reality of the thing is that it is not the Government's fault," said

Florentino Sanchez, who had spent the day digging with his bare hands for the bodies of four children of his cousin. The mother's body was found on Tuesday.

"We never believed the river would do this," he said.[29]

Soon after, in a "Week in Review" essay, the *Times* again suggested the governments were at fault. Rohter used the governments' responses to the flood to draw comparisons among nations. His premise was that a disaster "teaches a lot about the way a society does or does not work" and "the nations of the region always seem to respond in ways that illuminate their history and character."

Nicaragua, for instance, is still grappling with many of the same problems it could not resolve in the 1980's, when the Sandinista National Liberation Front was trying to fend off American-backed contra rebels in a bloody civil war. In that polarized political climate, the relief effort here last week was hampered by petty partisan squabbling; the conservative Government and the Sandinistas, who are now in opposition, even disagreed over whether it would be more appropriate to declare a "national disaster" or a "state of emergency."

Rohter compared that response with actions taken by a U.S. territory, Puerto Rico, during a previous hurricane, Georges. "In Puerto Rico, an American possession," Rohter said, with an important choice of words, "the government leaped into action as soon as the first hurricane watch was issued."[30] Rohter was making a contrast between Nicaraguan and U.S. society.

The *Times* returned to the theme on November 9 in a 2,800-word, front-page story that looked back on how the hurricane caused so much grief. The report acknowledged that much of the destruction resulted because the storm moved very slowly, allowing huge amounts of rain to fall. But the nations and people also bore responsibility, the *Times* said.

The freakish behavior of the storm is the major reason it caught governments and people off guard. But the high death toll also owes something to poverty and politics. Most working-class houses are poorly built, and many impoverished people erect their homes, often illegally but with a wink from local politicians, on marginal lands close to rivers or clinging to unstable mountain slopes that have been stripped of trees.[31]

Even two weeks later, the *Times* continued the theme. In a bylined editorial, a *Times* editor, Tina Rosenberg, focused specifically on government policies of deforestation. "Five days of torrential rain would have caused damage anywhere, but there would have been fewer lethal mud slides if the land in Honduras and Nicaragua had been covered with trees," she wrote. "Trees hold the soil together and help it absorb rain. When the land is stripped of trees, heavy rains sweep mud and minerals into the rivers, swelling and clotting the water and increasing its power to destroy."[32]

A letter to the editor saw government capitulation to corporations as part of the problem, a theme not emphasized in *Times* coverage. It said:

> The infrastructure that was destroyed was often created to meet the needs of the military and the multinational organizations. In Honduras, which is an oligarchy, the poor, who took the brunt of the storm, had been forced to live on the edges of banana plantations in flood-plain shantytowns or on hillsides that were of no economic value to the landowners. While aid efforts should continue, this disaster provides an opportunity for issues of basic justice and land reform to be addressed.[33]

Finally, some stories raised the idea that the flood could be interpreted as a punishment from the heavens. For example, a report on survivors explicitly offered the theme of punishment. It quoted Jose Antonio Amaya Garcia of Honduras.

> "It's a punishment from God," Mr. Amaya, an elderly carpenter, said late last week as he searched under an avalanche for what was left of his house. He is tiny and frail in his soiled shirt and pants, the last clothing he owns. "I am 73, and I've never seen a disaster like this."[34]

An essay on the *Times* op-ed page entitled "The Wrath of God?" offered a similar theme. Arturo J. Cruz Jr., a Nicaraguan professor, said that in the seventeenth century the people of Leon, Nicaragua, left the original site of the city, "believing that they were being punished by God for the sins of their ancestors, conquerors from Spain whose treatment of the native population was barbarous. Since then, doom has remained an indelible component of the Nicaraguan world view. To this day, many wonder if they have a pending 'bill' with God."[35]

MYTH, NEWS VALUES, AND DISASTER STORIES

On one level, the retelling of the Flood myth in the *Times* lends support to my thesis that myth has taken modern form in the news. *Times* reporting shows how *naturally* myth takes shape in news stories. *Times* coverage seemed so . . . normal. It is only on close examination that we can see the comparison to myth. As the writer and philosopher Roland Barthes wrote at the beginning of his book *Mythologies*, "The starting point of these reflections was usually a feeling of impatience at the sight of the *naturalness* with which newspapers, art and common sense constantly dress up a reality which, even though it is one we live in, is undoubtedly determined by history."[36]

Other insights can be gained into this mythic examination of *Times* coverage. For decades, gatekeeping studies have shown that U.S. news coverage of international affairs is dominated by stories of coups, crises, and catastrophes.[37] In tending the gates, in deciding what is "international news" and how it should be covered, U.S. news media often give priority to calamity. Nations and peoples around the globe merit U.S. news coverage in times of earthquakes, train wrecks, tidal waves, airline crashes, famines, and floods.

Research has also suggested why this is so. As we have seen in the previous chapter, scholars have argued persuasively that U.S. news media reaffirm U.S. political authority and superiority on the global stage. International news coverage, they suggest, is dictated by U.S. foreign policy. Coverage legitimizes global inadequacies, defends U.S. action or inaction, explains U.S. positions, and degrades the positions of other nations. Areas of U.S. interest become areas of U.S. news coverage. When do other areas of the world merit coverage? They become newsworthy only when they meet dramatic, attention-grabbing requisites: calamities. And even then, the portrayals of crises and catastrophes often can be understood to lay claim to U.S. superiority as they symbolically lay waste to a people or nation.[38]

Myth thus can provide an additional perspective to the distinguished literature on gatekeeping. International communication researchers have identified a mythic dimension to U.S. news coverage. As we have seen, myth has always affirmed the authority and superiority of the current social order. Myth legitimizes and justifies positions. Myth celebrates dominant beliefs and values. Myth degrades and demeans other beliefs that do not align with those of the storyteller. And myth has often fulfilled these roles through portrayals of disasters and calamities, such as the Flood. The Flood, again, can be seen as the ultimate morality tale. People who have done wrong or taken the wrong path or otherwise strayed are punished and swept away. Only the righteous are left alive and thereby confirmed in their position and place. Societies around the world have told themselves stories of the Flood to affirm their own status, to sanction their actions, to explain the fall of others, and to warn doubters and slackers.

In reporting global events, in tending the gates, U.S. news is doing what myth has always done. News is drawing upon the eternal story of calamity and crisis to uphold the social order and to affirm the superiority of a way of life. *Times* coverage of the 1998 Central American floods can be understood as fulfilling this mythic role. Months can go by without a single *Times* story from Guatemala, Honduras, or Nicaragua. With the onslaught of the hurricane and the resulting floods, the *Times* published daily, front-page stories chronicling the calamity and symbolically degrading the victims by suggesting that they and their nations were at fault.

The four themes of the Flood myth were quite clear. As the myth suggested, *Times* coverage averred that Central Americans had made social and political mistakes; the devastation of the flood was in part the result of those mistakes. The flood was complete in its devastation; entire communities were ravaged. Humans were helpless against its power. And survivors were left to rebuild society. These things seem natural and logical in *Times* coverage. But the *naturalness*—the structure and pattern and themes—derives from myth.

Again, the process must be mostly unconscious. Though journalists sometimes refer to "biblical proportions" and "mythic stories," they don't often see themselves as telling and retelling ancient tales of humankind. Yet like myth tellers of every age, journalists draw from archetypal stories to make sense of events. They draw from sacred, societal stories that celebrate shared values, counsel with lessons and themes, instruct and inform with exemplary models.

DAILY MYTHS OF DISASTER

Once more we should raise the question: Were the Central American floods too convenient as a case study of myth? The analysis suggests precisely otherwise. The mythic structure and themes identified in these stories actually appear often, almost daily, in the news. International news coverage is replete with stories of disasters, calamities, and catastrophes that are caused by the inadequacies of other nations, that are complete in their devastation, that humble humanity, and that leave chastened survivors to reflect on their fate and renew their society. News reports of floods, famines, tidal waves, plagues, volcanic eruptions, and countless other disasters regularly tell us the same story again and again, a story told since stories were first told. The litany of disaster brought to us in international news is a litany drawn from the fundamental stories of humankind. The gatekeepers of U.S. news open the gates for myth.

Conclusion

News, Myth, and Society

Twelve Propositions

Enlighten me now, O Muses, tenants of Olympian
homes.
For you are goddesses, inside on everything, know
everything.
But we mortals hear only the news, and know nothing
at all.

HOMER, the Iliad

As the twentieth century drew to a close, two dozen top journalists and educators gathered in Boston. Called together by the Nieman Foundation and the Project for Excellence in Journalism, the group was driven by concern over the state of journalism. "Concern" was the order of the day. The group called itself the Committee of Concerned Journalists. One primary result of the meeting: "A Statement of Concern." The statement called for journalists to engage in a period of national reflection; to read and sign the Statement of Concern; to participate in public forums around the country; to reflect on and define "the enduring purpose of journalism, along with its principles, responsibilities and aspirations."[1] To this day, committee members continue to make expressions of concern and proceed with individual efforts to define journalism's enduring purpose.

The concern, the committee, the conventions, commissions, and other commiserations affirm my starting point: The news is in crisis. People distrust the news. They despise journalists. They turn off the news and turn away. Newspaper publishers and broadcast conglomerates add to the problem. They chase profits not stories. They erode lines between advertising and news. They cut back bureaus and staffs. Journalists themselves flounder. They forsake significant news for criminal conflict and sexual spectacle. They chase readers and audiences. They try to entertain. They try to be outrageous. They try to be useful. They face a new century and a new technology with little understanding of both.

A primary reason for the crisis? The committee has it right: News lacks an enduring purpose. News lacks a defined social role. The confusion over purpose and role, however, seems quite strange. News has been produced for hundreds of years. Freedom of the press is enshrined in the First Amendment to the U.S. Constitution. How can its social role be unclear? Yet the confusion surrounding news is unmistakable. People no longer know, if they ever did know, what the news is *supposed to do*.

This book has offered an answer that might seem strange to those outside ivory-covered towers. I have argued that news has roots in humankind's eternal stories, that news can be understood as myth. I have contended that news media, such as the *New York Times*, can be seen as powerful mythmakers, as State Scribes not unlike Homer and Pindar, who tell us, daily, stories at the very heart of human life. I have maintained that these stories shape, but are also shaped by, the times in which they are told. Because the arguments might seem academic and abstract, I have identified seven master myths that appear regularly in the news. Through case studies of the *Times*, perhaps the world's most influential newspaper, I have set about trying to show—case by case, story by story, word by word—how news is myth.

What has been the use of all this? Certainly, after many years and pages, I have found the arguments interesting and appealing. But I also have found them useful. Myth has provided a very different way of looking at the news. Like finding a new vantage point at a parade, myth may help journalists and their audiences, educators and their students, to see better. Myth points out wonderful possibilities for news. Myth points out obvious pitfalls. Myth suggests paths to pursue. Myth warns of hazards ahead.

Twelve points in particular can be highlighted. With a deep and respectful bow to sociologist Hugh Duncan, who organized his work on symbols and social theory around a series of "axiomatic propositions," this chapter offers 12 propositions—some contradictory, some paradoxical—derived from my studies of news as myth. I don't know precisely how story and myth might ultimately be used to address the current crisis in journalism. I do know that any attempt to address the crisis that does not recognize the mythological role of journalism is destined to fail. Myth is part of the "enduring purpose" of journalism. And journalists, critics, readers, and nonreaders will benefit from acknowledging the influence of eternal stories on news and society.

1. AS MYTH, NEWS IS MOST IMPORTANT AS STORY, NOT AS INFORMATION

Traditional approaches to news, we saw, almost always begin from a model that sees news as information. The very word *news* suggests to us new information about an important event told in the form of a story. The emphasis, though, is placed decidedly on information, not on the story. Story is seen simply as a form or a vessel for conveying information. Journalists and readers accept and expect that the primary role of news is to convey information. Even grander, news is information for citizens. News is protected by the First Amendment because news provides information necessary for a democratic government.

But information simply does not fully explain—and probably never has explained—the news. Some of our most compelling news stories—floods and terrorist killings and home-run chases—bring us very little usable information for our daily lives. Other notable stories from past years too have little to do with information for democratic life: a baby fallen down a well, three whales trapped beneath Alaskan ice, the murder trial of a former football player, the death of a princess, the sexual escapades of White House denizens. As these stories rage and subside, the news appears to have careened off course. People angrily criticize the news and journalists engage in anxious self-reflection. The anger and angst may be partially misplaced. These stories are, in fact, an essential part of news. These stories are myths, compelling and enduring public stories that have long addressed the deep concerns of human existence.

This latest retelling of eternal stories, however, is complex. Modern society apparently has progressed enough to complicate simple storytelling. Because, in fact, news does more than tell stories. It does, sometimes, bring new information and break important developments. News not only tells us stories of sports heroes, it gives us the score of last night's game. News not only tells us about victims, it tells us that our neighbor is dead. Information is surely part of news. Information provides raw material from which the eternal stories are selected, shaped, recast, and retold.

The goal for any newsperson, then, is to strike a balance between story and information. News supplies confirmation as well as information. News offers drama as well as detail. Only through a studied blend of daily information and timeless stories will journalists find "the enduring purpose of journalism, along with its principles, responsibilities and aspirations."[2] A common business maxim is that railroad companies floundered because they kept building . . . railroads. Railroads thought they were in the *railroad* business. They actually were in the *transportation* business and were decimated by cars, trucks, and planes. Is news in a similar situation? Newspeople think they are in the *information* business. They keep inundating us with information. But newspeople are primarily in the *story* business. And news will remain a subject of crisis and concern as long as it strays from story.

2. AS MYTH, EACH NEWS STORY HAS A STORY

Sometimes reporters think their craft is simple. It is not brain surgery, they avow. They go to an event. They observe. They talk to people. They gather the facts. They try to spell the names right. If the event is complicated and a subject of dispute, they seek out views from both sides. They write a "balanced" story. They go for coffee. They return to the newsroom and get assigned another story.

But each news story, of course, turns out to be complicated and implicated in all kinds of entanglements. News, no doubt, is a complex form of storytelling. Every detail that is gathered, selected, and placed into words is shaped by a variety of influences. These influences can be direct, such as immediate conversations with editors, sources, and colleagues, or indirect, such as story forms, the education and experience of the storyteller, and the expectations of the audience. Even a seemingly simple story, such as a feature article on Mother Teresa, results from an interplay of forces, from the Roman Catholic Church to the archetype of the Good Mother.

Other stories, such as coverage of Haiti, can be highly contested, with readers and editors engaging in public debate over the choice of words, photographs, and interviews. Anthropologists, historians, philosophers, even scientists now appreciate the power of story in shaping their work. Journalists, of all people, should comprehend the implications of story and the many forces that ultimately shape the work they produce.

Objectivity, the tarnished but still enthroned god-term for some people in journalism, shadows this proposition. Journalists know the routine. The goal of objectivity has been bashed fairly well by even the weakest philosophers. Journalists say they know they can't be objective but they strive to be accurate and they "try to get the story right." Does embracing storytelling mean finally forsaking all attempts at accuracy and, much worse, accepting some fiction, some liberties with the facts for the sake of story? Not at all. Although storytelling is a subjective, creative exercise, news is not fiction and news is not false. News does not fail from a lack of objectivity. News fails from a lack of good storytelling.

3. AS MYTH, NEWS REQUIRES SCRUTINY AND STUDY

I have often returned to Roland Barthes's thought that myth works best when it seems completely natural, when the stories and their lessons appear transparent, obvious, unavoidable, and inevitable. Myth works best when it is not seen as myth. And so it is today. As we have seen, in its modern form, beneath the naturalness of the news story, myth does much work. In a story of a boxer, a Trickster is pilloried and humiliated. In feature articles about a nun, a Good Mother is lauded for virtue and compassion. In reports on the killing of a former black radical, a Scapegoat receives the ultimate justice for his social sins.

Because of this naturalness, news stories require scrutiny and analysis. The analysis need not be a byzantine hermeneutic inquiry. Doctoral candidates need those subjects for themselves. Journalists and readers alike need only pause to consider the language and pictures of news. Why was the widow of a terrorist victim on the front page of the *Times* three times in one week? Why did the *Times* publish a story on Christmas about voodoo rituals in Haiti? Why did a *Times* columnist imagine a situation where someone in prison might try to attack Mike Tyson "with a knife or a razor or a gun?" Why did the *Times* choose a front-page quote that said the

Central American floods were "a punishment from God?" Such questions lead, naturally, to appreciation and apprehension of the mythic quality of news.

At first it may seem the myth critic is looking too hard. After all, *it's just a news story*. But case after case, story after story, word after word, the implication is clear: Myth has taken shape in the words of the news and those words can have large social implications.

4. AS MYTH, NEWS STORIES MOST OFTEN SERVE AND PRESERVE SOCIAL ORDER

This proposition is darker than I would like. But there is no way to read the news regularly and not see how news most often affirms the status quo, confirms the way things are, and sustains the current social order. Many scholars take this further. They reduce culture and myth to ideology. For them, ideology is the starting point, the driving force that produces culture, society, myth, and news. For them, news and myth are told solely for the production of consent and the maintenance and support of ideology.

In the next proposition, I try to resist such reduction. But the devil must get his due. Social order—no abstract, static entity—is acted out and affirmed each day as people participate in dramas great and small. And news, as myth, participates decisively in social order. Myth not only offers order but also insists on order. Myth not only confirms beliefs but also constricts beliefs. Myth not only passes down traditions but also sanctions traditions. In support of social order, news as myth daily defends the dominant social consensus.

As myth, news stories herald values of sacrifice and service through the myth of the Good Mother. News stories demean Other Worlds, warn of their dark chaos and trumpet our own society's superiority. News stories celebrate modern versions of Heroes who embody social values. News stories degrade Scapegoats who transgress or protest too vigorously.

Our society seems to welcome dissent to social order. News, in particular, seems to have been established as a channel for such dissent. After all, didn't news bring down a president during Watergate? Isn't the news constantly criticizing public officials? But when studied carefully, news stories are shown to seldom challenge core values. They rarely question the very structure of society. They don't dispute the system of governance, the apportionment of power, the distribution of wealth, or other central features of U.S. society. News primarily tells stories that show U.S. society chugging along, through ups and downs, through changes in political parties, through wild swings in the stock market, and through natural disasters great and small. After years of watching dramatic spectacles and tumultuous accounts in the news, we lift our eyes and realize that things have pretty much stayed the same. Day after day, the news upholds the social order in which it holds, after all, a prominent position.

5. AS MYTH, NEWS STORIES HAVE THE CAPACITY TO CHANGE THE SOCIAL ORDER

We have seen much proof in the news of the power of ideology and social order. But we have also seen that news is messy and complicated and that each news story is a site of personal, social, and political struggle from its conception by a reporter to its understanding by a reader. News stories and their influence are not predetermined.

Thus, myth, thankfully, does not allow us to despair completely over the relationship between social order and news. As myth, news does not always manufacture consent, though it most often does. As myth, news cannot be reduced to ideology, though it often serves that role. Myth, although it throws all its weight to the protection and defense of social order, will survive the passage of any one order. The stories were told long before and will be told long after.

In fact, news can sometimes provide stories and exemplary models that can be used by groups to alter or shape social order. The work of independent journalist I. F. Stone, an icon to many on the political left, exemplified the ability of news to challenge the social order. For decades, Stone produced a weekly newsletter that offered a radical perspective on the news. As the *New York Times* and other mainstream media faithfully echoed early official explanations for U.S. involvement in Vietnam, for example, Stone mined new information from government documents. He placed that information into stories—mythic stories—that not only opposed the dominant explanation but also offered an alternative perspective on the mendacity of government, the military, and U.S. global goals. On the political right, radio commentator Rush Limbaugh performs a similar role. His daily show offers myths that oppose segments of the social order, contest the stories of the *Times* and other media elite, and dispute official administration explanations.

Alternative news outlets on the political right and left assure us that news will not always serve social order. Challenging dominant social values and assumptions is difficult. But it can be done. Myth upheld long-ago regimes—but myth also helped overthrow them.

6. AS MYTH, NEWS ADDRESSES THE PUBLIC IN DEEP AND PROFOUND WAYS

Many attempts to address the current crisis in journalism look for new ways of reaching the public. "Public journalism" is only the most obvious example. Other strategies include "service" journalism, "news you can use," and coverage derived from focus groups. These strategies strive to connect news with the public. Myth, however, reframes our understanding of news—and our understanding of news and public life.

Put simply, journalists and audiences conceive of public life too narrowly. Some see public life in terms of civic affairs. People are seen as citizens and voters, and journalism is cast in hallowed terms as a great informer and trustee for this public. Others see public life in more cynical terms as consumer affairs. People are understood as buyers, and journalism is cast as a great informer and trustee for a purchasing and investing public.

News as myth restores a broader view of public life. Myth suggests that news is intimately entwined with *all* the wide-ranging issues and concerns of human existence, not just civic duties or purchasing problems. As myth, news confronts death as well as taxes, evil as well as crime, fate as well as elections, souls as well as sickness, salvation as well as sales. Myth argues that journalism must greatly expand its view of stories and public life.

Newspeople ignore obvious evidence. Newspaper sales, magazine circulation, television news ratings, and web site traffic all surge during dramatic and sensational events: schoolyard killings, royal weddings, hurricanes, assassinations, airline crashes, and inaugurations. What are people seeking? They're not going to use these stories to vote for a candidate. They want compelling dramas. They want satisfying stories that speak to them of history and fate and the fragility of life. They want myth.

"Service" journalism or "news you can use" deserves special consideration. The concept has been employed by many news magazines and television networks. Most often, the notion means stories about purchasing, saving, investing, and "making choices." The concept is supposed to free journalists and audiences from the tyranny of political information and involve news in the day-to-day decisions made by regular people.

Myth, however, would expand "news you can use" in ways unrecognizable to the marketing department. Myth would offer people news they can use to comprehend the hand of history and fate; news they can use to understand hatred and fear; news they can use to consider the possibilities and shortfalls of their own lives. Myth means that the most complex phenomena of public life, from birth to death, will be captured in the dramatically compelling narratives of news.

7. AS MYTH, NEWS WILL BE ABSORBED WITHIN RITUALS

The routines of reading and watching the news may be as important as the content of the stories. Many people make time for the news every day. They partake of the news almost ritualistically, incorporating newspapers or network broadcasts into their daily schedules. Reassurance and comfort reside in the rhythmic attention to the news: the morning paper at the kitchen table or on the train, the magazine over lunch, the nightly news shows over dinner. Researchers have studied people's reactions when newspapers are shut down due to labor strife. Many readers find their lives and routines seriously disrupted. Some people even begin reading month-old copies of newspapers. They rely not only on the stories but on the *rituals* of news. We learned back in childhood: There is stability and structure in story time. An emphasis on myth helps us understand the rituals surrounding news.

Myth can also shed light on other readers' ritualistic feelings about the news. Many people claim to hate the news. They hate the power of the news, its apparent ability to sway and influence events. They hate the politics they see in the news. They see it as liberal and outdated. Or they see it as conservative and cruel. They hate the news for its hypocrisy, arrogance, and hubris. They hate the news for taking a stand, for violating standards of objectivity. They hate the news for not taking a stand, for serving as a conduit for those in power. They hate the news for its dependence on official sources. They hate the news for its independence. They hate the news for being stuffy and grey. They hate the news for its attempts at style and color.

Conversely, some readers greatly admire and glorify the news. Journalists, especially television journalists, have become bona fide celebrities. They are paid large sums to speak at conferences and conventions. They are speakers of choice for university commencements. They leave journalism for prestigious posts in government, industry, and education. They are lauded and respected for their work in the news.[3]

Myth brings a historical perspective to readers' complex stormy relationship with the news. The myth teller has always been a conflicted social figure, a voice hated but heeded. "Don't kill the messenger!" journalists sometimes cry in mock fear when they bring bad news. There is truth in the cry. The messenger often has been feared, fooled, honored, ridiculed, trusted, and despised. The rituals surrounding attention to—and degradation of—the news, is part of myth.

8. AS MYTH, THE NEWS STORY IS IRRELEVANT TO MOST OF THE PEOPLE MOST OF THE TIME

Given this book's emphasis on the language of news and eternal, essential stories, this proposition may seem perplexing. But I must admit that the words of the news story are most often . . . ignored. This proposition is not easy to accept for one who has spent most of his life writing, teaching, and studying the news. But it is unavoidable. And it is not as cynical as it seems. As stories, myth and news have always been matters for interpretation. A story means different things to different people. Human nature will ensure that no matter what happens or how the news covers it, most people will interpret the story so that it reinforces their own view of the world. That's why humans have stories in the first place: to make sense of the world. Yet that sense of the world is shaped very early by genes, parents, families, friends, schools, churches, temples, playgrounds, and maybe even words heard in the womb. A news story is not easily going to change all that. Stories most often *confirm* a view of the world.

And so we are left with the unsettling proposition that the specific content of a news story is in large measure irrelevant. Reporters actually understand this better than the public. They know a story will be seen as harshly negative by one reader, as positive puff by another—and blithely ignored by still others. The story is the same. The readers are different. As myth, news provides forms in which people can reaffirm and reconfirm their views of the world. Some people probably understood news reporting of Huey Newton as I did, as stories of the Scapegoat, demeaned as a social outcast. Other people undoubtedly read the reporting on Newton with satisfaction that the "black thug" got what he deserved. Many other people probably never even glanced at the stories.

Stories become sites for people to catch and comprehend their experiences of the world. Life can be hard, difficult to apprehend. People take from the stories what they need. They see what they've already seen. They learn what they've already been taught. They take what they bring. They understand what they've already understood.

9. AS MYTH, NEWS OFFERS BRIDGES ACROSS TIME AND SPACE TO A SELF-ABSORBED SOCIETY

Throughout this book, we've seen that myth is especially interesting because it must combine the timeless and the historically specific. Archetypes and myths don't exist somewhere in some "original state" without history or culture. Myths exist only in the telling, and that telling always takes place in a particular time and place and bears traces of that time and place. Context is as important as text.

And so the comparison of news and myth allows us to see bridges across eras and cultures. Stories of Mark McGwire, Paul Bunyan, and Samson offer more than curious, superficial similarities. They show us aspects of human experience that have persisted for centuries. They allow us to appreciate the human need for heroes and for stories about prodigious feats and marvelous deeds. Stories of Leon Klinghoffer and other innocent victims remind us that cruel happenstance and terrible fate always have been part of the human condition. All human societies need structures and stories to deal with death. Our suffering links us with the suffering of others around the world and throughout time.

This social and historical understanding is a good thing. Our time seems particularly susceptible to self-conscious, self-absorbed superiority. No time, we tell ourselves, is quite like our own. No society has built what we have built. But in many ways, our time is very much like other times. Our news stories daily provide evidence, if we learn to look, of our common humanity with others across time and place. The great Hero myth, told throughout time, echoes again in our modern stories of a somewhat cranky, nutrient-swilling, power-hitting first baseman. We can be rightfully awed by the marriage of the sacred and the profane, the eternal stories and the daily news. We may even ruefully acknowledge the shallowness of our cynical, skeptical, modern heroes in relation to those towering figures of the past. We may question our superiority.

10. AS MYTH, NEWS FROM STATE
SCRIBES HAS HIGH STATUS—AT A COST

This book has acknowledged the influence and importance of elite media, especially the *New York Times*. The stories of the *Times* are read in the White House, Congress, the Supreme Court, foreign capitals, executive suites, publishing houses, and network news offices—as well as in kitchens, diners, and pancake houses. Such status seems singular and unique. Has there ever been anything like the *Times*?

There has. Myth has given us a new way of understanding and talking about the *Times*'s status. By seeing the *Times* as State Scribe, a highly positioned mythmaker, we can situate the *Times* as the latest in a long line of privileged storytellers with access and influence. Societies have always had potent and persuasive storytellers. Social life seems to require select scribes who gain the ear of the privileged and the powerful. Sometimes scribes are supported through literary patronage. Pindar enjoyed such a post. Other times scribes are installed in institutionalized positions, such as those filled by chief priests. Rather than a unique institution, the *Times*, through myth, can be seen as having attained a most traditional position as national dramatist and social scribe.

Myth thus gives another perspective to Harrison Salisbury's argument that the *Times* and other elite media have emerged as leading representatives of a fourth estate, a fourth branch of government that reports upon the other three.[4] The fourth estate can be understood as state scribes that take their place of power alongside those of the federal, representative, and judicial estates.

Yet myth helps us see more deeply. The fourth estate is a position of compromise as well as capacity. The State Scribe can be compromised by its own prominence, made infirm by its own influence. As state scribes, the *Times*, CNN, the Associated Press, the *Wall Street Journal*, and the television networks may prove unwilling to critique fundamental principles of the state. As fourth estate, the state scribes may prove unable truly to scrutinize the other estates—or the system that keeps such estates in place. The scribes, after all, have received power, prominence, and privilege within the current social, economic, and political system. They cannot be expected to turn on or to tear down a system that bequeaths them such access and influence.

Success therefore has been purchased at a price. State scribes become preeminent voices in national and international circles—and they step into those circles. State scribes record news of administrations and authorities—and they become administrative and authoritative. State scribes share and shape—rather than scrutinize and criticize—assumptions, values, and beliefs of those in power. The heady power to select "all the news that's fit to print" can also be debilitating.

The *Times*, in particular, can be understood in this manner. In real ways, the *Times*'s success leads to its failures. As it records events in business and political circles, the *Times* enters those circles. As it provides news for the influential and the elite, the *Times* becomes influential and elite. The paradox seems certain to mark the *Times* in our times, making it damnable to its detractors, praiseworthy to its supporters. As the *Times* succeeds, so shall it fail. As it succeeds at being the paper of record, the chronicler of the day's events, the *Times* will fail to report on moments and acts—not yet news events—shaping tomorrow. It will fail to hear those without power and position who do not contribute for the record. It will record the authoritative voices of those with economic and political power and fail to record the whispers of change, the rant of defiance, the cry of the poor. It will overlook many who falter and fall, fit for salvation, unfit for print.

11. AS MYTH, NEWS WILL BE CRUCIAL BUT CONFLICTED IN AN ONLINE WORLD

Myth and the new technology may seem to be an unlikely pair. But we have already seen that myth has adapted to every storytelling medium—from tribal tales to cable television. The new technology is no different. The combination of myth and online news, though, will produce intriguing, paradoxical, perhaps ominous, results.

The information model of journalism, already in great disrepair, will be dismantled by the marriage of myth and new media. News is losing whatever franchise it had on whatever information is. Information is no longer some scarce resource, a commodity that newspeople can cull and sell. Our society rapidly moved from information explosion to information overload. Information is everywhere. From online events calendars to live, continuous congressional coverage, anyone can give and get information online. If news is only information, news is nothing.

Yet information overload offers opportunities to news: as myth. In the throes of all this information, the need for myth increases. People grapple with the meaning of rapidly changing times. People seek out ways in which they can organize and explain the world. People need stories. Myth has long played these roles. Myth has identified and organized important events in the lives of individuals and societies. Myth has interpreted and explained the meaning of the past, the portents of the future. Myth has offered the stability of story in unstable times.

Decades ago, Marshall McLuhan foresaw the increasing need for myth to organize experience in the face of information overload. "You cannot cope with vast amounts of information in the old fragmentary classified patterns," he told literary critic Frank Kermode in a 1964 interview.[5] "You tend to go looking for mythic and structural forms in order to manage such complex data, moving at very high speeds.

"So the electric engineers often speak of pattern recognition as a normal need of people processing data electrically and by computers and so on—the need for pattern recognition," McLuhan said. "It's a need which the poets foresaw a century ago in their drive back to mythic forms of organizing experience." And so myth and new technology offer opportunities to one another. In a modern, wired world, the news provides *pattern recognition*—mythic forms of organizing experience.

State scribes stand poised to exploit these opportunities—perhaps to the detriment of society. Amid the chaos of the information explosion, the authority of the storyteller seems likely to increase. In the din of a million voices, the voice of an established storyteller, for better or worse, attains even more status. We have already seen evidence of this power in the infancy of online news. Dramatic events—the election of a president, a terrorist killing, a celebrity trial, a devastating flood—bring a rush of readers to the web sites of traditional news outlets, the established "brands," the state scribes.

And the power of the state scribes is being enhanced, politically and economically, as they join together in huge global conglomerates. As previous propositions affirmed, it's always been dangerous to have storytelling power invested in a select social few. Power corrupts. And in our times of consolidation of new and news media, the danger looms larger. State scribes, long beholden to privileged and powerful rulers, now are also compromised by their responsibilities to stockholders, corporate owners, and even to other scribes to whom they have been married and merged. It is a perilous world in which a very few voices, so compromised, can signal to society what is important and what is not, how to act and how not, who is worthy and who is not.

The web, though, is terribly tangled. Myth and new technology may actually pose threats to the state scribes as well. People are increasingly able to seek out stories and storytellers who challenge and reject views of the state scribes. People have the ability to find others who share and confirm their views of the world, bypassing the communication of the scribes.

For example, people with disabilities can find each other online and organize to challenge their exclusion from positions, power, and print. Political candidates unaffiliated with the two major parties have a means to reach a larger audience. Hate groups, isolated in their own communities, can seek support from around the world. What happens online in all these different connections? *People share stories.* They sustain each other with stories that draw from archetypal figures and forms to offer exemplary models and meaning for human life. They tell each other news—as myth. Through these disparate online stories, the status of state scribes quite possibly can be challenged. Digital technology thus has the possibility to nourish a far-reaching medley of voices and stories—or to impose the crushing conformity of a few global scribes.

12. AS MYTH, NEWS WILL
"DREAM THE MYTH ONWARDS"

Eliade, Jung, and other students of myth recognized that people of all times, including modern times, need myth to live. Our physical, biological selves could not long endure in a chaotic, nameless landscape without reason or meaning. Humans need meaning and sense to live, and myth has been one of the central ways that humans make meaning and sense of the world. Adapting its images to every age, in myriad forms, from Greek dramas to today's news stories, myth must be ceaselessly modern. "Mythological motifs frequently appear, but clothed in modern dress," Jung said, "for instance, instead of the eagle of Zeus, or the great roc, there is an airplane; the fight with the dragon is a railway smash; the dragon-slaying hero is an operatic tenor; the Earth Mother is a stout lady selling vegetables; the Pluto who abducts Persephone is a reckless chauffeur, and so on."[6]

In an evocative phrase, Jung concluded that myth must always be a part of the present, central to human experience: "The most we can do," he said, "is to *dream the myth onwards* and give it a modern dress."[7] As we start the twenty-first century, with information plentiful, with news distrusted, with journalists despised, Jung's words can offer a fundamentally different way of understanding news. The news still serves as messenger, the news still brings information from near and far. But the news does far more. News offers eternal stories that give meaning and value to life. News dreams the myth onward and gives myth modern dress.

Notes

INTRODUCTION

1. James C. McKinley Jr., with William K. Stevens, "The Life of a Hurricane, the Death that It Caused," *New York Times*, November 9, 1998, pp. A1, A8.

2. Don Cameron Allen, *The Legend of Noah* (Urbana: University of Illinois Press, 1963); Arthur C. Custance, *The Flood: Local or Global?* (Grand Rapids, MI: Zondervan, 1979); Alan Dundes, ed., *The Flood Myth* (Berkeley and Los Angeles: University of California Press, 1988); J. F. Bierlein, *Parallel Myths* (New York: Ballantine Books, 1994), pp. 121–135; Leonard Woolley, "Stories of the Creation and the Flood," in Dundes, ed., *The Flood Myth*, pp. 89–100.

3. James W. Carey, "In Defense of Public Journalism," in Theodore L. Glasser, ed., *The Idea of Public Journalism* (New York: Guilford Press, 1999), p. 51; also see Davis Merritt, *Public Journalism and Public Life: Why Telling the News Is Not Enough*, 2nd ed. (Mahwah, NJ: Erlbaum, 1998); Jay Rosen, *Getting the Connections Right: Public Journalism and the Troubles in the Press* (New York: Twentieth Century Fund Press, 1996); Jay Rosen and Paul Taylor, *The New News Versus the Old News: The Press and Politics in the 1990s* (New York: Twentieth Century Fund Press, 1992).

4. See James Fallows, *Breaking the News: How the Media Undermine American Democracy* (New York: Pantheon Books, 1996); John Maxwell Hamilton and George A. Krimsky, *Hold the Press: The Inside Story on Newspapers* (Baton Rouge: Louisiana State University Press, 1996); Michael

Schudson, *The Power of News* (Cambridge, MA: Harvard University Press, 1995); Daniel C. Hallin, *We Keep America on Top of the World: Television Journalism and the Public Sphere* (New York: Routledge, 1994); Howard Kurtz, *Media Circus: The Trouble with America's Newspapers* (New York: Times Books, 1993); Larry J. Sabato, *Feeding Frenzy: How Attack Journalism Has Transformed American Politics* (New York: Free Press, 1991); and Doug Underwood, *When MBAs Rule the Newsroom: How the Marketers and Managers Are Reshaping Today's Media* (New York: Columbia University Press, 1993).

5. See PBS television journalist Jim Lehrer's comments to the International Center for Journalists 1998 awards dinner in "Why Journalists Rate with Lawyers, Politicians, Pornographers," *International Journalist*, Winter 1998–1999, pp. 1, 2, 5. A 1998 study by the American Society of Newspaper Editors found that 78 percent of respondents believed the news is biased. A 1994 Times Mirror survey found that 71 percent of respondents believed that the news media "stand in the way of America solving its problems." In regular measurements by Yankelovich Associates of people's confidence in social institutions, confidence in newspapers dropped from 51 to 20 percent from 1988 to 1993. See Dylan Loeb McClain, "More Journalists Are Critical of the Media," *New York Times*, April 5, 1999, p. C9; David Noack, "ASNE: How to Make Friends and Win Back Skeptical Readers," *Editor & Publisher*, December 19, 1998, pp. 9, 45; Linda Fibich, "Can the Media Win Back the Public?", *American Journalism Review*, September 1995, pp. 16–23; and Paul Starobin, "A Generation of Vipers," *Columbia Journalism Review*, March–April 1995, pp. 25–32. Also see David H. Weaver and G. Cleveland Wilhoit, *The American Journalist in the 1990s: U.S. News People at the End of an Era* (Hillsdale, NJ: Erlbaum, 1996).

6. See Michael Janeway, *Republic of Denial: Press, Politics, and Public Life* (New Haven, CT: Yale University Press, 1999); Jay Rosen, *What Are Journalists For?* (New Haven, CT: Yale University Press, 1999); Bruce W. Sanford, *Don't Shoot the Messenger: How Our Growing Hatred of the Media Threatens Free Speech for All of Us* (New York: Free Press, 1999); and Bartholomew H. Sparrow, *Uncertain Guardians: The News Media as a Political Institution* (Baltimore: Johns Hopkins University Press, 1999). Also see Fallows, *Breaking the News*; Glasser, *The Idea of Public Journalism*; Schudson, *The Power of News*; Hallin, *We Keep America on Top of the World*; Kurtz, *Media Circus*; and Sabato, *Feeding Frenzy*.

7. An in-depth discussion of much of this literature can be found in a work by the French philosopher Paul Ricoeur, *Time and Narrative*, 3 vols., trans. Kathleen McLaughlin and David Pellauer (Chicago: University of Chicago Press, 1984).

8. Richard Zoglin, "The Last Great Newspaper," *Time*, September 29, 1997, p. 68.

9. For a classic study that counted the number of times the *Times* was cited, see Craig H. Grau, "What Publications Are Most Frequently Quoted in the Congressional Record?", *Journalism Quarterly*, 53, 1976, 716–719.

10. The relationship between the *Times* and Washington policymakers is discussed throughout J. Herbert Altschull, *Agents of Power: The Media and Public Policy*, 2nd ed. (White Plains, NY: Longman, 1996); R. O. Blanchard, *Congress and the News Media* (New York: Hastings House, 1978); Stephen Hess, *The Government–Press Connection* (Washington, DC: Brookings Institute Press, 1984); Martin Linsky, *Impact: How the Press Affects Federal Policy Making* (New York: Norton, 1986); Michael Parenti, *Inventing Reality: The Politics of the News Media*, 2nd ed. (New York: St. Martin's Press, 1993); Mark J. Rozell, *In Contempt of Congress: Postwar Press Coverage on Capitol Hill* (New York: Praeger, 1996); and Carol H. Weiss, "What America's Leaders Read," *Public Opinion Quarterly*, 38, 1974, 1–22. Mark Lasswell, however, has noted the increasing influence of the *Wall Street Journal* in comparison to the *Times*; see his "Beating the Paper of Record," online at http://www.salon.com, July 24, 1997.

11. Research that touches on the relationship between *Times* reporting and U.S. foreign policy includes Nicholas Berry, *Foreign Policy and the Press: An Analysis of the "New York Times" Coverage of U.S. Foreign Policy* (New York: Greenwood Press, 1990); Russ Braley, *Bad News: The Foreign Policy of the "New York Times"* (Chicago: Regnery Gateway, 1984); Edward Herman and Noam Chomsky, *Manufacturing Consent: The Political Economy of the Mass Media* (New York: Pantheon Books, 1988); Stephen Hess, *International News and Foreign Correspondents* (Washington, DC: Brookings Institute Press, 1996); Jarol B. Manheim, *Strategic Public Diplomacy and American Foreign Policy* (New York: Oxford University Press, 1994); Patrick O'Heffernan, *Mass Media and American Foreign Policy* (Norwood, NJ: Ablex, 1991); and Philip Seib, *Headline Diplomacy: How News Coverage Affects Foreign Policy* (Westport, CT: Greenwood Press, 1996).

12. The influence of the *Times* on the agendas of other news media has been noted in Berry, *Foreign Policy and the Press*, pp. xi–xix; Don Campbell, *Inside the Beltway: A Guide to Washington Reporting* (Ames: Iowa State University Press, 1991), pp. 4, 13, 48; Doris Graber, *Mass Media and American Politics*, 5th ed. (Washington, DC: Congressional Quarterly Press, 1997), pp. 44, 340–341; Hess, *International News and Foreign Correspondents*, pp. 47–50; and Manheim, *Strategic Public Diplomacy*, pp. 148–171.

13. Roland Barthes, *Mythologies*, trans. Annette Lavers (London: Cape, 1972); Marshall McLuhan, "Myth and Mass Media," in Henry Murray, ed., *Myth*

and *Mythmaking* (New York: Braziller, 1960), pp. 288–299 (originally published in *Daedalus*, *88*, 1959, 339–348).

14. See W. Lance Bennett, "Myth, Ritual and Political Control," *Journal of Communication*, *30*, Autumn 1980, 166–179; S. Elizabeth Bird and Robert W. Dardenne, "Myth, Chronicle and Story: Exploring the Narrative Qualities of News," in James W. Carey, ed., *Media, Myths, and Narratives* (Newbury Park, CA: Sage, 1988), pp. 67–86; Myles Breen and Farrel Corcoran, "Myth in the Television Discourse," *Communication Monographs*, *49*, June 1982, 127–136; Richard Campbell, *"60 Minutes" and the News: A Mythology for Middle America* (Urbana: University of Illinois Press, 1991); Howard Davis and Paul Walton, "Death of a Premier: Consensus and Closure in International News," in Howard Davis and Paul Walton, eds., *Language, Image, Media* (Oxford, UK: Blackwell, 1983), pp. 8–49; Graham Knight and Tony Dean, "Myth and the Structure of News," *Journal of Communication*, *32*, Spring 1982, 144–158; John Lawrence and Bernard Timberg, "News and Mythic Selectivity," *Journal of American Culture*, *2*, Summer 1979, 321–330; David L. Paletz, John Z. Ayanian, and Peter A. Fozzard, "Terrorism on TV News: The IRA, the FALN, and the Red Brigades," in William C. Adams, ed., *Television Coverage of International Affairs* (Norwood, NJ: Ablex, 1982), pp. 143–165; and Robert Rutherford Smith, "Mythic Elements in Television News," *Journal of Communication*, *29* Winter 1979, 75–82.

    Also see Sarah R. Hankins, "Archetypal Alloy: Ronald Reagan's Rhetorical Image," *Central States Speech Journal*, *34*, 1983, 3–43; Paul Heyer, *Titanic Legacy: Disaster as Media Event and Myth* (Westport, CT: Praeger, 1995); Jack Lule, "The Myth of My Widow: A Dramatistic Analysis of News Portrayals of a Terrorist Victim," in A. Odasuo Alali and Kenoye Kelvin Eke, eds., *Media Coverage of Terrorism* (Newbury Park, CA: Sage, 1991), pp. 86–111; and J. A. F. Van Zyl, *Media and Myth: The Construction of Television News* (Mowbray, South Africa: IDASA, 1991).

15. Heyer, *Titanic Legacy*; Christopher P. Campbell, *Race, Myth and the News* (Thousand Oaks, CA: Sage, 1995); Campbell, *"60 Minutes" and the News*.

CHAPTER 1

1. Jack Lule, "Death and Defiance on Cedar Avenue," *Today—The Inquirer Magazine*, July 11, 1982, p. 10.

2. Carl G. Jung, *Archetypes and the Collective Unconscious*, trans. R.F.C. Hull (New York: Pantheon Books, 1959); Mircea Eliade, *Patterns in Comparative Religion*, trans. Rosemary Sheed (New York: Sheed & Ward, 1958); Northrop Frye, "The Archetypes of Literature," *Kenyon Review*, *12*, Winter

1951, 92–110; Northrop Frye, *Anatomy of Criticism* (Princeton, NJ: Princeton University Press, 1957).

3. Jung, *Archetypes and the Collective Unconscious*; Carl G. Jung, ed., *Man and His Symbols* (New York: Dell, 1964); Carl G. Jung, *Symbols of Transformation*, 2nd ed., trans. R. F. C. Hull (Princeton, NJ: Princeton University Press, 1976).

4. Eliade, *Patterns in Comparative Religion*, pp. 58–59.

5. Mircea Eliade, *Myth and Reality*, trans. Willard R. Trask (New York: Harper & Row, 1963), pp. 1–2.

6. Eliade, *Myth and Reality*, p. 8.

7. Eliade, *Patterns in Comparative Religion*, pp. 410–411; emphasis in original.

8. Eliade, *Myth and Reality*, pp. 183–184.

9. Mircea Eliade, *Myths, Dreams and Mysteries*, trans. Philip Mairet (New York: Harper & Brothers, 1960), pp. 31–32.

10. Joseph Campbell, "The Historical Development of Mythology," in Henry Murray, ed., *Myth and Mythmaking* (New York: Braziller, 1960), pp. 1–2.

11. Jung, *Symbols of Transformation*, p. 25.

12. Eliade, *Myths, Dreams and Mysteries*, p. 33.

13. Eliade, *Myth and Reality*, p. 162.

14. Mircea Eliade, *The Sacred and the Profane*, trans. Willard R. Trask (New York: Harcourt, Brace & World, 1959), p. 205; Joseph Campbell, *The Hero with a Thousand Faces* (New York: Bollingen Foundation/Pantheon Books, 1949); Joseph Campbell, *Myths to Live By* (New York: Viking Press, 1972); John G. Cawelti, *The Six-Gun Mystique*, 2nd ed. (Bowling Green, OH: Bowling Green State University Popular Press, 1984); Marshall Fishwick, *American Heroes: Myth and Reality* (Washington: Public Affairs Press, 1954).

15. Such news conventions are discussed in Robert Darnton, "Writing News and Telling Stories," *Daedalus, 104,* Spring 1975, 175–194; David L. Eason, "Telling Stories and Making Sense," *Journal of Popular Culture, 15,* Fall 1981, 125–129; Michael Schudson, "The Politics of Narrative Form: The Emergence of News Conventions in Print and Television," *Daedalus, 111,* Fall 1982, 97–112.

16. Eliade, *Patterns in Comparative Religion*, p. 430.

17. Eliade, *Myth and Reality*, p. 19.

18. Eliade, *Myth and Reality*, p. 19; emphasis in original.

19. Eliade, *Myth and Reality*, p. 6; emphasis in original.

20. Ernst Cassirer, *The Myth of the State* (New Haven, CT: Yale University Press, 1946), p. 57; emphasis in original. Henry Tudor too noted that "the myth-maker does not invent his facts; he interprets facts that are already given in the culture to which he belongs." Myth's "success as a practical ar-

gument," he argued, "depends on its being accepted as true, and it is generally accepted as true if it explains the experience of those to whom it is addressed." See Henry Tudor, *Political Myth* (London: Pall Mall Press, 1972), p. 138.

21. Mitchell Stephens, *The History of News: From the Drum to the Satellite* (New York: Viking Press, 1988).

22. Eliade, *Patterns in Comparative Religion*, p. 426; Joseph Henderson, "Ancient Myths and Modern Man," in Carl G. Jung, ed., *Man and His Symbols* (New York: Dell, 1964), p. 101; Jung, *The Archetypes and the Collective Unconscious*, pp. 367, 376. Also see Jung, *Symbols of Transformation*.

23. Joseph Campbell, "Mythological Themes in Creative Literature and Art," in Joseph Campbell, ed., *Myths, Dreams and Religion* (New York: Dutton, 1970), pp. 138–144.

24. Sir James George Frazer, *The Golden Bough, Vol. 9: The Scapegoat* (New York: Macmillan, 1951).

25. Thomas Carlyle, *Sartor Resartus: On Heroes and Hero-Worship* (New York: Dutton, 1908); Campbell, *The Hero with a Thousand Faces*; Dorothy Norman, *The Hero: Myth/Image/Symbol* (New York: Anchor Books, 1990); Lord Fitzroy Richard Raglan, *The Hero: A Study in Tradition, Myth, and Drama* (New York: Vintage Books, 1956).

26. J. J. Bachofen, *Myth, Religion and Mother Right* (Princeton, NJ: Princeton University Press, 1967); Joseph Campbell, *The Masks of God: Primitive Mythology* (New York: Viking Press, 1959); Carl G. Jung, *Four Archetypes: Mother, Rebirth, Spirit, Trickster* (London: Routledge & Kegan Paul, 1972); Erich Neumann, *The Great Mother: An Analysis of the Archetype* (Princeton, NJ: Princeton University Press, 1963); James J. Preston, ed., *Mother Worship: Theme and Variations* (Chapel Hill: University of North Carolina Press, 1982); Kathryn Allen Rabuzzi, *Motherself : A Mythic Analysis of Motherhood* (Bloomington: Indiana University Press, 1988); Marina Wagner, *Alone of All Her Sex: The Myth and the Cult of the Virgin Mary* (New York: Knopf, 1976).

27. William J. Hynes and William G. Doty, eds., *Mythical Trickster Figures: Contours, Contexts, and Criticisms* (Tuscaloosa: University of Alabama Press, 1993); Paul Radin, *The Trickster: A Study in American Indian Mythology* (New York: Schocken Books, 1955).

28. Jean-Pierre Vernant, *Myth and Society in Ancient Greece*, trans. Janet Lloyd (Atlantic Highlands, NJ: Humanities Press, 1980); Eliade, *Myth and Reality*, p. 145.

29. Don Cameron Allen, *The Legend of Noah* (Urbana: University of Illinois Press, 1963); Arthur C. Custance, *The Flood: Local or Global?* (Grand Rapids, MI: Zondervan, 1979); Alan Dundes, ed., *The Flood Myth* (Berkeley and Los Angeles: University of California Press, 1988); J. F. Bierlein, *Parallel Myths* (New York: Ballantine Books, 1994), pp. 121–135.

CHAPTER 2

1. Jack Lule, "Bruce Springsteen: Rock's Future Is Now," *Today: The Inquirer Magazine*, December 7, 1980, pp. 16–21, 48. Years later, Springsteen included a wry song, "Local Hero," on a new collection. I take no credit—nor earn any royalties—for the Springsteen song. He and I had simply drawn from a story as old as humankind.

2. Stith Thompson, *Motif-Index of Folk-Literature* (Bloomington: Indiana University Press, 1955). The first sections of the index catalog myths. Later sections catalog folktales and other forms of folk literature. Other scholars of myth have recognized and identified recurring myths. See James Frazer, *The Golden Bough* (New York: Macmillan, 1951); Joseph Campbell, *The Hero with a Thousand Faces* (New York: Meridian, 1956); and Mircea Eliade, *Patterns in Comparative Religion*, trans. Rosemary Sheed (New York: Sheed & Ward).

3. Martin S. Day, *The Many Meanings of Myth* (Lanham, MD: University Press of America, 1984), pp. 1–32; also see Ivan Strenski, *Four Theories of Myth in Twentieth-Century History* (Iowa City: University of Iowa Press, 1987).

4. Carl G. Jung, *Archetypes and the Collective Unconscious*, trans. R. F. C. Hull (New York: Pantheon Books, 1959); Carl G. Jung, ed., *Man and His Symbols* (New York: Dell, 1964); Carl G. Jung, *Symbols of Transformation*, 2nd ed., trans. R.F.C. Hull (Princeton, NJ: Princeton University Press, 1976).

5. Robert Darnton, "Writing News and Telling Stories," *Daedalus, 104*, Spring 1975, 175–194, quote on 191.

6. Darnton, "Writing News and Telling Stories," p. 189.

7. David L. Eason, "Telling Stories and Making Sense," *Journal of Popular Culture, 15*, Fall 1981, 125–129, quote on 125.

8. S. Elizabeth Bird and Robert W. Dardenne, "Myth, Chronicle, and Story: Exploring the Narrative Qualities of News," in James W. Carey, ed., *Media, Myths and Narratives: Television and the Press* (Newbury Park, CA: Sage, 1988), pp. 67–86.

9. Michael Schudson, "The Politics of Narrative Form: The Emergence of News Conventions in Print and Television," *Daedalus, 111*, Fall 1982, 97–112, quote on 98.

10. Herbert J. Gans, *Deciding What's News: A Study of "CBS Evening News," "NBC Nightly News," "Newsweek," and "Time"* (New York: Pantheon Books, 1979), pp. 39–69.

11. Richard Campbell, *"60 Minutes" and the News: A Mythology for Middle America* (Urbana: University of Illinois Press, 1991), pp. 137–157.

12. Bronislaw Malinowski, "Myth in Primitive Psychology," in *Magic, Science and Religion* (Garden City, NY: Doubleday & Company, 1954), p. 101.

13. They argue that "the 'societal purpose' of the media is to inculcate and defend the economic, social, and political agenda of privileged groups that

dominate the domestic society and the state." See Edward S. Herman and Noam Chomsky, *Manufacturing Consent: The Political Economy of the Mass Media* (New York: Pantheon Books, 1988), p. 298.

14. Maxwell E. McCombs and Donald L. Shaw, "The Agenda-Setting Function of Mass Media," *Public Opinion Quarterly, 36,* 1972, 176–187; Donald L. Shaw and Maxwell E. McCombs, *The Emergence of American Political Issues: The Agenda-Setting Function of the Press* (St. Paul, MN: West, 1977).

15. Harold Lasswell, "The Structure and Functions of Communication in Society," in Lyman Bryson, ed., *The Communication of Ideas* (New York: Harper, 1948), pp. 37–51.

16. John Dewey, *The Public and Its Problems* (New York: Holt, 1927).

17. Charles Cooley, *The Two Major Works: "Human Nature and the Social Order" and "Social Organization"* (Glencoe, IL: Free Press, 1956); George Herbert Mead, *Mind, Self, and Society* (Chicago: University of Chicago Press, 1934); Robert Park, "Morale and the News," *American Journal of Sociology, 47,* 1941, 360–377; also see Daniel J. Czitrom, *Media and the American Mind: From Morse to McLuhan* (Chapel Hill: University of North Carolina Press, 1982).

18. See Kenneth Burke, *The Philosophy of Literary Form* (Baton Rouge: Louisiana State University Press, 1941); *Language as Symbolic Action* (Berkeley and Los Angeles: University of California Press, 1966), and *Permanence and Change,* rev. ed. (Berkeley and Los Angeles: University of California Press, 1984).

19. Walter Lippmann, in his critiques of news, also saw news dramatically. "The audience must participate in the news, much as it participates in the drama, by personal identification," he argued; see his *Public Opinion,* p. 355. The philosopher George Herbert Mead echoed Lippmann. Mead saw news reports as dramatic narratives. The news recounts "situations through which one can enter into the attitude and experience of other persons," Mead wrote. "The drama has served this function in presenting what have been felt to be important situations." See Mead, *Mind, Self, and Society,* p. 257.

James W. Carey has tied together the work of Burke with a McLuhan-like emphasis on technology and the Chicago school emphasis on symbolic systems.

> We create, express, and convey our knowledge of and attitudes toward reality through the construction of a variety of symbol systems: art, science, journalism, religion, common sense, mythology. How do we do this? What are the differences between these forms? What are the historical and comparative variations in them?

See Carey, "A Cultural Approach to Communication," *Communication, 2,* 1975, 17. Reading a newspaper, for example, Carey said, should be seen "less as sending or gaining information and more like attending a mass: a situation in which nothing new is learned but in which a particular view of the world is portrayed and confirmed" (p. 8).

20. Northrop Frye, *The Educated Imagination* (Bloomington: Indiana University Press, 1964), p. 63.

CHAPTER 3

1. Discussions of news, terrorism, and public policy can be found in A. Odasuo Alali and Kenoye Kelvin Eke, eds., *Media Coverage of Terrorism: Methods of Diffusion* (Newbury Park, CA: Sage, 1991); Yonah Alexander and Robert Picard, eds., *In the Camera's Eye: News Coverage of Terrorist Events* (New York: Brassey's, 1991); and Robert Picard and Rhonda Sheets, *Terrorism and the News Media Research Bibliography* (Boston: Emerson College and The Terrorism and the News Media Research Project, 1986).
2. Mircea Eliade, *Patterns in Comparative Religion*, trans. Rosemary Sheed (New York: Sheed & Ward, 1958), p. 426.
3. Eliade, *Patterns in Comparative Religion*, p. 426.
4. Joseph Henderson, "Ancient Myths and Modern Man," in Carl G. Jung, ed., *Man and His Symbols* (New York: Dell, 1964), p. 101.
5. Mircea Eliade, *Birth and Rebirth*, trans. Willard R. Trask (New York: Harper & Brothers, 1958), p. 136.
6. Sara Rimer, "To Hostage Families, Waiting Back Home Is Also a Nightmare," *New York Times*, October 9, 1985, p. A1.
7. Rimer, "To Hostage Families, Waiting Back Home Is Also a Nightmare," p. A10.
8. Sara Rimer, "Cheers, Then Heartbreak at Apartment on 10th Street," *New York Times*, October 10, 1985, p. A1.
9. E. J. Dionne Jr., "Hostage's Death: 'A Shot to Forehead,'" *New York Times*, October 11, 1985, p. A1.
10. Sara Rimer, "Wife Calls Victim of Hijackers a Hero," *New York Times*, October 11, 1985, p. A13.
11. Sara Rimer, "Aged Victim, Portrayed as Helpless, Is Recalled as a Strong, Happy Man," *New York Times*, October 12, 1985, p. A8.
12. Robert D. McFadden, "15 Passengers, on Return to U.S., Tell of Terror on the Cruise Liner," *New York Times*, October 13, 1985, p. A1.
13. George James, "For 15 Achille Lauro Passengers, Cruise Ends in Newark," *New York Times*, October 13, 1985, p. A24.
14. Sara Rimer, "Slain Hostage's Widow Tells Reagan She Spat in the Faces of the Hijackers," *New York Times*, October 13, 1985, p. A26.

15. "Transcript of President's Talk with Marilyn Klinghoffer," *New York Times*, October 13, 1985, p. A26.

16. Eric Pace, "A Somber Homecoming for Leon Klinghoffer," *New York Times*, October 21, 1985, p. A1.

17. Pace, "A Somber Homecoming for Leon Klinghoffer," p. A6.

18. Sara Rimer, "Klinghoffer Eulogized as Public and Private Hero," *New York Times*, October 22, 1985, p. A10.

19. Eliade, *Patterns in Comparative Religion*, p. 419.

20. Eliade, *Patterns in Comparative Religion*, p. 426.

21. Carl G. Jung, *The Archetypes and the Collective Unconscious*, trans. R. F. C. Hull (New York: Pantheon Books, 1959), pp. 367, 376; also see Carl G. Jung, *Symbols of Transformation*, trans. R. F. C. Hull (Princeton, NJ: Princeton University Press, 1976).

22. Erich Neumann, *The Origins and History of Consciousness*, trans. R. F. C. Hull (Princeton, NJ: Princeton University Press, 1970), p. 380.

23. Kenneth Burke, *The Rhetoric of Religion* (Berkeley and Los Angeles: University of California Press, 1970), p. 217.

24. Neumann, *The Origins and History of Consciousness*, p. 378.

25. The myth-like manner in which the *Times* reports used personal details to invoke the symbol of the self can also be seen in literature, such as James Joyce's novel *Ulysses*. That book is crammed with the staggering details of Leopold Bloom's life until finally the details collapse and Bloom is revealed as the hero Ulysses and Ulysses is revealed as the symbol of the self.

26. Sigmund Freud, *Civilization and Its Discontents*, in James Strachey, ed. and trans., *The Standard Edition of the Complete Psychological Works of Sigmund Freud*, Vol. 21 (London: Hogarth Press, 1961), p. 122.

27. The phrase "pornography of grief" is often credited to the *Washington Post* columnist and television commentator George Will. Discussions of ethics, privacy, and news coverage of victims can be found in Clifford G. Christians, Mark Fackler, and Kim B. Rotzoll, *Media Ethics: Case and Moral Reasoning*, 4th ed. (White Plains, NY: Longman, 1995), pp. 115–131; Philip Patterson and Lee Wilkins, eds., *Media Ethics: Issues and Cases* (Dubuque, IA: Brown, 1994), pp. 109–135; and H. J. McCloskey, "Privacy and the Right to Privacy," in Anthony Serafini, ed., *Ethics and Social Concern* (New York: Paragon Books, 1989), pp. 664–690.

CHAPTER 4

1. Much of the following biographical information is taken from Gilbert Stuart Moore, *A Special Rage: A Black Reporter's Encounter with Huey P. Newton's Murder Trial, the Black Panthers and His Own Destiny* (New York:

Harper & Row, 1971); Bobby Seale, *Seize the Time: The Story of the Black Panther Party and Huey P. Newton* (New York: Random House, 1970); and Huey P. Newton, *Revolutionary Suicide* (New York: Harcourt Brace Jovanovich, 1973).

2. Malcolm X, *Malcolm X Speaks: Selected Speeches and Statements* (New York: Merit, 1965), p. 8. The line has continued to inspire debate, crowning, for example, the finale of Spike Lee's film of racial politics, *Do the Right Thing.*

3. Tom Wolfe, *Radical Chic and Mau-Mauing the Flak Catchers* (New York: Farrar, Straus, 1970).

4. Excellent accounts of Newton's trial are given in Moore, *A Special Rage,* and in Michael Arlen, *An American Verdict* (Garden City, NY: Doubleday, 1973). Also see Murray Kempton, *The Briar Patch: The People of the State of New York v. Lumumba Shakur et al.* (New York: Dutton, 1973).

5. See Paul Chevigny, *Cops and Rebels: A Study of Provocation* (New York: Pantheon Books, 1972). Edward Epstein discusses press coverage of confrontations between police and the Panthers and the evidence of a conspiracy between the FBI and state police against the Panthers in "The Panthers and the Press," *Between Fact and Fiction: The Problem of Journalism* (New York: Vintage, 1975, pp. 33–77). COINTELPRO, the FBI plan to disrupt the Panthers and other U.S. oppositional groups, is discussed in William Keller, *The Liberals and J. Edgar Hoover* (Princeton, NJ: Princeton University Press, 1989); Athan Theoharis, *The Boss: J. Edgar Hoover and the Great American Inquisition* (Philadelphia: Temple University Press, 1988); and Richard Gid Powers, *Secrecy and Power: The Life of J. Edgar Hoover* (New York: Free Press, 1987). Also see David Garrow, *The FBI and Martin Luther King, Jr.: From "Solo" to Memphis* (New York: Norton, 1981).

6. Kenneth Burke also saw myth involved with the construction and defense of consensus. Even within myths that tell the origins of a society, Burke astutely observed the defense of social order. He argued that "an account of *origins* is also a way of establishing *sanctions.* Its narrative stating how things *were* in the past thereby substantiates the principles of governance to which the faithful *should* be vowed in the present." See Burke, *Language as Symbolic Action* (Berkeley and Los Angeles: University of California Press, 1966), p. 390.

7. A simple but classic definition, offered by the scholar Bronislaw Malinowski, states that myth is a social charter. That is, myth provides a preferred way to think and act in society. It offers rules and norms. See Malinowski, *"Magic, Science and Religion" and Other Essays* (Garden City, NY: Doubleday, 1954), p. 144.

Walter Burkert, following Malinowski, also stressed that myth justifies and defends: "Institutions or presentations of family, clan, or city are explained and justified by tales—'charter myths,' in Malinowski's term." See

Burkert, *Structure and History in Greek Mythology and Ritual* (Berkeley and Los Angeles: University of California Press, 1979), p. 23. And Joseph Campbell argued that one of the primary functions of myth was to shape individuals to the aims and ideals of particular social groups. See Campbell, "Mythological Themes in Creative Literature and Art," in Joseph Campbell, ed., *Myths, Dreams and Religion* (New York: Dutton, 1970), pp. 138–144.

8. Sir James George Frazer, *The Golden Bough, Vol. 9: The Scapegoat* (New York: Macmillan, 1951), p. 109.

9. Frazer, *The Golden Bough: The Scapegoat*, p. 212.

10. Frazer, *The Golden Bough: The Scapegoat*, pp. 250–264.

11. Kenneth Burke, *Permanence and Change*, rev. ed. (Berkeley and Los Angeles: University of California Press, 1984), p. 285.

12. Previous discussions that touch on media coverage of Newton and the Panthers can be found in Earl Anthony, *Picking Up the Gun: A Report on the Black Panthers* (New York: Dial, 1970); Arlen, *An American Verdict*; Black Panther Party, *All Power to the People: The Story of the Black Panther Party* (Oakland, CA: People's Press, 1970); and Epstein, "The Panthers and the Press."

    Also see G. Louis Heath, *Off the Pigs! The History and Literature of the Black Panther Party* (Metuchen, NJ: Scarecrow Press, 1976); Gene Marine, *The Black Panthers* (New York: Signet Books, 1969), pp. 67–76; Moore, *A Special Rage*; Seale, *Seize the Time*; and Gail Sheehy, *Panthermania: The Clash of Black against Black in One American City* (New York: Harper & Row, 1971).

13. Herbert J. Gans, *Deciding What's News* (New York: Pantheon Books, 1979), p. 295; Carolyn Martindale, "Selected Newspaper Coverage of Causes of Black Protest," *Journalism Quarterly*, 66, Winter 1989, 964. Also see J. Herbert Altschull, *Agents of Power*, 2nd ed. (White Plains, NY: Longman, 1995).

14. Classic work in this area includes *Report of the National Advisory Commission on Civil Disorders* (Washington, DC: U.S. Government Printing Office, March 1968); George P. Hunt, "The Racial Crisis and the News Media: An Overview," in Paul Fisher and Ralph Lowenstein, eds., *Race and the News Media* (New York: Praeger, 1967), pp. 11–20; William L. Rivers and Wilbur Schramm, "The Negro and the News: A Case Study," in Rivers and Schramm, *Responsibility in Mass Communication*, rev. ed. (New York: Harper & Row, 1969), pp. 175–189; Jack Lyle, ed., *The Black American and the Press* (Los Angeles: Ward Ritchie Press, 1968); and Vernon A. Stone, "Trends in the Status of Minorities and Women in Broadcast News," *Journalism Quarterly*, 65, Summer 1988, 288–293.

15. Peter Braham, "How the Media Report Race," in Michael Gurevitch, Tony Bennett, James Curran, and Janet Woollacott, eds. *Culture, Society and the*

Media (New York: Methuen, 1982), pp. 268–286; Jannette L. Dates and William Barlow, eds., *Split Image: African Americans in the Mass Media* (Washington, DC: Howard University Press, 1990); Robert Entman, "Modern Racism and the Images of Blacks in Local Television News," *Critical Studies in Mass Communication, 7*, 1990, 332–345; Robert Entman, "Blacks in the News: Television, Modern Racism and Cultural Change," *Journalism Quarterly, 69*, Summer 1992, 341–361; Carolyn Martindale, *The White Press and Black America* (Westport, CT: Greenwood Press, 1986).

16. Well-respected work in this area includes Stuart Hall, "Deviance, Politics, and the Media," in P. Rock and M. McIntosh, eds. *Deviance and Social Control* (London: Tavistock, 1974); Paula Johnson, David Sears, and John McConahay, "Black Invisibility, the Press and the LA Riot," *American Journal of Sociology, 76*, January 1971, 713–717; Richard Lentz, *Symbols, the News Magazines, and Martin Luther King* (Baton Rouge: Louisiana State University Press, 1990); and David Paletz and Robert Dunn, "Press Coverage of Civil Disorders: A Case Study of Winston-Salem, 1967," *Public Opinion Quarterly, 33*, 1969–1970, 340–345.

    Also see Todd Gitlin, *The Whole World Is Watching* (Berkeley and Los Angeles: University of California Press, 1980), pp. 290–291; David L. Paletz and Robert M. Entman, *Media, Power, Politics* (New York: Free Press, 1981); and Pamela J. Shoemaker, "Media Treatment of Deviant Political Groups," *Journalism Quarterly, 61*, Spring 1984, 66–75, 82.

17. Dennis Hevesi, "Huey Newton Symbolized the Rising Black Anger of a Generation," *New York Times*, August 23, 1989, p. A15.

18. "Huey Newton, Head of Black Panthers, Found Shot to Death," *New York Times*, August 23, 1989, p. A1.

19. Theodore L. Glasser and James S. Ettema in particular have focused attention on the use of irony in news. See Theodore L. Glasser and James S. Ettema, "When the Facts Don't Speak for Themselves: A Study of the Use of Irony in Daily Journalism," *Critical Studies in Mass Communication, 10*, December 1993, 322–338; and James S. Ettema and Theodore L. Glasser, "The Irony in—and of—Journalism: A Case Study in the Moral Language of Liberal Democracy," *Journal of Communication, 44*, Spring 1994, 5–28.

20. "Black Panthers Leader Dies on Turf Where Work Began," *Kansas City Times*, August 23, 1989, p. A1.

21. Paul Clancy, "Ex-'Panther' Slain," *USA Today*, August 23, 1989, p. A2.

22. "Huey Newton Slain; He Was '60s Apostle of Black Militancy," *Atlanta Constitution*, August 23, 1989, p. A1.

23. Harry Harris, "The Final Chapter: Police Suspect Drugs Involved," (Oakland) *Tribune*, August 23, 1989, p. A1.

24. Lori Olszewski and Rick DelVecchio, "Huey Newton Shot to Death in West Oakland," *San Francisco Chronicle*, August 23, 1989, p. A1.

25. Olszewski and DelVecchio, "Huey Newton Shot to Death in West Oakland."
     San Francisco Chronicle, August 23, 1989, p. A1.
26. "Huey Newton, Head of Black Panthers, Found Shot to Death," *New York Times*, August 23, 1989, p. A1.
27. Mark A. Stein and Valarie Basheda, "Black Panther Founder Huey Newton Is Killed," *Los Angeles Times*, August 23, 1989, p. A1.
28. Clancy, "Ex-'Panther' Slain."
29. Harris, "The Final Chapter: Police Suspect Drugs Involved."
30. Cynthia Gorney, "Huey Newton, Cofounder of Black Panthers, Slain in Oakland," *Washington Post*, August 23, 1989, p. A6.
31. "Huey Newton Slain; He Was '60s Apostle of Black Militancy."
32. "Huey Newton Slain; Led Black Panthers," *St. Louis Post-Dispatch*, August 23, 1989, p. 1.
33. Harris, "The Final Chapter: Police Suspect Drugs Involved."
34. Olszewski and DelVecchio, "Huey Newton Shot to Death in West Oakland."
35. Olszewski and DelVecchio, "Huey Newton Shot to Death in West Oakland"; "Huey Newton Slain; Led Black Panthers."
36. Gorney, "Huey Newton, Cofounder of Black Panthers, Slain in Oakland."
37. Gorney, "Huey Newton, Cofounder of Black Panthers, Slain in Oakland."
38. "Huey Newton, Head of Black Panthers, Found Shot to Death."
39. "Huey P. Newton," *Wall Street Journal*, August 23, 1989, p. A1.
40. Stein and Basheda, "Black Panther Founder Huey Newton Is Killed."
41. Hevesi, "Huey Newton Symbolized the Rising Black Anger of a Generation."
42. Martin Lee and Norman Solomon also charge U.S. news media with ignoring state harassment of the Panthers. See their *Unreliable Sources: A Guide to Detecting Bias in News Media* (New York: Carol, 1990), p. 56.
43. Gorney, "Huey Newton, Cofounder of Black Panthers, Slain in Oakland"; William Brand and Larry Spears, "Friends and Foes Remember Newton: 'Visionary,' 'Thug,'" (Oakland) *Tribune*, August 23, 1989, p. A2; "Huey Newton Slain; Led Black Panthers."
44. Olszewski and DelVecchio, "Huey Newton Shot to Death in West Oakland."
45. Brand and Spears, "Friends and Foes Remember Newton: 'Visionary,' 'Thug.'"
46. Clancy, "Ex-'Panther' Slain." The report was making a caustic allusion to the Panthers' support from liberal groups in the 1970s and Tom Wolfe's satirizing of that support in *Radical Chic and Mau-Mauing the Flak Catchers*. The disenchanted member of the "radical chic" is identified in the report as David Horowitz, former editor of *Ramparts* and author of *Destructive Generation: Second Thoughts about the '60s* (New York: Collier, 1989).
47. Gorney, "Huey Newton, Cofounder of Black Panthers, Slain in Oakland."

48. "Black Panthers Co-Founder Newton Dies in Shooting," *Houston Post*, August 23, 1989, p. A1.

49. "Huey Newton Slain; He was '60s Apostle of Black Militancy."

50. "Troubled Life of Huey Newton," *San Francisco Chronicle*, August 23, 1989, p. A12.

51. The site description is taken from the *Los Angeles Times*, the only newspaper to report the memorial scene. See Stein and Basheda, "Black Panther Founder Huey Newton Is Killed."

52. "A Passerby Pauses by Some Flowers That Had Been Left at the Spot Where Huey Newton Was Slain in Oakland," *San Francisco Chronicle*, August 23, 1989, p. A1; the Oakland *Tribune* ran a small, one-column, uncaptioned photograph of a similar scene on August 23, 1989, p. A3.

53. Jacqueline Cutler, "People Remember Leadership and His Past," (Oakland) *Tribune*, August 23, 1989, p. A2.

54. Stein and Basheda, "Black Panther Founder Huey Newton Is Killed."

55. "Unidentified Man Lays Flowers at Spot Where Huey Newton Was Slain," *Los Angeles Times*, August 23, 1989, p. A3.

56. Stein and Basheda, "Black Panther Founder Huey Newton Is Killed."

57. Gitlin, *The Whole World Is Watching*, p. 2. Also see Stokely Carmichael and Charles Hamilton, *Black Power: The Politics of Liberation in America* (New York: Random House, 1967), pp. 2–32; and Robert F. Williams, "Every Freedom Movement Is Labeled 'Communist,'" in Thomas Wagstaff, ed., *Black Power: The Radical Response to White America* (Beverly Hills, CA: Glencoe Press, 1969), pp. 105–111.

58. Gans, *Deciding What's News*, p. 295.

59. Gitlin's, *The Whole World Is Watching* discusses media coverage of student protest in the 1960s.

60. Marine, *The Black Panthers*, p. 69.

61. Moore, *A Special Rage*, p. 258.

62. Heath, *Off the Pigs*, p. ix.

CHAPTER 5

1. Jack Curry, "A Reluctant Home-Run Hitter, a Reluctant Hero," *New York Times*, September 9, 1998, p. D3.

2. Thomas Carlyle, *Sartor Resartus: On Heroes and Hero-Worship* (New York: Dutton, 1908); Joseph Campbell, *The Hero with a Thousand Faces* (New York: Bollingen Foundation/Pantheon Books, 1949); Dorothy Norman, *The Hero: Myth/Image/Symbol* (New York: Anchor Books, 1990); Lord Fitzroy Richard Raglan, *The Hero: A Study in Tradition, Myth, and Drama* (New York: Vintage Books, 1956).

3. Mircea Eliade, *Myths, Dreams and Mysteries*, trans. Philip Mairet (New York: Harper & Brothers, 1960), p. 32.
4. Mircea Eliade, *Myth and Reality*, trans. Willard R. Trask (New York: Harper & Row, 1963), p. 2.
5. Campbell, *The Hero with a Thousand Faces*; Raglan, *The Hero*; Robert A. Segal, "Introduction," *In Quest of the Hero* (Princeton, NJ: Princeton University Press, 1990), pp. vii–xii.
6. Marshall Fishwick, *The Hero, American Style* (New York: McKay, 1969).
7. Carlyle, *Sartor Resartus*, p. 312.
8. Campbell, *The Hero with a Thousand Faces*.
9. Hans Lenk, "Herculean 'Myth' Aspects of Athletics," in David L. Vanderwerken and Spencer K. Wertz, eds., *Sport Inside Out: Readings in Literature and Philosophy* (Fort Worth: Texas Christian University Press, 1985), pp. 435–446; Peter Williams, *The Sports Immortals: Deifying the American Athlete* (Bowling Green, OH: Bowling Green State University Popular Press, 1994).
10. Daniel Boorstin, *The Image: A Guide to Pseudo-Events in America* (New York: Atheneum, 1987), p. 51.
11. Campbell, *The Hero with a Thousand Faces*, p. 387.
12. Walter J. Ong, *The Presence of the Word* (Minneapolis: University of Minnesota Press, 1981), pp. 204–205.
13. Boorstin, *The Image*, p. 54.
14. Boorstin, *The Image*, p. 60.
15. Susan J. Drucker, "The Mediated Sports Hero," in Susan J. Drucker and Robert S. Cathcart, *American Heroes in a Media Age* (Cresskill, NJ: Hampton Press, 1994), p. 93.
16. Allen Guttmann, *From Ritual to Record: The Nature of Modern Sports* (New York: Columbia University Press, 1978), p. 55.
17. Claire Smith, "Thomas Isn't Appreciated by Baseball," *New York Times*, February 25, 1998, p. C1.
18. Murray Chass, "1998 Baseball Preview," *New York Times*, March 29, 1998, p. H11.
19. "Play Ball," *New York Times*, March 31, 1998, p. A22.
20. Jack Curry, "All Eyes Remain on Slugger after He Launches No. 47," *New York Times*, August 12, 1998, p. C2.
21. Murray Chass, "A Smile, a Stance, a Swing," *New York Times*, August 21, 1998, p. C1.
22. Associated Press, "The Teams That Made Milwaukee Famous," *New York Times*, April 1, 1998, p. C5.
23. Ira Berkow, "A Classic: Maddux Stymies McGwire," *New York Times*, August 29, 1998, p. C2.
24. Ira Berkow, "Take That! McGwire Has a 500-Foot Reply," *New York Times*, August 31, 1998, p. C1.

25. "One Swing Away," *New York Times*, September 4, 1998, p. A23.

26. "McGwire Does It!," *New York Times*, September 9, 1998, p. A24.

27. George Vecsey, "A Sport Is Reborn—The Home Run, America's Signature Feat, Invigorates Baseball; September's Aura Restored to Fans," *New York Times*, September 4, 1998, p. D1.

28. Murray Chass, "Ultimate Sports Goal Lures McGwire and Sosa and Fans," *New York Times*, September 4, 1998, p. A1.

29. Jack Curry, "Take Me Out to Batting Practice; McGwire's Blasts Bring Fans Out Early, Clutching Gloves and Dreaming of a Souvenir," *New York Times*, August 13, 1998, p. C1.

30. Jack Curry, "3 Strikeouts Continue McGwire's Frustration," *New York Times*, August 11, 1998, p. C2.

31. Claire Smith, "Expectations Still Soar a Mile High," *New York Times*, July 1, 1998, p. C2.

32. Curry, "All Eyes Remain on Slugger after He Launches No. 47."

33. Chass, "A Smile, a Stance, a Swing."

34. Bill Dedman, "He's Chasing Record, Too, but Where Is Sosa-Mania?", *New York Times*, August 28, 1998, p. C3.

35. Associated Press, "Sosa's Feats Providing Worthy Counterpoint," *New York Times*, August 25, 1998, p. C3.

36. David W. Chen, "Dominicans' Favorite Son: Sammy Sosa, Home Run Hitter," *New York Times*, September 5, 1998, p. B3.

37. Ira Berkow, "With 3 Swings, Sluggers Trade Lead in Homers," *New York Times*, August 20, 1998, p. A1.

38. Associated Press, "Quiet Night for McGwire and Sosa," *New York Times*, August 19, 1998, p. C6.

39. Joe Drape, "McGwire Admits Taking Controversial Substance," *New York Times*, August 22, 1998, p. C3.

40. Harvey Araton, "The News Is Out: Popeye Spikes His Spinach," *New York Times*, August 23, 1998, sec. 8, p. 1.

41. Associated Press, "Sosa's Feats Providing Worthy Counterpoint."

42. Ira Berkow, "Over Fence Came Before Over Counter," *New York Times*, August 27, 1998, p. C1

43. Araton, "The News Is Out: Popeye Spikes His Spinach."

44. William C. Rhoden, "Baseball's Pandora's Box Cracks Open," *New York Times*, August 25, 1998, p. C1.

45. Alan Olshan, "Home Run Chase Needs No Asterisk," *New York Times*, August 30, 1998, sec. 4, p. 12.

46. Dave Anderson, "Two Votes for McGwire to Hit 62," *New York Times*, July 7, 1998, p. C1.

47. Jack Curry, "A Reluctant Home-Run Hitter, A Reluctant Hero," *New York Times*, September 9, 1998, p. D3.

48. Curry, "A Reluctant Home-Run Hitter, A Reluctant Hero."

49. Curry, "A Reluctant Home-Run Hitter, A Reluctant Hero."
50. Buster Olney, "McGwire Gets Better, and a Record Looks More Vulnerable," *New York Times*, July 9, 1998, p. A1.
51. Murray Chass, "It's Sosa's Day, but Night Belongs to McGwire," *New York Times*, September 3, 1998, p. D1.
52. Vecsey, "A Sport Is Reborn."
53. Dave Anderson, "Baseball's Godzilla Has a Bat," *New York Times*, May 26, 1998, p. C1.
54. Richard Sandomir, "Marketing Clout: The Fans Flock to See McGwire," *New York Times*, July 22, 1998, p. C1.
55. Ira Berkow, "Home Run Derby Hits Wrigley; Battle between Familiar Neighbors Has Fans Lining Up," *New York Times*, August 18, 1998, p. C1.
56. Olney, "McGwire Gets Better, and a Record Looks More Vulnerable."
57. Selena Roberts, "No Homers, No Relief for a Silent McGwire," *New York Times*, September 25, 1998, p. D2.
58. Claire Smith, "Expections Still Soar a Mile High," *New York Times*, July 1, 1998, p. C2.
59. Claire Smith, "The Power and the Glory; Mark McGwire Cracks Home Runs and Creates Expectations," *New York Times*, May 7, 1998, p. C1.
60. Murray Chass, "A Smash Hit: McGwire Clouts His 60th," *New York Times*, September 6, 1998, sec. 1, p. 1.
61. Murray Chass, "McGwire Grabs Share of Maris's Mark," *New York Times*, September 8, 1998, p. A1.
62. Jack Curry, "Goodbye, Ruth; Hello, Maris; And Now the Wait for No. 62; A Family Celebration for a Historic Moment," *New York Times*, September 8, 1998, p. D1.
63. Curry, "Goodbye, Ruth; Hello, Maris."
64. George Vecsey, "Many Joys of a Home Run Lovefest," *New York Times*, September 8, 1998, p. D1.
65. Murray Chass, "Just Clearing the Wall, McGwire Claims the Record," *New York Times*, September 9, 1998, p. A1.
66. George Vecsey, "A Mighty Swing, a Grand Record; After 37 Years, McGwire Passes Maris," *New York Times*, September 9, 1998, p. D1.
67. Curry, "A Reluctant Home-Run Hitter, A Reluctant Hero."
68. "McGwire Does It!"
69. Thomas L. Friedman, "Foreign Affairs; Bringing Out the Best," *New York Times*, September 11, 1998, p. A27.
70. "McGwire Punches Up the Story," *New York Times*, September 16, 1998, p. D1.
71. Selena Roberts, "McGwire Responds in the Fifth," *New York Times*, September 26, 1998, p. D1.
72. Alan Schwarz, "Ideas & Trends: Big-Bang Theory; A Blast from the Past Makes Baseball a Current Event," *New York Times*, September 13, 1998, sec. 4, p. 4.

73. One story said, "It does not take long for the vexing issues of race and national origin to creep onto the field. In Atlanta or Boston, in Houston or Miami, awkward pauses and disagreements renew the long, uncomfortable relationship between the national pastime and the national enigma." See Bill Dedman, "It's a Race for the Record, but Is It Also about Race?", *New York Times*, September 20, 1998, sec. 8, p. 3.

74. Roberts, "No Homers, No Relief for a Silent McGwire."

75. Murray Chass, "McGwire's Grand Finale Makes It 70," *New York Times*, September 28, 1998, p. A1.

76. Philip M. Boffey, "Post-Season Thoughts on McGwire's Pills," *New York Times*, September 30, 1998, p. A16.

77. Curry, "A Reluctant Home-Run Hitter, A Reluctant Hero."

78. Friedman, "Foreign Affairs; Bringing Out the Best."

79. Boffey, "Post-Season Thoughts on McGwire's Pills."

80. Friedman, "Foreign Affairs; Bringing Out the Best."

81. Olney, "McGwire Gets Better, and a Record Looks More Vulnerable."

82. Anderson, "Baseball's Godzilla Has a Bat."

83. Nick Trujillo, *The Meaning of Nolan Ryan* (College Station: Texas A & M University Press, 1994), pp. 98, 109.

84. Don Sabo and Sue Curry Jansen, "Prometheus Unbound: Constructions of Masculinity in Sports Media," in Lawrence A. Wenner, ed., *MediaSport* (London: Routledge, 1998), p. 204.

85. Don Sabo, Sue Curry Jansen, et al., "Televising International Sport: Race, Ethnicity, and Nationalistic Bias," *Journal of Sport and Social Issues*, 20, 1996, 7–21.

86. Red Smith, *The Red Smith Reader* (New York: Random House, 1982), p. 16.

87. Tom Boswell, *Game Day* (New York: Doubleday, 1990), p. xvii.

88. Eliade, *Myth and Reality*, p. 185.

89. Campbell, *The Hero with a Thousand Faces*, p. 388.

90. Leah R. Vande Berg, "The Sports Hero Meets Mediated Celebrityhood," in Lawrence Wenner, ed., *MediaSport* (New York: Routledge, 1998), p. 152.

91. Leah R. Vande Berg and Nick Trujillo, "From Wild Western Prodigy to the Ageless Wonder: The Mediated Evolution of Nolan Ryan," in Susan J. Drucker and Robert S. Cathcart, eds., *American Heroes in a Media Age* (Cresskill, NJ: Hampton Press, 1994), pp. 240–241.

CHAPTER 6

1. Anne Hanley, "But Even She Must Wait Her Turn for Sainthood," (London) *Independent*, August 30, 1998, p. 16; Pamela Constable, "Mother Teresa Mourned on Anniversary of Death," *Washington Post*, September 6, 1998, p. A29.

2. J. J. Bachofen, *Myth, Religion and Mother Right* (Princeton, NJ: Princeton University Press, 1967); Joseph Campbell, *The Masks of God: Primitive Mythology* (New York: Viking Press, 1959); Carl G. Jung, *Four Archetypes: Mother, Rebirth, Spirit, Trickster* (London: Routledge & Kegan Paul, 1972); Erich Neumann, *The Great Mother: An Analysis of the Archetype* (Princeton, NJ: Princeton University Press, 1963); James J. Preston, ed., *Mother Worship: Theme and Variations* (Chapel Hill: University of North Carolina Press, 1982); Kathryn Allen Rabuzzi, *Motherself: A Mythic Analysis of Motherhood* (Bloomington: Indiana University Press, 1988); Marina Wagner, *Alone of All Her Sex: The Myth and the Cult of the Virgin Mary* (New York: Knopf, 1976).

3. James Freeman, "Introduction: The Crosscultural Study of Mother Worship," in Rebuzzi, *Mother Worship*, p. xv.

4. Neumann, *The Great Mother.*

5. Mircea Eliade, *Myths, Dreams and Mysteries*, trans. Philip Mairet, (New York: Harper & Brothers, 1960), p. 161.

6. Mircea Eliade, *The Sacred and the Profane*, trans. Willard R. Trask (New York: Harcourt, Brace & World, 1959), pp. 141–144.

7. Michael Atkinson, "Robert Bly's *Sleepers Joining Hands*: Shadow and Self," in Richard P. Sugg, ed., *Jungian Literary Criticism* (Evanston, IL: Northwestern University Press, 1992), pp. 83–102; Karin J. Billions, "Phyllis Schlafly: Great Mother, Heroine and Villain," in Susan J. Drucker and Robert S. Cathcart, eds., *American Heroes in a Media Age* (Cresskill, NJ: Hampton Press, 1994), pp. 149–167; Karen Elias-Button, "Journey into an Archetype: The Dark Mother in Contemporary Women's Poetry," in Richard P. Sugg, ed., *Jungian Literary Criticism* (Evanston, IL: Northwestern University Press, 1992), pp. 355–366; Meredith Powers, *The Heroine in Western Literature: The Archetype and Her Reemergence in Modern Prose* (Jefferson, NC: McFarland, 1991); Janice H. Rushing, "Evolution of 'The New Frontier' in Alien and Aliens: Patriarchal Cooptation of the Feminine Archetype," *Quarterly Journal of Speech*, 75, 1989, pp. 1–24.

8. The total number of news items on Mother Teresa for the three decades was 33. The method for compiling early *Times* coverage of Mother Teresa deserves mention. Electronic databases were useless because they began their searches in the mid-1970s or later. Thus, I used the *New York Times* annual index for this study. However, even this index is not wholly reliable, particularly if individuals are not well known when they are mentioned in the paper. Searches thus were also done under listings for "India," "Calcutta," "Roman Catholic Church," and "Missionary." Even the spelling of names must be scrutinized. In various years, Mother Teresa appeared in the *Times* index under "Theresa" and "Teresa," as well as under "Mother."

9. Biographical details are taken from Mother Teresa, *A Simple Path* (New York: Ballantine Books, 1995); Malcolm Muggeridge, *Something Beautiful*

for God (New York: Harper & Row, 1971); and Robert Serrou, *Teresa of Calcutta* (New York: McGraw-Hill, 1980).

10. "Mother Teresa, A Disaster for India," *Free Inquiry, 13*, 1992, 44.

11. Christopher Hitchens, "Minority Report: Mother Teresa of Calcutta," *Nation*, April 13, 1992, p. 474; also see Christopher Hitchens, "Minority Report: Mother Teresa on a Roll," *Nation*, March 17, 1997, p. 8.

12. Christopher Hitchens, *The Missionary Position: Mother Teresa in Theory and Practice* (New York: Verso, 1995).

13. Hitchens, "Minority Report: Mother Teresa of Calcutta," p. 474.

14. Matt Cherry, "An Interview with Christopher Hitchens on Mother Teresa," *Free Inquiry, 16*, Fall 1996, 53.

15. Hitchens, "Minority Report: Mother Teresa on a Roll."

16. Christopher Hitchens, "Saint of the Rich," online at http://www.salon.com, September 5, 1997.

17. A. M. Rosenthal, "India's Great Adventure, Ten Years Later," *New York Times Magazine*, August 11, 1957, p. 9.

18. Paul Grimes, "Reds Still Strong in Calcutta Despite China Border Dispute," *New York Times*, December 28, 1959, p. 3.

19. Paul Grimes, "Calcutta a City of Frustrations," *New York Times*, December 27, 1959, p. 13.

20. Joseph Lelyveld, "Sidewalk Is Home for Kishan Babu Family in Calcutta," *New York Times*, September 8, 1967, p. 3.

21. Joseph Lelyveld, "A Calcutta Nun Softens Death for the Poor," *New York Times*, April 13, 1968, p. A2.

22. Lelyveld, "A Calcutta Nun Softens Death for the Poor."

23. Serrou, *Teresa of Calcutta*, pp. 84–85; Hitchens, "Mother Teresa on a Roll," p. 8.

24. "Mother Teresa, the Good Samaritan of Calcutta, Talks with a Visitor at Her Nursery," *New York Times*, April 13, 1968, p. A2.

25. "Caring for a Youngster in Her Refuge in Calcutta," *New York Times*, July 24, 1973, p. 2.

26. Michael Kaufman, "The World of Mother Teresa," *New York Times Magazine*, December 9, 1979, pp. 42–111.

27. Lelyveld, "A Calcutta Nun Softens Death."

28. Bernard Weinraub, "Monsoon Is Season of Death in the Slums of Calcutta," *New York Times*, July 24, 1973, p. 2.

29. "Friend of the World's Poor," *New York Times*, December 23, 1970, p. 3.

30. "From Calcutta with Love," *New York Times*, December 25, 1973, p. 28.

31. Michael Kaufman, "A Day with Mother Teresa: Kindness Is Her Theme," *New York Times*, October 25, 1979, p. A2.

32. Kaufman, "The World of Mother Teresa."

33. Paul Hofmann, "Pope Deplores Criticism by Intellectual in Church," *New York Times*, December 23, 1970, p. 3.

34. Paul Hofmann, "A Nun from India Is Extolled by Pope at Peace Prize Rite," *New York Times*, January 7, 1971, p. 14.
35. Kenneth Briggs, "Spiritual Parley Hears 'Living Saint,'" *New York Times*, October 25, 1975, pp. 31, 36.
36. Kenneth Briggs, "Catholic Hunger Fight Dramatized," *New York Times*, August 3, 1976, p. 14.
37. "Because of Her Compassionate Concern," *New York Times Magazine*, December 9, 1979, p. 45.
38. Frank Prial, "Mother Teresa of Calcutta Wins Peace Prize," *New York Times*, October 18, 1979, p. A1.
39. "A Secular Saint," *New York Times*, October 19, 1979, p. A34.
40. "Mother Teresa, Receiving Nobel, Assails Abortion," *New York Times*, December 11, 1979, p. A3.
41. Roland Barthes, *Mythologies*, trans. Annette Lavers (London: Cape, 1972), p. 155; emphasis added.
42. Helen Hughes, *News and the Human Interest Story* (Chicago: University of Chicago Press, 1940).
43. Michael Schudson, *Discovering the News* (New York: Basic Books, 1978), p. 27.
44. Herbert Gans, *Deciding What's News* (New York: Pantheon Books, 1979), p. 156.
45. Murray Edelman, *Constructing the Political Spectacle* (Chicago: University of Chicago Press, 1988), p. 99.
46. James Curran, Angus Douglas, and Garry Whannel, "The Political Economy of the Human-Interest Story," in Anthony Smith, ed., *Newspapers and Democracy* (Cambridge, MA: MIT Press, 1980), p. 306.
47. W. Lance Bennett, *News: The Politics of Illusion*, 2nd ed. (New York: Longman, 1988), p. 26.
48. Curran, Douglas, and Whannel, "The Political Economy of the Human-Interest Story," p. 306.

CHAPTER 7

1. Tyson served more than three years in prison. Not long after his release, he returned to the ring. His career continued to be surrounded in controversy, including a bizarre 1997 fight in which Tyson was disqualified for biting the ear of Evander Holyfield.
2. Henry McNulty, "Did the Tyson Trial Belong in the Sports Section?", *Editor & Publisher*, February 29, 1992, pp. 5, 34; Evelyn Nussenbaum, "Tyson Trial Coverage" (letter to the editor), *New York Times*, February 19, 1992, p. A20; Ann-Marie Paley, "Tyson's Trial Isn't Sports News" (letter to the edi-

tor), *New York Times*, March 15, 1992, p. H9; Tom Witosky, "Tyson Trial Belonged on Sports Pages" (letter to the editor), *New York Times*, March 4, 1992, p. A22.

3. William J. Hynes and William G. Doty, eds., *Mythical Trickster Figures: Contours, Contexts, and Criticisms* (Tuscaloosa: University of Alabama Press, 1993), p. 1.

4. Paul Radin, *The Trickster: A Study in American Indian Mythology* (New York: Schocken Books, 1955), p. 155.

5. Joseph Henderson, "Ancient Myths and Modern Man," in Carl G. Jung, ed., *Man and His Symbols* (New York: Dell, 1964), pp. 103–104.

6. Walter Lippmann, *Public Opinion* (New York: Harcourt, Brace & Company, 1922), p. 81.

7. See Ash Corea, "Racism and the American Way of Media," in John Downing, ed., *Questioning the Media*, 2nd ed. (Newbury Park, CA: Sage, 1995), pp. 345–361; Janette L. Dates and William Barlow, *Split Image: African Americans in the Mass Media* (Washington, DC: Howard University Press, 1990); Robert Entman, "Modern Racism and the Images of Blacks in Local Television News," *Critical Studies in Mass Communication*, 7(4), 1990, 332–345; and Robert Entman, "Blacks in the News: Television, Modern Racism and Cultural Change," *Journalism Quarterly*, 69(2), 1992, 341–361.

   Also see Paul Fisher and Ralph Lowenstein, *Race and the News Media* (New York: Praeger, 1967); J. Fred MacDonald, *Blacks and White TV*, 2nd ed. (Chicago: Nelson-Hall, 1992); Carolyn Martindale, "Coverage of Black Americans in Five Newspapers since 1950," *Journalism Quarterly*, 62(2), 1985, 321–328, 438; Carolyn Martindale, *The White Press and Black America* (Westport, CT: Greenwood Press, 1986); and *Report of the National Advisory Commission on Civil Disorders* (Washington, DC: U.S. Government Printing Office, 1968), pp. 362–386.

8. Harry Edwards, *Sociology of Sport* (Homewood, IL: Dorsey Press, 1973); Leonard Koppett, *Sports Illusion, Sports Reality* (Boston: Houghton Mifflin, 1981); Jack Scott, *The Athletic Revolution* (New York: Free Press, 1971), pp. 80–88.

9. Al-Tony Gilmore, *Bad Nigger: The National Impact of Jack Johnson* (London: Kennikat Press, 1975), pp. 133–154; John M. Hoberman, *Sport and Political Ideology* (Austin: University of Texas Press, 1984), pp. 16–19, 166–174; Joyce Carol Oates, "Rape and the Boxing Ring," *Newsweek*, February 24, 1992, pp. 60–61; Jeffrey T. Sammons, *Beyond the Ring: The Role of Boxing in American Society* (Urbana: University of Illinois Press, 1988).

10. Distinctions are made in the social science literature between modern racism and the similarly focused symbolic racism. See John B. McConahay, "Modern Racism, Ambivalence, and the Modern Racism Scale," in John

F. Dovidio and Samuel L. Gaertner, eds., *Prejudice, Discrimination and Racism* (Orlando, FL: Academic Press, 1986), pp. 91–125; and David O. Sears, "Symbolic Racism," in Phyllis A. Katz and Dalmas A. Taylor, eds., *Eliminating Racism* (New York: Plenum Press, 1988), pp. 53–84. Also see Daniel Bell, *Faces at the Bottom of the Well: The Permanence of Racism* (New York: Basic Books, 1992); and Andrew Hacker, *Two Nations: Black and White, Separate, Hostile, Unequal* (New York: Scribners, 1992).

11. McConahay, "Modern Racism," pp. 92–93.

12. Entman, "Modern Racism," p. 343; Entman, "Blacks in the News," p. 346.

13. bell hooks, *Black Looks: Race and Representation* (Boston: South End Press, 1992), p. 6.

14. Looking back, some observers have concluded that the rape trial provided the pivotal moment of Tyson's life, altering his career and celebrity status. See Tom Friend, "Seven: The Sins of Tyson," *ESPN: The Magazine*, November 2, 1998, pp. 70–74.

15. McNulty, "Did the Tyson Trial Belong in the Sports Section?", p. 5; also see Tom Witosky, "Beyond the Games," *Nieman Reports*, Spring 1992, pp. 25–28, 37.

16. Both press portraits also draw from other racist stereotypes for African Americans. See Donald Bogle, *Toms, Coons, Mulattoes, Mammies and Bucks: An Interpretive History of Blacks in American Films*, 3rd ed. (New York: Continuum, 1994); Sterling A. Brown, *The Negro in American Fiction*, 2nd ed. (New York: Atheneum, 1972); and Dates and Barlow, *Split Image*.

17. Ira Berkow, "The 'Animal' in Mike Tyson," *New York Times*, February 11, 1992, p. B11.

18. Bob Verdi, "Tyson Need Not Look Far for Blame," *Chicago Tribune*, February 13, 1992, p. C1.

19. Earl Gustkey, "Bad Image Is Good Box Office," *Los Angeles Times*, September 10, 1991, p. C1.

20. Ira Berkow, "A Champ Named Desiree," *New York Times*, February 25, 1992, p. B9.

21. Verdi, "Tyson Need Not Look Far for Blame."

22. Ira Berkow, "Tyson Is a Role Model in Reverse," *New York Times*, August 11, 1991, sec. 8, p. 2.

23. George Vecsey, "Don't Blame Boxing for Tyson," *New York Times*, September 12, 1991, p. A15.

24. Jim Murray, "Boxing's Soiled Image Suffers Another Blow," *Los Angeles Times*, September 12, 1991, p. C1.

25. Bernie Lincicome, "Tyson a Brute?: So What's New?", *Chicago Tribune*, August 13, 1991, p. C1.

26. Fuller attempted to inject another stereotype into the trial: He requested that an expert testify about the size of Tyson's genitalia as a possible explanation for injuries to the accuser. The request was denied but became the basis for a raucous *Saturday Night Live* television comedy skit. See Sonja Steptoe, "A Damnable Defense," *Sports Illustrated*, February 24, 1992, p. 92.

27. Berkow, "The 'Animal' in Mike Tyson."

28. John Kass, "Defense Depicts Tyson Accuser as Gold Digger," *Chicago Tribune*, February 7, 1992, p. C1.

29. Bernie Lincicome, "Olympic Stars Can Learn from Tyson," *Chicago Tribune*, February 12, 1992, p. C1.

30. Berkow, "Tyson Is a Role Model in Reverse."

31. Vecsey, "Don't Blame Boxing for Tyson."

32. Anna Quindlen, "Public & Private: Tyson Is Not Magic," *New York Times*, February 9, 1992, sec. 4, p. 17.

33. Lincicome, "Tyson a Brute?: So What's New?"

34. DeWayne Wickham, "If Tyson Is a Hero, We Need No More," *USA Today*, February 20, 1992, p. A7.

35. "The Tyson Years," *New York Times*, February 11, 1992, p. B15.

36. "Mike Tyson Chronology," *Los Angeles Times*, February 11, 1992, p. C1.

37. "Tracing Major Events of Heavyweight's Life," *USA Today*, September 10, 1991, p. C8.

38. Tom Boswell, "A One-Sided Bout against Trouble," *Washington Post*, September 11, 1991, p. G1.

39. Robert Lipsyte, "Who Is Tyson, and What May Happen Next?", *New York Times*, September 13, 1991, p. B11.

40. Mike Royko, "Race Has Nothing to Do with Tyson," *Chicago Tribune*, February 13, 1992, p. A3.

41. "The Mike Tyson Verdict," *Washington Post*, February 13, 1992, p. A22.

42. Earl Gustkey, "Don't Blame Boxing, Don't Blame Ghetto—Blame Him," *Los Angeles Times*, February 11, 1992, p. C1.

43. Michael Wilbon, "Entitled to Everything He Got," *Washington Post*, February 12, 1992, p. B1.

44. Dave Anderson, "10 Years, 10 Years, 10 Years," *New York Times*, March 27, 1992, p. B7.

45. John Kass, "Ex-Champ Tyson Convicted of Rape," *Chicago Tribune*, February 11, 1992, p. A1.

46. E. R. Shipp, "Tyson Gets 6-Year Prison Term for Rape Conviction in Indiana," *New York Times*, March 27, 1992, p. A1.

47. John Kass, "Tyson Exchanges His Gloves for Cuffs—For at Least 3 Years," *Chicago Tribune*, March 27, 1992, p. A1.

48. Alison Muscatine, "Tyson Gets 6 Years in Prison for Rape," *Washington Post*, March 27, 1992, p. A1.

49. "Mike Tyson Leaving Court Yesterday," *New York Times*, February 11, 1992, p. A1; "Mike Tyson Arriving at the Diagnostic Reception Center in Plainville, Ind., Yesterday after He Was Sentenced," *New York Times*, March 27, 1992, p. B12; also see "Law Enforcement Officials Escort Mike Tyson," *Chicago Tribune*, February 11, 1992, p. A1.

50. "In Former Heavyweight Champion Mike Tyson's New Entourage There Are a Lot of People Wearing Badges," *Washington Post*, February 12, 1992, p. B1.

51. Al Neuharth, "A Heartland Lesson for New York Brat," *USA Today*, February 14, 1992, p. A7.

52. Vecsey, "Don't Blame Boxing for Tyson."

53. Fred Mitchell, "Tyson Could Become a Marked Man in Prison," *Chicago Tribune*, March 27, 1992, p. C9.

54. Dave Anderson, "The Humiliation of No. 922335 Mike Tyson," *New York Times*, March 29, 1992, sec. 8, p. 4.

55. Shipp, "Tyson Gets 6-Year Prison Term for Rape Conviction in Indiana."

56. Clarence Page, "Blaming 'Jezebel' Ignores the Violent Truth about Tyson," *Chicago Tribune*, February 12, 1992, p. C17.

57. William Raspberry, "The Real Victim in Indianapolis," *Washington Post*, February 14, 1992, p. A25.

58. Bill Brubaker, "Tyson Maintains Innocence, Lifestyle," *Washington Post*, September 15, 1991, p. D1.

59. Jon Saraceno, "Tyson Book Paints Boxer as Victim," *USA Today*, September 10, 1991, p. C1.

60. Boswell, "A One-Sided Bout against Trouble."

61. Robert Lipsyte, "Who Is Tyson, and What May Happen Next?"

62. Verdi, "Tyson Need Not Look Far for Blame."

63. Page, "Blaming 'Jezebel' Ignores the Violent Truth about Tyson."

64. Arthur Ashe, "Heroes: Thomas vs. Tyson," *Washington Post*, September 15, 1991, p. C2.

65. Boswell, "A One-Sided Bout against Trouble."

66. Jim Murray, "Patterson Heard Cus Teach Class," *Los Angeles Times*, February 13, 1992, p. C1.

67. Lipsyte, "Who Is Tyson, and What May Happen Next?"

68. William C. Rhoden, "Creating a New Standard," *New York Times*, March 1, 1992, p. D1.

69. William Gildea, "Many Expect Tyson's Return," *Washington Post*, March 27, 1992, p. D1.

70. Kass, "Ex-Champ Tyson Convicted of Rape"; "Ministers Circulate Petitions to Keep Tyson Out of Prison," *Chicago Tribune*, February 18, 1992, p. A2.

71. Rhoden, "Creating a New Standard."

72. Julie Cart, "Sports Heroes, Social Villains," *Los Angeles Times*, February 2, 1992, p. C3.

73. Robert Lipsyte, "The Manly Art of Self-Delusion," *New York Times*, August 4, 1991, sec. 8, p. 1.

74. Rhoden, "Creating a New Standard."

75. Julianne Malveaux, "Women, Men and Tyson," *USA Today*, February 12, 1992, p. A6.

76. Barbara Reynolds, "In Battle of Good vs. Evil, Ministers Choose Tyson," *USA Today*, February 21, 1992, p. A7.

77. Allan Johnson, "Tyson Rape Case Strikes a Nerve among Blacks," *Chicago Tribune*, March 29, 1992, p. C1.

78. Page, "Blaming 'Jezebel' Ignores the Violent Truth about Tyson."

79. Megan Rosenfeld, "After the Verdict, the Doubts; Black Women Show Little Sympathy for Tyson's Accuser," *Washington Post*, February 13, 1992, p. D1.

80. Lipsyte, "Who Is Tyson, and What May Happen Next?"

81. Mike Penner, "Boxing, the Public Are Not Blameless," *Los Angeles Times*, February 12, 1992, p. C1.

82. Bogle, *Toms, Coons, Mulattoes, Mammies and Bucks*; Kenneth W. Goings, *Mammy and Uncle Mose: Black Collectibles and American Stereotyping* (Bloomington: Indiana University Press, 1994); D. Hamilton and T. Trolier, "Stereotypes and Stereotyping: An Overview of the Cognitive Approach," in John F. Dovidio and Samuel L. Gaertner, eds., *Prejudice, Discrimination and Racism* (Orlando, FL: Academic Press, 1986), pp. 91–125; MacDonald, *Blacks and White TV.*; Patricia A. Turner, *Ceramic Uncles and Celluloid Mammies: Black Images and Their Influence on Culture* (New York: Anchor Books, 1994).

83. Entman, "Blacks in the News," p. 346.

84. Entman, "Blacks in the News," p. 345.

85. Hamilton and Trolier, "Stereotypes and Stereotyping"; Turner, *Ceramic Uncles and Celluloid Mammies.*

86. Lippmann, *Public Opinion*, p. 81.

87. Lippmann, *Public Opinion*, p. 119.

88. Michael Schudson, "The Politics of Narrative Form: The Emergence of News Conventions in Print and Television," *Daedalus*, *111*(1), 1982, 98.

89. Stuart Hall, "The Rediscovery of 'Ideology': Return of the Repressed in Media Studies," in Michael Gurevitch, Tony Bennett, James Curran, and Janet Woollacott, eds., *Culture, Society and the Media* (London: Methuen, 1982), p. 88.

90. Entman, "Blacks in the News," p. 345.

91. Carl G. Jung, "Approaching the Unconscious," in Carl G. Jung, ed., *Man and His Symbols* (New York: Dell, 1964), p. 75.

92. Claude Lévi-Strauss, *Structural Anthropology*, trans. Claire Jacobson and Brooke Grundfest Schoepf (New York: Basic Books, 1963), p. 229; Mircea Eliade, *Patterns in Comparative Religion*, trans. Rosemary Sheed (New York: Sheed & Ward, 1958), p. 418. Also see Claude Lévi-Strauss, *The Raw and the Cooked*, trans. John Weightman and Doreen Weightman (New York: Harper & Row, 1969).
93. hooks, *Black Looks*, p. 4.

CHAPTER 8

1. Catherine Orenstein, "Haiti and the Mainstream Press," *Lies of Our Times*, October 1993, pp. 18–19; Catherine Orenstein, "Haiti's Curse," *Lies of Our Times*, December 1993, pp. 3–5; Noam Chomsky, "The 'Truth' about Haiti," *Lies of Our Times*, January–February 1993, pp. 5–8.
2. John Hess, "Haiti and the French Connection," *Lies of Our Times*, January–February 1994, pp. 21–22.
3. See S. J. Taylor, *Stalin's Apologist: Walter Duranty, New York Times's Man in Moscow* (New York: Oxford University Press, 1990); and James William Crowl, *Angels in Stalin's Paradise: Western Reporters in Soviet Russia, 1917 to 1937. A Case Study of Louis Fischer and Walter Duranty* (Washington, DC: University Press of America, 1982). Also see Whitman Bassow, *The Moscow Correspondents: Reporting on Russia from the Revolution to Glasnost* (New York: Morrow, 1988).
4. David Halberstam, *The Making of a Quagmire* (New York: Random House, 1965); David Halberstam, *The Powers That Be* (New York: Knopf, 1979), pp. 445–446; John Galloway, *The Kennedys and Vietnam* (New York: Facts on File, 1971), pp. 46–47. Also see John Hohenberg, *Foreign Correspondence: The Great Reporters and Their Times*, 2nd ed. (Syracuse, NY: Syracuse University Press, 1995), p. 275; and Gay Talese, *The Kingdom and the Power* (New York: World, 1969), p. 443.
5. Edwin Diamond, *Behind the Times: Inside the New "New York Times"* (Chicago: University of Chicago Press, 1995), p. 244.
6. The story of El Mozote is told by Mark Danner, in *The Massacre at El Mozote: A Parable of the Cold War* (New York: Vintage Books, 1994).
7. J. Herbert Altschull, *Agents of Power*, 2nd ed. (New York: Longman, 1995); Nicholas Berry, *Foreign Policy and the Press: An Analysis of the "New York Times" Coverage of U.S. Foreign Policy* (New York: Greenwood Press, 1990); Johan Galtung and Richard Vincent, *Global Glasnost: Toward a New World Information and Communication Order* (Cresskill, NJ: Hampton Press, 1992); Philip Gaunt, *Choosing the News* (New York: Greenwood Press, 1990); James Hoge, "The End of Predictability," *Media Studies Journal*, 7(4), 1993, 1–9; Patrick O'Heffernan, *Mass Media and American For-*

eign Policy: Insider Perspectives on Global Journalism and the Foreign Policy Process (Norwood, NJ: Ablex, 1991).

8. Daniel Hallin, "Hegemony. The American News Media from Vietnam to El Salvador: A Study of Ideological Change and Its Limits," in D. L. Paletz (ed.), *Political Communication Research: Approaches, Studies, Assessments* (Norwood, NJ: Ablex, 1987), p. 23.

9. Hoge, "The End of Predictability," p. 1.

10. Jon Vanden Heuvel, "For the Media, a Brave (and Scary) New World," *Media Studies Journal, 7*(4), 1993, 12, 19.

11. Bernard Gwertzman, "Memo to the *Times* Foreign Staff," *Media Studies Journal, 7*(4), 1993, 33.

12. Gwertzman, "Memo to the *Times* Foreign Staff," pp. 37–38.

13. Galtung and Vincent, *Global Glasnost*; Michael Traber, "Communication Ethics," in G. Gerbner, H. Mowlana, and K. Nordenstreng, eds., *The Global Media Debate* (Norwood, NJ: Ablex, 1993), pp. 151–159.

14. Clifford G. Christians, John P. Ferre, and Mark P. Fackler, *Good News: Social Ethics and the Press* (New York: Oxford University Press, 1993), p. 93.

15. "Policy seems to follow the media spotlight," Vanden Heuvel writes, citing U.S. actions in Somalia and Bosnia as examples; see his "For the Media, a Brave (and Scary) New World," p. 12.

16. Hoge, "The End of Predictability," p. 6.

17. See Altschull, *Agents of Power*; and Hallin, "Hegemony." Also see Daniel Hallin, *We Keep America on Top of the World* (London: Routledge, 1994).

18. Chomsky affirms: "Case by case, we find that conformity is the easy way, and the path to privilege and prestige; dissidence carries personal costs that may be severe, even in a society that lacks such means of control as death squads, psychiatric prisons, or extermination camps. The very structure of the media is designed to induce conformity to established doctrine." See his *Necessary Illusions: Thought Control in Democratic Societies* (Boston: South End Press, 1989), p. 10.

19. Hallin, *We Keep America on Top of the World*, p. 76.

20. Campbell, *The Hero with a Thousand Faces*, p. 79.

21. Jean-Pierre Vernant, *Myth and Society in Ancient Greece*, trans. Janet Lloyd (Atlantic Highlands, NJ: Humanities Press, 1980), p. 134.

22. "It is through myth, as we said before, that the ideas of *reality, value, transcendence* slowly dawn," Eliade wrote. "Through myth, the World can be apprehended as a perfectly articulated, intelligible, and significant Cosmos." See Mircea Eliade, *Myth and Reality*, trans. Willard R. Trask (New York: Harper & Row, 1963), p. 145.

23. The brief account of recent United States–Haiti relations has been derived from Paul Farmer, *The Uses of Haiti* (Monroe, ME: Common Courage Press, 1994); and North American Congress on Latin America, *Haiti: Dangerous Crossroads* (Boston: South End Press, 1995).

24. Jim Naureckas, "The Demonization of Jean-Bertrand Aristide," *Extra!*, November–December 1994, pp. 6–7.

25. In May 1994, perhaps in response to the hunger strike of civil rights activist Randall Robinson, Clinton did change U.S. policy on returning refugees. Still not permitted entry to the United States, they were placed in offshore "safe havens."

26. Joanne Landy, "Born-Again Interventionists," *Progressive*, September 1994, p. 23; Jane Regan, "Haiti on the Brink," *Progressive*, September 1994, pp. 20–24.

27. The biography of Larry Rohter was supplied by the *New York Times* foreign desk.

28. Larry Rohter, "No Choice But to Withdraw Offer, Panamanian Says," *New York Times*, July 8, 1994, p. A6.

29. Larry Rohter, "Despite Talk of Invasion, Haiti's Terror Continues," *New York Times*, July 17, 1994, sec. 1, p. 6.

30. Larry Rohter, "Number of Haitians Fleeing by Sea Drops Off Abruptly," *New York Times*, July 20, 1994, p. A3.

31. Larry Rohter, "Haiti Attacks Critics and Restricts Civil Rights," *New York Times*, August 3, 1994, p. A9.

32. Larry Rohter, "Haitian Military Greets Invasion Vote with Defiance," *New York Times*, August 2, 1994, p. A3.

33. Rohter, "Haitian Military Greets Invasion Vote with Defiance."

34. Larry Rohter, "U.S. Weighs Options; Haiti's Latest Tactic Sends Monitors Packing," *New York Times*, July 17, 1994, sec. 4, p. 2.

35. Larry Rohter, "In Port-au-Prince, the Signs of Invasion Are in the Air," *New York Times*, September 15, 1994, p. A8.

36. Larry Rohter, "Haiti Holding Up Relief Supplies as a Bargaining Chip to Regain Recognition," *New York Times*, July 21, 1994, p. A10.

37. Larry Rohter, "Haiti Plans Ballot Likely to Yield a Replacement for Aristide," *New York Times*, July 27, 1994, p. A3.

38. Rohter, "Haitian Military Greets Invasion Vote with Defiance."

39. Larry Rohter, "Invasion that Never Comes Has Many Haitians Skeptical," *New York Times*, August 10, 1994, p. A1.

40. Larry Rohter, "Military Leader in Haiti Resigns, Vowing to Leave," *New York Times*, October 11, 1994, p. A1.

41. Larry Rohter, "Aristide Calls for Reconciliation on His Own Radio Station," *New York Times*, July 16, 1994, sec. 1, p. 4.

42. Larry Rohter, "Liberal Wing of Haiti's Catholic Church Resists Military," *New York Times*, July 24, 1994, sec. 1, p. 3.

43. Larry Rohter, "Joyous Haitians Decorate the Capital for Aristide," *New York Times*, October 15, 1994, sec. 1, p. 6.

44. Larry Rohter, "Aristide Can Speak, But Can the U.S. Hear?", *New York Times*, October 16, 1994, sec. 4, p. 5.

45. Larry Rohter, "After the Homecoming, the Hard Part," *New York Times*, October 16, 1994, sec. 1, p. 1.

46. Rohter, "Aristide Can Speak, But Can the U.S. Hear?"

47. Larry Rohter, "Some Aristide Supporters Seek Abolition of Military," *New York Times*, November 22, 1994, p. A8.

48. Larry Rohter, "Haiti's Prime Minister Resigns After Disputes Over Economy," *New York Times*, October 14, 1995, sec. 1, p. 2.

49. Larry Rohter, "Privatization Starts Feud in Haiti," *New York Times*, October 19, 1995, p. A9.

50. Larry Rohter, "Aristide Decides to Quit as Priest," *New York Times*, November 17, 1994, p. A1.

51. Larry Rohter, "Call Me 'Mister,' Aristide Says," *New York Times*, November 20, 1994, sec. 4, p. 2.

52. Larry Rohter, "Haitian Leader's Angry Words Unnerve Elite and Worry Allies," *New York Times*, November 19, 1995, sec. 1, p. 1.

53. Larry Rohter, "In or Out of Presidency, Aristide Is Still the Issue," *New York Times*, February 9, 1996, p. A6.

54. Allan Nairn, "The Eagle Is Landing: U.S. Forces Occupy Haiti," *Nation*, October 3, 1994, pp. 344–354; Allan Nairn, "Behind Haiti's Paramilitaries: Our Man in FRAPH," *Nation*, October 24, 1994, pp. 458–463; Allan Nairn, "Haiti under the Gun: How U.S. Backed Paramilitaries Rule through Fear," *Nation*, January 8–15, 1996, pp. 11–15.

55. Larry Rohter, "Haiti Parliament Meets, but Delays an Amnesty Vote," *New York Times*, September 29, 1994, p. A16.

56. Larry Rohter, "Violence by Paramilitary Groups in Haiti Raises Pressure on U.S.," *New York Times*, October 1, 1994, sec. 1, p. 1.

57. Rohter, "Violence by Paramilitary Groups in Haiti Raises Pressure on U.S."

58. Larry Rohter, "Haiti's Attaches: Deadly Heirs to the Tontons Macoute," *New York Times*, October 4, 1994, p. A10.

59. Larry Rohter, "Beyond the U.S. Raid: Haiti Is Still a Minefield," *New York Times*, October 4, 1994, p. A10.

60. Larry Rohter, "Haiti's Military Power Structure is Showing Signs of Falling Apart," *New York Times*, October 5, 1994, p. A1.

61. Larry Rohter, "The Iron Fist in Haiti Begins to Lose Its Grip," *New York Times*, October 9, 1994, sec. 4, p. 5.

62. Larry Rohter, "U.S. Inaction on Gunmen Upsets Haitians," *New York Times*, October 19, 1994, p. A3.

63. Larry Rohter, "Some Haitians No Longer View G.I.'s as Saviors," *New York Times*, January 17, 1995, p. A3.

64. Larry Rohter, "Mystery of the Missing Haitian Bully," *New York Times*, February 14, 1995, p. A8.

65. Larry Rohter, "Haiti Is a Land without a Country," *New York Times*, August 14, 1994, sec. 4, p. 3.

66. Larry Rohter, "Mission in Haiti: Grim Shadow of Economic Reality," *New York Times*, September 25, 1994, sec. 1, p. 16.

67. Rohter, "Aristide Can Speak, But Can the U.S. Hear?"

68. Larry Rohter, "So Far at Least, Inept Is the Kindest Word for Haitian Democracy," *New York Times*, July 2, 1995, sec. 4, p. 3.

69. Larry Rohter, "High Spirits in Haiti, Even with Many to Mourn," *New York Times*, November 2, 1994, p. A4.

70. Larry Rohter, "In a Harsh Land, Faith at Christmas," *New York Times*, December 25, 1994, sec. 4, p. 1.

71. Rohter, "Haitian Military Greets Invasion Vote with Defiance."

72. Galtung and Vincent, *Global Glasnost*, p. 24. Traber also has seen the opportunity for renewed news values. "One of the biggest challenges of the new international information order," he wrote, "is to develop new and different criteria for newsworthiness"; see his "Communication Ethics," p. 156. In this human, humane journalism, Christians and his coauthors suggested, reporters can "specialize in truthful narratives about justice, covenant, and empowerment"; see Christians, Ferre, and Fackler, *Good News*, p. 116.

73. Hallin sees "an extended period of public confusion and uncertainty about world politics, and a passive, sometimes grudging consent to the decisions of the foreign policy establishment"; see his "Hegemony," p. 23. Others too have seen no reason for hope in post-cold war news. Altschull notes the possibilities offered the news media in "the age of globalization." Yet despite his hope that "the press will turn away from its historic role as blind chronicler of conflict and search out a different role, that of conflict resolver," his first law of journalism remains: "In all press systems, the news media are agents of those who exercise political and economic power." See Altschull, *Agents of Power*, pp. 442, 440.

74. Vernant, *Myth and Society in Ancient Greece*, p. 134.

75. Joseph Campbell, *The Masks of God: Creative Mythology* (New York: Viking Press, 1968), p. 611.

76. Hallin, *We Keep America on Top of the World*, p. 76.

CHAPTER 9

1. Don Cameron Allen, *The Legend of Noah* (Urbana: University of Illinois Press, 1963); Alan Dundes, ed., *The Flood Myth* (Berkeley and Los Angeles: University of California Press, 1988); J. F. Bierlein, *Parallel Myths* (New York: Ballantine Books, 1994), pp. 121–135.

2. Stith Thompson, *Motif-Index of Folk-Literature* (Bloomington: Indiana University Press, 1955).

3. Dundes, *The Flood Myth*, p. 2.

4. Allen, *The Legend of Noah*; Arthur C. Custance, *The Flood: Local or Global?* (Grand Rapids, MI: Zondervan, 1979); Leonard Woolley, "Stories of the Creation and the Flood," in Dundes, ed., *The Flood Myth*, pp. 89–100.

5. "32 Killed in Major Hurricane, Honduras Says," *New York Times*, October 29, 1998, p. A5.

6. "Death Toll from Storm Hits 450 after Mudslides in Nicaragua," *New York Times*, November 1, 1998, p. A6.

7. Larry Rohter, "Flood Toll Estimate Rises Above 1,000 in Central America," *New York Times*, November 2, 1998, pp. A1, A6.

8. Larry Rohter, "Officials Predict Hurricane's Toll Will Exceed 7,000," *New York Times*, November 3, 1998, p. A1.

9. Rohter, "Officials Predict Hurricane's Toll Will Exceed 7,000."

10. Larry Rohter, "Nicaragua's Main Highway Is a Flow of Human Misery," *New York Times*, November 4, 1998, p. A1.

11. Larry Rohter, "For Nicaraguan Victims, Not Even a Grave," *New York Times*, November 6, 1998, p. A1.

12. Philip Shenon, "U.S. Says Storm Aid Could Cost Billions," *New York Times*, November 7, 1998, p. A3.

13. Mirta Ojito, "Central Americans in New York Scramble to Help Hurricane Victims," *New York Times*, November 4, 1998, p. D7.

14. "Hurricane Threatens 4 Caribbean Nations," *New York Times*, October 27, 1998, p. A14.

15. "Hurricane Hits Coasts of Honduras and Belize," *New York Times*, October 28, 1998, p. A11.

16. "Storm's Floods Rise in Honduras and Nicaragua," *New York Times*, October 31, 1998, p. A3.

17. Larry Rohter, "Flood Toll Estimate Rises Above 1,000 in Central America."

18. Larry Rohter, "Now Ruined Economies Afflict Central America," *New York Times*, November 13, 1998, p. A12.

19. Rohter, "Officials Predict Hurricane's Toll Will Exceed 7,000."

20. Rohter, "Officials Predict Hurricane's Toll Will Exceed 7,000."

21. James C. McKinley Jr., "Relief Effort in Honduras in Dire Need of Resources," *New York Times*, November 4, 1998, p. A6.

22. Larry Rohter, "How Nations Run: Disasters as a Guide," *New York Times*, November 8, 1998, p. K6.

23. "1 House Left in Sea of Mud," *New York Times*, November 3, 1998, p. A13.

24. "Leveled by Storm," *New York Times*, November 10, 1998, p. A16.

25. James C. McKinley Jr., "Honduras's Capital: City of the Dead and the Dazed," *New York Times*, November 5, 1998, p. A3.

26. Rohter, "Nicaragua's Main Highway Is a Flow of Human Misery."

27. Rohter, "For Nicaraguan Victims, Not Even a Grave."

28. Larry Towell, "Rebuilding Honduras," *New York Times Magazine*, December 6, 1998, p. 67.

29. McKinley, "Honduras's Capital: City of the Dead and the Dazed."

30. Rohter, "How Nations Run: Disasters as a Guide."

31. James C. McKinley Jr., with William K. Stevens, "The Life of a Hurricane, the Death that It Caused," *New York Times*, November 9, 1998, p. A1.

32. Tina Rosenberg, "Trees and the Roots of a Storm's Destruction," *New York Times*, November 26, 1998, p. A38.

33. Ronald Patterson, "Hurricane Relief is Just a Band-Aid" (letter to the editor), *New York Times*, November 14, 1998, p. A12.

34. McKinley, with Stevens, "The Life of a Hurricane, the Death That It Caused."

35. Arturo J. Cruz Jr., "The Wrath of God?", *New York Times*, November 16, 1998, p. A21.

36. Roland Barthes, *Mythologies*, trans. Annette Lavers (London: Cape, 1972), p. 11.

37. The gatekeeping literature is voluminous and includes Kurt Lewin, "Channels of Group Life: Social Planning and Action Research," *Human Relations*, *1*, Summer 1947, 145–146; David Manning White, "The 'Gate Keeper:' A Case Study in the Selection of News," *Journalism Quarterly*, *27*, Fall 1950, 383–396; James W. Markham, "Foreign News in the United States and South American Press," *Public Opinion Quarterly*, *25*, Summer 1961, 249–262; Paul B. Snider, "Mr. Gates Revisited: A 1966 Version of the 1949 Case Study," *Journalism Quarterly*, *44*, Fall 1967, 419–427; John Dimmick, "The Gate-Keeper: An Uncertainty Theory," *Journalism Monographs*, *37*, 1974; Sophie Peterson, "Foreign News Gatekeepers and Criteria of Newsworthiness," *Journalism Quarterly*, *56*, Spring 1979, 116–125; Richard M. Brown, "The Gatekeeper Reassessed: A Return to Lewin," *Journalism Quarterly*, *56*, Autumn 1979, 595–601; D. Charles Whitney and Lee Becker, "Keeping the Gates for Gatekeepers: The Effects of Wire News," *Journalism Quarterly*, *59*, Spring 1982, 60–65; Glen Bleske, "Ms. Gates Takes Over," *Newspaper Research Journal*, *12*, 1991, 88–97; and Pamela Shoemaker, *Gatekeeping* (Newbury Park, CA: Sage, 1991).

38. See, e.g., Bernard C. Cohen, *The Press and Foreign Policy* (Princeton, NJ: Princeton University Press, 1963); Johan Galtung and Mari Holmboe Ruge, "The Structure of Foreign News," *Journal of Peace Research*, *2*, Spring 1965, 64–91; Mort Rosenblum, *Coups and Earthquakes: Reporting the Third World for America* (New York: Harper & Row, 1979); Annabelle Sreberny-Mohammadi, "The 'World of the News,'" *Journal of Communication*, *34*, Winter 1984, 121–134; Herman and Chomsky, *Manufacturing Consent*; Daniel C. Hallin, *We Keep America on Top of the World: Television Journalism and the Public Sphere* (London: Routledge, 1994); Altschull, *Agents of Power*; and Edward S. Herman and Robert W. McChesney, *The*

Global Media: The New Missionaries of Global Capitalism (London: Cassell, 1997).

Also see Jonathan Benthall, *Disasters, Relief and the Media* (London: Tauris, 1995); Brookings Institution, *From Massacres to Genocide: The Media, Public Policy, and Humanitarian Crises* (Washington, DC: Brookings Institution Press, 1996); Paul Heyer, *Titanic Legacy: Disaster as Media Event and Myth* (Westport, CT: Praeger, 1995); Susan D. Moeller, *Compassion Fatigue: How the Media Sell Disease, Famine, War and Death* (New York: Routledge, 1999); and Robert Rotberg, *The Media, Humanitarian Crises, and Policy-Making* (Cambridge, MA: World Peace Foundation, 1995).

CONCLUSION

1. "Committee of Concerned Journalists," *Poynter Report*, Fall 1997, p. 3; also see "Committee of Concerned Journalists," online at: http://www.journalism.org/concern
2. Sociologist Michael Schudson has arrived at a similar conclusion. Schudson has argued that news is first and foremost "a form of culture" that contributes to "public knowledge." News media, Schudson says, first identify an event as newsworthy and give that event "public legitimacy." They provide a hierarchy of importance and salience. "What they produce and reproduce is not information—if there is such a thing; it is what is recognized or accepted as public knowledge given certain political structures and traditions," he says. The news media contribute as producers of meanings, symbols, and messages. "The news serves a vital democratic function whether in a given instance anyone out there is listening or not," he says. "The news constructs a symbolic world that has a kind of priority, a certification of legitimate importance. And that symbolic world, putatively and practically, in its easy availability, in its cheap, quotidian, throw-away material form, becomes the property of all of us." See Michael Schudson, *The Power of News* (Cambridge, MA: Harvard University Press, 1995), pp. 3, 31, 33.
3. Arthur Ochs Sulzberger Jr. enjoys telling a story about people's feelings of loyalty for the *Times*. The paper, he told *Time* magazine, was preparing for changes in the 1990s. Trying to gauge public reaction in advance, staff members showed proposed changes to focus groups. One horrified woman said, "I don't read the paper, but it can't change." Sulzberger's bemused reaction: "Even our nonreaders are loyal to us." See Richard Zoglin, "The Last Great Newspaper," *Time*, September 29, 1997, p. 68.
4. Harrison E. Salisbury, *Without Fear or Favor: The "New York Times" and Its Times* (New York: Times Books, 1980), p. ix.

5. Marshall McLuhan, "BBC Interview by Frank Kermode, 1964," *The Video McLuhan* (Toronto, Canada, 1996).
6. Carl G. Jung, *The Spirit in Man, Art, and Literature*, trans. R. F. C. Hull (London: Routledge & Kegan Paul, 1966), p. 97.
7. Carl G. Jung, *The Archetypes and the Collective Unconscious*, trans. R. F. C. Hull (New York: Pantheon Books, 1959), p. 160.

Index

239

About the Author

Jack Lule, PhD, is Professor and Chair in the Department of Journalism and Communication at Lehigh University in Bethlehem, Pennsylvania. He is the author of more than 50 articles, book chapters, essays, and reviews and has won numerous awards for excellence in research and teaching. He also serves on the editorial board of *Journalism and Mass Communication Quarterly*. A former reporter, Dr. Lule continues to be a frequent contributor to newspapers and periodicals.